Lucy M. J. Garnett, John S. Stuart-Glennie

Greek Folk-Songs from the Turkish Provinces of Greece

Albania, Thessaly - not yet wholly free - and Macedonia, literal and metrical translations

Lucy M. J. Garnett, John S. Stuart-Glennie

Greek Folk-Songs from the Turkish Provinces of Greece

Albania, Thessaly - not yet wholly free - and Macedonia, literal and metrical translations

ISBN/EAN: 9783337247904

Printed in Europe, USA, Canada, Australia, Japan

Cover: Foto ©Thomas Meinert / pixelio.de

More available books at **www.hansebooks.com**

GREEK FOLK-SONGS

FROM

THE TURKISH PROVINCES OF GREECE,

'Η ΔΟΥΛΗ ῾ΕΛΛΑΣ:

*ALBANIA, THESSALY, (NOT YET WHOLLY FREE,)
AND MACEDONIA:*

Literal and Metrical Translations

BY

LUCY M. J. GARNETT,

CLASSIFIED, REVISED, AND EDITED, WITH AN

HISTORICAL INTRODUCTION ON THE SURVIVAL OF PAGANISM.

BY

JOHN S. STUART GLENNIE, M.A.,
OF THE MIDDLE TEMPLE, BARRISTER-AT-LAW.

LONDON:
ELLIOT STOCK, 62, PATERNOSTER ROW, E.C.
1885.

'*Thug e doibh sgeul air Rìgh na Gréige, agus mar a bha Nighean an Rìgh air a gleidheadh 'san Dùn, 's nach robh aon air bith gu* AILLIDH, *Nighean Rìgh na Gréige, fhaotainn ri phòsadh, ach aon a bheircadh a mach i le sàr ghaisge.*'—SGEUL CHONUIL GHUILBNICH.

'*And he told them the Tale of the King of Greece, and how his Daughter was kept in the Dun, and that no one at all was to get* BEAUTY, *Daughter of the King of Greece, to marry, but one who could bring her out by great valour.*'—CAMPBELL, West Highland Tales, Vol. III., *p.* 258.

To
THE HELLENES
OF
ENSLAVED GREECE
(ALBANIA, THESSALY, NOT YET WHOLLY FREE,
AND MACEDONIA),
THESE
GREEK FOLK-SONGS
ARE DEDICATED,

WITH THE EARNEST WISH OF
THE TRANSLATOR AND EDITOR,
THAT THEIR JOINT WORK—

IN GIVING SOME BETTER KNOWLEDGE OF,

AND KEENER SYMPATHY WITH,
A PEOPLE
WHOSE SPIRIT AND SENTIMENT

ARE STILL CLASSICAL—

MAY GAIN HELP FOR A LAST AND SUCCESSFUL STRUGGLE

FOR THE COMPLETION

OF
HELLENIC INDEPENDENCE.

GENERAL TABLE OF CONTENTS.

PREFACE.

PAGE
REMARKS, POLITICAL AND LINGUISTIC - - xvii

HISTORICAL INTRODUCTION.
THE SURVIVAL OF PAGANISM.

SECTION I.—THE FACT OF THE SURVIVAL OF PAGANISM 3
„ II.—PAGAN SANCTUARIES AND FOLK-SONG
         SCENES - - - - - 20
„ III.—THE CAUSE OF THE SURVIVAL OF
         PAGANISM - - - - 42
NOTE BY THE TRANSLATOR - - - - 65

METRICAL TRANSLATIONS.
CLASS I.—MYTHOLOGICAL FOLK-SONGS.

SECTION I.—IDYLLIC - - - - - 69
„ II.—CHRISTIAN - - - - 94
„ III.—CHARONIC - - - - 111

CLASS II.—AFFECTIONAL FOLK-SONGS.

SECTION I.—EROTIC - - - - - 133
„ II.—DOMESTIC - - - - 157
„ III.—HUMOURISTIC - - - - 184

CLASS III.—HISTORICAL FOLK-SONGS.

SECTION I.—PASHALIC - - - - 199
„ II.—SOULIOTE - - - - - 216
„ III.—HELLENIC - - - - 240

APPENDIX.
BIBLIOGRAPHY OF GREEK FOLK-LORE - - 259

ANALYTICAL TABLE OF CONTENTS.

PREFACE.
REMARKS, POLITICAL AND LINGUISTIC.

                                                                            PAGE

1. The bearing of the Study of Folk-life and Folk-lore on Historical Theory, and the Influence of the latter on Political Forces - - - xvii
2. The importance for Civilization of the Resurrection of the Greeks, and the completion of Hellenic independence - - - - - xix
3. The 'Policy of the European Concert,' and the two chief actual objects of that 'Concert' with respect to Europe - - - - xx
4. The suggested New Policy of a Greco-Albanian Confederation - - - - - xxi
5. The relation of Modern to Classical Greek, and the causes of the different histories of the Greek and Latin Languages - - - - xxiii
6. The Greek *Patois* of Southern Albania, and English *Patois* of Southern Scotland, and the characteristics of the former in relation to Athenian Modern Greek - - - - - xxvii
7. The Gaelic 'Tale of the King of Greece,' a legendary reminiscence explained by the facts of Keltic History - - - - xxix

HISTORICAL INTRODUCTION.
THE SURVIVAL OF PAGANISM.

SECTION I.

THE FACT OF THE SURVIVAL OF PAGANISM.

		PAGE
1.	The Plutarchian Legend of the Death of Pan	3
2.	The symbolic meaning given to this Legend, and its untruth	4
3.	Testimonies to this untruth by Christian students of Folk-lore	6
4.	The essential and surviving characteristics of Paganism	8
5.	Illustrations in our Folk-songs of the feeling of Oneness with Nature, and of direct Personalizing of its phenomena	8
6.	Illustrations of the indirect Personalizing of Nature in the creation of Gods and Demi-gods	10
7.	Illustrations of unconsciousness of sin in Sexual Love, and of nonbelief in a supernatural state of Rewards and Punishments	13
8.	Illustrations of the feeling of Family kinship, and of patriotic devotion to the Fatherland	15
9.	What was the origin of the Legend of which the symbolic truth is thus disproved?	16
10.	A suggestive proximity of localities, and synchronism of dates	17
11.	The fact of survival to be more fully illustrated before investigating the cause	18

SECTION II.

PAGAN SANCTUARIES AND FOLK-SONG SCENES.

The sites of the Ancient Sanctuaries, centres of origin of the Modern Songs - - - - 20

Analytical Table of Contents.

SUB-SECTION I.—ALBANIA.

		PAGE
1.	The Glen of Dodona, and its ruined later Temples	21
2.	The primitive Sanctuary imaginatively restored	22
3.	The Holy Places of Epeiros, and their systematic relations	23
4.	The Acherusian Plain, and the Vergilian localities of the New Ilion	24
5.	The strath of Ioánnina, the Hellopía of Hesiod, and Hellas of Aristotle	25

SUB-SECTION II.—THESSALY.

1.	Roumanian Mézzovo, and the Zygos Pass from Illyria into Thessaly	27
2.	The Mid-air Monasteries as Historical Monuments	28
3.	The Upper and Lower Plains of Thessaly and their enclosing Hills	29
4.	Olympus on its Thessalian and Macedonian sides	31
5.	The Seat of two Races of Men and Sanctuary of two Orders of Gods	32

SUB-SECTION III.—MACEDONIA.

1.	The range of Olympus, and the variety of its aspects as seen from Salonica	34
2.	Salonica, and the Homeric Rhapsodist of its Kallameriá Gate	35
3.	The original Macedonia, the upland Glens west of the Axius	36
4.	The Promontory of the Holy Mountain and its Monasteries	37
5.	Samothrace, and surviving relics of the worship of the Kábeiri	39

The wonder and interest of the survival of Paganism above illustrated - - - - 41

SECTION III.

THE CAUSE OF THE SURVIVAL OF PAGANISM.

1. The history of professed Creeds not the history of Religion - - - - 42
2. The problem presented by the Overthrowal, yet Survival and Revival of Paganism - - - 44
3. The New Theory of the 'Unity of History,' and of European-Asian Civilization - - - 45
4. The Sixth Century B.C. the true division between Ancient and Modern History - - - 47
5. The general explanation given of the origin of Christianity by the facts of the Revolution of the Sixth Century B.C. - - - - 49
6. The five elements of contemporary sentiment and thought which Christianity succeeded in combining - - - - - - 52
7. The general philological and historical proof of the Semitic character of the Christian God-idea - 54
8. This proved also by the difference between the Christian and the Neo-Platonic Trinity, and struggle of the Neo-Platonists against Christianity 56
9. And by the history of the influence of Neo-Platonism on Christian Theology - - - - 58
10. Further verifications indicated of the suggested cause of Survival - - - - 60
11. The provisional utility of the Semitic God-idea of Christianity, but return now to the God of our Aryan Forefathers - - - - 62

NOTE BY THE TRANSLATOR - - - - 65

Analytical Table of Contents. xi

METRICAL TRANSLATIONS.

CLASS I.—MYTHOLOGICAL FOLK-SONGS.

SECTION I.

IDYLLIC.

	PAGE
The Sunborn and Hantseri	69
The Siren and the Seamen	74
The Shepherd and the Lamia	75
The Stoicheion and the Widow's Son	76
The Stoicheion and Yanni	78
Yanni and the Drakos	79
The Witch of the Well	80
The Witch Mother-in-Law	81
The Bridge of Arta	81
The Enchanted Deer	83
The Sun and the Deer	85
The Black Racer	86
The Shepherd and the Wolf	87
The Swallows' Return	88
The Bird's Complaint	89
The First of May	90
The Soldier and the Cypress Tree	91
The Apple Tree and the Widow's Son	92
The River and the Lover	92
Olympos and Kissavos	93

SECTION II.

CHRISTIAN.

For the Feast of the Christ-Births	94
Saint Basil, or the New Year	96
The Feast of the Lights, or Epiphany	97
Vaia, or Palm Sunday	98

	PAGE
Ode to the Seven Passions	99
For the Great Friday	101
The Resurrection	104
The Miracle of St. George	104
The Vow to St. George	107
Procession for Rain	108
The Visit to Paradise and Hell	109

SECTION III.

CHARONIC.

The Moirai	111
Charon and his Mother	111
Charon's Wedding-Feast for his Son	112
Charon and the Souls	113
Charon and the Young Wife	114
Charon and the Shepherd	115
The Jilted Lover and Charon	116
Zahos and Charon	117
The Rescue from Charon	118
The River of the Dead	119
Dirge for a Father	120
Dirge for a House-Mistress	121
Dirge for a Son	121
Dirge for a Daughter	122
Dirge for a Sister	123
Dirge for a Young Husband	124
The Young Widow	124
The Dead Son to his Mother	125
The Vampire	126
Thanásé Vághia	129

CLASS II.—AFFECTIONAL FOLK-SONGS.

SECTION I.

EROTIC.

	PAGE
The Fruit of the Apple-Tree	133
The Neglected Opportunity	134
The Wooer	135
The Lover's Dream	136
The Nuns	137
The Despairful One	138
Elenáki, the Nightingale	138
The Last Request	139
The Lover's Return	140
The Widow's Daughter	140
The Partridge	141
The Discovered Kiss	142
The Rake	143
The Woman-Hunter	143
The Forsaken One	144
The Vlach Shepherdess Unkind	145
The Vlach Shepherdess Kind	146
The Black-Eyed One	146
The Lover	147
Fair Ones and Dark Ones	148
Blue-Eyed and Dark-Eyed Ones	149
The Blue-Eyed Beauty	149
The Garden	150
Yanneótopoula	150
The Little Bird	151
The Cypress	152
The Broken Pitcher	152
Distichs	153
The Bulgarian Girl and the Partridge	153
The Rose-Tree	154
The Green Tree	155

SECTION II.

DOMESTIC.

SUB-SECTION I.—EARLY MARRIED LIFE.

	PAGE
For the Throning of the Bride	157
For the Bride's Departure	158
For the Young Bridegroom	159
The Wife's Dream	159
The Husband's Departure	160
The Exiled Bird	161
The Absent Husband	162
The Husband's Return	163

SUB-SECTION II.—LULLABIES AND NURSERY RHYMES.

Lullabies I.—IX.	165
Nursery Rhymes I.—VIII.	170

SUB-SECTION III.—LATER MARRIED LIFE.

The Parson's Wife	175
The Forsaken Wife	176
The Sale of the Wife	177
Maroúla, the Divorced	178
The Old Man's Bride	179
The Old Man's Spouse	180
Yannakos, or the Assassinated Husband	180
The Child Slayer	182

SECTION III.

HUMOURISTIC.

The Dance of the Maidens	184
The Feast	185
The Janissary	186
The Tree	186
The Wineseller	187
The Gallants	188

Analytical Table of Contents. xv

	PAGE
The Dream	188
The Refusal	189
The Lemon-Tree	190
The Hegoumenos and the Vlach Maiden	191
The Bulgarian Girl	191
The Wooer's Gift	192
The Shepherd's Wife	193
The Klephts	194
The Thief turned Husbandman	196

CLASS III.—HISTORICAL FOLK-SONGS.

SECTION I.

PASHALIC.

The Sack of Adrianople	199
The Capture of Constantinople	200
The Child-Tax	201
Dropolitissa	202
Night-School Song	202
The Sea-Fight and the Captive	203
Serapheim of Phanári	204
The Slave	206
Metsoïsos	207
Christos Milionis	209
Syros	210
Satir Bey	212
The Capture of Lárissa and Tírnavo	213
Soulieman Pashína	214
Noutso Kontodemos	214

SECTION II.

SOULIOTE.

Koutsonika	216
Lambros Tzavelas	217

Analytical Table of Contents.

	PAGE
The Capture of Preveza	219
The Monk Samuel	220
Evthymios Vlachavas	228
Moukhtar's Farewell to Phrosýne	233
The Capture of Gardiki	234
The Klepht Vrykolakas	236
Despo of Liakatá	237
The Exile of the Parghiots	238

SECTION III.
HELLENIC.

Zito Hellas!	240
Kostas Boukoválas	241
The Klepht's Farewell to his Mother	243
The Klepht's Wintering	245
The Klephts Awaiting the Spring	246
Haidee	247
The Lovelorn Klepht	248
The Death of the Klepht	248
Sabbas the Armatole	250
Diákos the Armatole	250
The Siege of Missolonghi	252
Nasos Mantalos	253
The Battle of Kalabáka	254
Kapitan Basdékis	255
Themistocles Doumouzos	257

APPENDIX.

BIBLIOGRAPHY OF GREEK FOLK-LORE - - 259

ERRATA.

P. xxviii. *For* ῎χω, *read* ἴχω ; *and for* νά, νὰ.
P. 8. love, that is, not mere lust—*delete* second comma.
P. 8, n. 13. *For* Bulgaresa, *read* Bulgares.
P. 21, n. 2. *For* δυσχειμέρον, *read* δυσχειμέρου.
P. 23. *For* κλιήζετε, *read* κλήζετε.
P. 44, n. 1. *After* DEMOSTHÉNES, *insert* (*in Neær*. 1504, 157, Bekker) ; *for* Τὰς ἑταίρας ἔχομεν ἡδονῆς ἕνεκα, *read* Τὰς μὲν γὰρ ἑταίρας ἡδονῆς ἕνεκ' ἔχομεν ; *and add to end of sentence* γνησίως.
P. 65. *For* 'Ολίμπου, *read* 'Ολύμπου.
P. 90. Third line from foot, *for* his, *read* her.
P. 104. *For* ἀνέστι, *read* ἀνέστη.
P. 115. *For* young levente, *read* strapping shepherd ; *and for* levente, *further down, read* young hero.
P. 153. *For* ootprint, *read* footprint.
In the BIBLIOGRAPHY *insert*—
BENT.—*The Cyclades, or Life among the Insular Greeks*, 1885.
For PASHELY, *read* PASHLEY ; *and insert*—
POLITES.—Νεοελλήνικη Μυθολογία.
THIERSCH.—*Das Volksleben der Neugriechen*.
WACHSMUTH.—*Hellenischer Alterthumskunde*.

Histories, but of the General History of Civilization. Nor is this an inference merely from the greater scope of the New Antiquarianism. Invaluable as the greater

b

generalizations of the New Philosophy of History may be as suggestive hypotheses, they have always been more or less influenced by the conventional views of the educated class to which the Philosopher has belonged. Historical generalizations, therefore, thus influenced, and yet dealing with large historical facts of Belief and Conduct, cannot but be importantly corrected, if not altogether recast, if the evidence as to Belief and Conduct is sought, not merely, as usually hitherto, in Literature, but also, and even more assiduously, in the realities of Folk-life, and the records of Folk-lore. It is this view and aim, less or more distinctly defined, that has always guided my historical studies, and that has recently led me to the study more especially of Greek Folk-songs. And some results of this study will be found indicated in the following Historical Essay on *The Survival of Paganism.*

But those Nationalist Antiquarian Researches had results far more important than even the rewriting of National Histories. It is to these Researches that are due, if not the kindling, certainly all the consuming power, of those aspirations to National Freedom and National Unity, which have been the most revolutionary Political Forces of the century, and which are certainly not even yet played out. Nor will the New Antiquarianism which, in the intellectual sphere, will cause the rewriting, not of mere National Histories, but of the General History of Civilization, be wanting in results correspondingly great in the political sphere. Histories of Civilization which take due account of the results of the Comparative Science of Folk-life and Folk-lore, will be distinctively theories of Economic Development ; and the Political Forces, to which these theories will give at once revolutionary heat and determined direction, will aim not merely at National Resurrections, but at Economic Reconstructions. The former must precede the latter; and it is, I confess, but for the sake of the latter that I would do what in me lies to promote the former.

Now, of all National Resurrections, that one which will, I believe, most profoundly aid general Economic Reconstruction, is the Resurrection of the Greeks. Nor do I think so only because of the position occupied by the Greeks in the Levant, their progressive spirit, and their great commercial and administrative ability. I think so because general Economic Reconstruction there cannot be without general Intellectual Progress; and because the Greeks—admirably Pagan still as their Folk-songs prove—are, beyond all other East-European peoples, imbued with that spirit of synthetic Intuition and sceptic Curiosity which alone emancipates from enslaving Superstition; that Classic Spirit of which a Greek formulated the immortal axioms: 'Nature is not episodic in its phenomena, like a bad tragedy' (Οὐκ ἔοικε δ' ἡ φύσις ἐπεισοδιώδης οὖσα ἐκ τῶν φαινομένων ὥσπερ μοχθηρὰ τραγουδία—*Metaph.* XIII. iii.); and 'All men by nature reach forth to know' (Πάντες Ἄνθρωποι τοῦ εἰδέναι ὀρέγονται φύσει. — *Ibid.* I. i.). These are the grounds which should, I think, make Philhellenes of all who desire that general Intellectual Progress which is the condition of general Economic Reconstruction. Nor can the political advantage to Great Britain of so considerable a commercial and naval ally in the Mediterranean as a reconstituted Greece might be— nor can this political advantage be, for a British citizen, either an unimportant or unworthy additional reason for Philhellenism, if he has any due conception either of the Imperial duties of Great Britain, or of the position which England may take in the van of the Economic Revolution. These are the equally large and solid grounds of Philhellenism, and especially of British Philhellenism. And hence, not only would I hope, by this work, to contribute some further suggestions, at least, to the New Philosophy of History, the theory of the General History of Civilization; but to contribute also, in some degree, to the renewal of British Philhellenism, and to the completion of Hellenic Independence.

Such being the philosophical, and more particularly the political aim of the Book, as, indeed, indicated by its *Dedication,* a few remarks may, perhaps, be desirable with respect to the Policy that should, as I venture to think, be followed in giving political effect to Philhellenic sympathies. And first of all, negatively to define this Policy. It will certainly not be the Policy hitherto of 'Liberals'—the Policy of the 'European Concert.' No doubt, there does exist a 'European Concert.' But this 'Concert' is very far as yet from being of a 'millennial' character. Its two chief actual objects, so far as Europe is concerned, are these: first, to suppress the Socialist Revolution menacing, and justly menacing, the very foundations of our present ' Social Order ;' and secondly, what here chiefly concerns us, to prevent such an enlargement of Greece, however just, as would be inimical to the diverse, yet, in this, common interests, not indeed of the Peoples, but of the Governing Factions, of Germany and Austria, of Russia, of Italy, and of France. Never, therefore—never, at least, till all other imbecilities were outdone by the Egyptian blindness and blundering of a Government tolerated only with the hope of Home Reforms—never was there such a piece of contemptible sentimentalism, or still more contemptible hypocrisy, as the pretence of being able to obtain justice for Greece

Political and Linguistic. xxi

through the 'European Concert.' The events of the spring of 1881 verified what I wrote to this effect in the autumn of 1880. The Powers who hope to benefit by the expulsion of Pashas from Europe were, notwithstanding their treacherous 'invitation,' as opposed as the Porte itself to conceding to Greece more than, at most, the Plains of Thessaly, and these only with an indefensible frontier. The 'Naval Demonstration' was, therefore, a grotesque, saved only from becoming a tragical farce, by complete abandonment of the boundary about which this futile bounce was made. And our sentimental or hypocritical statesmen were only too glad to get out of their difficulties by accepting a slight enlargement of Turkey's long-offered concessions in the Thessalian Plains.

In a long series of Letters contributed, in 1880 and 1881, to the *Manchester Guardian* and the *Glasgow Herald*, I endeavoured to show that the true solution of the Greek Question was to be found, not in that proposed annexation of Epeiros to the Kalamas which, as my inquiries proved, would certainly have excited strong anti-Hellenic feeling, and been resisted by the Albanians; but in such a Greco-Albanian Confederation as I had already suggested in 1879 in my *Europe and Asia*, and illustrated in the politico-ethnographical map published therewith. Such a Confederation I maintained to be the first condition of the enfranchisement of Northern Greece from the Turkish, and of its salvation from a Slavonic yoke. For it would not only give at once to Greece an army of hereditary fighters, and a position on the flank of every anti-Hellenic movement in Macedonia; but ultimately, as north-western frontier, not the Kalamas, which cuts in half the Greek-speaking population of Albania, but such a true ethnographical boundary as, uniting the racially and linguistically akin Greeks and Albanians of a New Hellas, would divide them from the racially and linguistically alien Montenegrins and Bosnians of a Great Servia. The encouragement and support, therefore, of Greek efforts towards such a Greco-Albanian Confederation—and, first of all, by the re-establishment of the Consulates at Ioánnina and Monastír, abolished by 'Liberal' economy—should be the first plank of a British Philhellenic Policy. And, as in keeping only with that shameful ignorance of knowable, or still more shameful denying of known facts, which has characterized the whole history of that disastrous Foreign Policy of the Gladstone Administration which—not only when we think of the Transvaal, of Egypt, and of the Soudan, but of what this Gladstonian Policy has tolerated, and of what it has prepared—may be summed up in three words, *War with Dishonour*—as in keeping only with such a Policy of imbecility, the Policy of the 'European Concert,' as a means of obtaining justice for Greece, will be dismissed with deserved contempt, while maintaining, however, of course, as long as possible the European Peace.

With reference to the Policy of a Greco-Albanian Confederation, one or two notes on the ethnographical relations of Greeks and Albanians may not be out of place. North of Tepeléni—famous as the original lordship of the great Albanian hero, Alí Pashá—we find pure Albanian spoken, with but one or two small districts in which Greek is the common language, and a few Vlach villages in which Roumanian as well as Albanian is spoken. But the whole country south of Tepeléni is Greek-speaking with certain large districts in which Albanian as well as Greek, and certain small districts in which Roumanian as well as Greek, is spoken.

Political and Linguistic. xxiii

The more usual, or tripartite division of Albania and the Albanians, is a tribal, rather than, like that by a line through Tepeléni, a linguistic division. Upper or Northern Albania is the country of the Ghegs, with Scodra, or Scútari as their capital. Middle Albania is the country of the Tosks, with Berat as their capital. And Lower or Southern Albania—the ancient *Epeiros*, or 'Continent,' of the inhabitants of the islands lying off it—is the country of the Tzames with—but here one comes on a burning question: for of Southern Albania, in its general sense, Ioánnina is, geographically, the capital, but ethnographically, it is a Greek rather than Albanian town. Those of the Albanians who are Muslims belong, for the most part, to the exceedingly rationalistic order of the Bektashí Dervishes. And finally, Albanian bears a closer relation to Greek than to any other language; nor is the difference between them comparable to that between the Gaelic and Scotch of the Highlanders and Lowlanders of that Keltic Albania (*Albain* or *Albanach*) which, in the eleventh century—the same, very singularly, in which the former Illyrians were first spoken of as Albanians (τὸ τῶν Ἀλϛανων ἔθνος)—first began to be called Scotland.

Having thus defined the philosophical aim, and indicated the policy by which, as I think, effect may best be given to the political aim, of this Collection of Greek Folk-songs, I would now make a few remarks, not indeed on the *Translations*, of which Miss Garnett will herself say all that is necessary, but on the Language of which they are renderings.

The Originals are in a *patois* of which some of the characteristics will presently be noted. But it is important, first, to point out that, as spoken by an educated contemporary Greek, the Language, of which this *patois* is a rustic dialect, differs less, in its grammatical forms, from that of the Homeric Rhapsodists of nearly three millenniums ago, than the Language of an educated contemporary Englishman differs from that of Chaucer, only half a millennium ago. There are, it is true, great and important differences between Classical and Modern Greek, both in vocabulary and in syntax—differences which I shall presently state, or rather summarize (p. xxviii.), and which the student, who cares to go into more detail, will easily find out for himself by comparing the Alexandrian Greek of the *New Testament* with Attic Greek on the one side, and Romaic Greek on the other. But it is now more than thirty years since Professor Blackie first forcibly pointed out that the Neo-Hellenic of Tricoupis is but such a Dialect of Greek as the Ionic of Homer, or Doric of Theocritus; and that, great as are the changes in English pronunciation since even Chaucer's time, the accent in Greek is still on the very syllables accented by the grammarians of the days of the Ptolemies, more than two thousand years ago. Not even yet, however, is this fact generally realized, if indeed, known. This is chiefly due, I believe, to the thoroughly false views of European History generally prevalent. And hence it is by indicating, at least, what will, as I think, be found to be somewhat truer historical views, that the reader will be most readily enabled to understand, and hence realize the fact that, while Italian, for instance, differs from Latin, as a new Language, or new *genus*, Modern differs from Classical Greek as but a new Dialect, or new *species*.

The unity which, as shown in the *Introduction* is, for the first time, given to European-Asian History by the substitution of the natural Epoch of the General Revolution of the Sixth Century B.C. for the supernatural Era of the birth of Jesus—this unity, like every unity of Evolution, is a unity, not of identity, but of correlative differences. For if the Sixth Century B.C. shows a general similarity in the great movements of Human Development both in Asia and in Europe, it shows also, as pointed out in the *Introduction* (p. 49), the origination then of a profound difference between the Civilizations of Europe and of Asia. And so it is also in the case of European Civilization considered by itself. Immortal as the *Decline and Fall* must be, the history of Europe is not truly, as to Gibbon, the history of the Roman Empire. No sooner had a general European Civilization been constituted—a civilization, not merely, as in the Classical Period (500 B.C.—1 A.C), of two European peninsulas, but, as in the succeeding Neo-Aryan Half-millennium (1 A.C.—500 A.C.), a Civilization extending from Britain to the Bosphorus—no sooner had such a general European Civilization been constituted than, under the nominal unity of the Roman Empire, there arose two distinctly different Civilizations—the Civilizations of Eastern and Western Europe, the Civilizations of the Greek and the Latin tongue : Civilizations different in every regard, economical and political, moral and religious, philosophical and literary. It is in the interaction of these two clearly differentiated Civilizations, and not in an appellation which, for nearly a thousand years, was little more than a mere vain and empty name, that the true unity is to be found of European Civilization. And the recognition of this differentiation and interaction may at least prepare us, if not to expect, to accept the fact of the utmost contrast between the history of the Greek, and the history of the Latin Language.

How it was that Greek remained a Living, while Latin became a Dead Tongue—how it was that the one lived on in a new Dialect, while the other gave place to a new Language, will be further clear on consideration of the following facts. Though, after the fall of the Western (470), the Eastern Empire was still called 'Roman,' so little was it in race and language 'Roman,' that the *Institutes* of Justinian had already, in the Sixth Century A.C., to be translated into Greek for popular use. During the thousand years between the fall of Rome and the fall of Constantinople (470—1453) Classical Greek continued to be the literary language of a State which, through the very loss of its provinces, became so much more nationally Greek that, when Constantine IX. died gloriously in the breach, defending not only his capital, but Christendom, from Mohammed the Conqueror, he was, though in name a Roman Emperor, in fact a Greek King. And just as the conditions of the Slavonian, and of the Frankish invasions and conquests had formerly been, so the conditions of the Ottoman invasions and conquests were now, such as to foster and fan rather than stifle and quench the flame of distinctive Greek life, and so prepared the Greeks to lead the way in those heroic movements of National Resurrection which made illustrious the close of the Eighteenth Century. For whereas, in the time of the Emperors, the polite was very different from the popular dialect—as we know from the two poems in that dialect which the monk Theodore Ptochoprodromos addressed to the Emperor Manuel (1143)—and no effort was made to approximate them; yet now, in the general enslavement, such an effort was vigorously made by patriotic Greeks, and its success was greatly aided by the invention, at this time, of printing.

Among the results of these patriotic exertions to amalgamate the Greeks by assimilating their polite and popular dialects may be mentioned the *Church History* of Meletius, Bishop of Athens (d. 1714); the Romance of Kornaro entitled *Erotocritus* (1737); and the translation of the *Arabian Nights* (1792). This movement was brought to a climax by Adamantinos Koraes of Smyrna (b. 1748). Since the establishment of the Greek Kingdom, there has been a sustained effort, in the reverse direction, towards the reclassicalising of the Language. But still, by poets not of the people, and notably by Valaorites (b. 1824), the popular dialects, and especially the Epirote *patois*, have been largely used for poetry. Such are some of the general facts which may enable the reader not only to recognise, but in some degree also, perhaps, to understand, that identity of Modern, with Classical, Greek speech, which not only connects, as with a living bond, the Present with the Classical Period, but serves also to explain that wonderful identity of Modern with Classical Greek sentiment which he will find in the following Translations.

And now with respect more particularly to that *patois* of Modern Greek of which these Translations are renderings. It is in the Epirote *patois* that most of the Folk-songs here translated have been composed. For among rustic dialects of Greek, that of Southern Albania holds much the same place as, among rustic dialects of English, that of Southern Scotland. There is this difference, however, between the two cases: to Burns, who made the English *patois* of Southern Scotland classical, this *patois* was his mother tongue; while to Valaorites, who made the Greek *patois* of Southern Albania classical, it was, from the circumstances of his birth and education, rather his nurse's than his mother's tongue, and hence his acquaintance with it had, in after life, to be perfected by special effort. By no means, however, on this account, is the Epirote of Valaorites more easy than that of the nameless popular bards who spontaneously utter in that dialect their 'native woodnotes wild.' On the contrary, it is so labouredly rustic as to be more difficult than the genuinely rustic speech itself. But M. de Queux de St. Hilaire, in his Introduction to M. Blancard's Translations of Valaorites' *Poèmes Patriotiques*, goes, perhaps, too far when he says of his author's poetical language that it is as remote from the true popular, as from the new literary language—' Cette langue populaire s'éloigne autant de la langue littéraire .... que de la langue aussi factice et idiomatique que Valaorites voulait remettre en honneur.'

The *patois* of these Folk-songs may be generally characterized as simply carrying a stage or two further those differences which distinguish from Classical Greek, the Modern Greek of educated speakers. The latter, as is well known, differs from the former in the loss of tenses by the verb—the use of the auxiliaries $\theta \acute{\epsilon} \lambda \omega$ and $\H{\chi}\omega$ for the future and perfect, and of $\nu \acute{a}$ ($\mathit{i}\nu a$) instead of the infinitive—and the loss of cases by the noun—the genitive and dative being confused with the accusative. And not only thus, as to grammar, but as to words, Modern differs from Classical Greek in these various ways: in the ordinary use of what were formerly poetical words; in the use of old words with new meanings; in the curtailment of words; in the lengthening of words, particularly for diminutives; and in the importation of new words from all the languages with which the Greeks as a people have been brought into contact—Latin, Slavonian, Italian, Albanian, and Turkish.

Now, in the *patois* of these Folk-songs all these differences as to grammar and as to words between ordinary Modern and Classical Greek are exaggerated, and there are besides some interesting peculiarities of pronunciation rather than of words. These consist either in the elision, or in the change, not only of vowels, but of consonants. In certain districts ν, and in others ρ, is elided; in certain districts, κ is substituted for τ, and in others, ρ for λ. And particularly remarkable in this respect is the difference between the *patois* of the storm-secluded old Pelasgian island of Samothrace; and the *patois* of the adjoining mainland of Thrace and Macedonia, where Greeks are mixed with Bulgarians. In Samothrace, there is an elision of the harsh ρ in the words in which it usually occurs; while on the mainland a rasping ρ seems to be preferred to a liquid λ, and one hears the natives address each other as ἀδερφέ, instead of ἀδελφέ! The result of these peculiarities, added to the exaggeration of all the differences that distinguish educated Modern from Classical Greek, is, that one who can read the Modern Greek of Athens with ease, may find very great difficulty with the Greek of the Folk-songs; while one who can easily read the Greek of the Folk-songs may be almost wholly unable to understand the Literary Greek of Athens. But just so a foreigner, perfectly familiar with Literary English, would be unable to understand Broad Scotch, or the Lancashire, or East Anglian Dialects, either spoken, or written phonetically with all their elisions and transmutations.

One word, in conclusion, with reference to the *motto* I have chosen from the Gaelic *Sgeulachan*, translated by the late Mr. Campbell of Islay. It may, perhaps, be found to be not without appropriateness. For the occurrence in Gaelic Folk-stories of the ' Tale of the King of

Greece' has, I believe, an historical, as well as poetic, significance. Philologists have now proved that Keltic has the closest affinities with Greek and Latin—Kymric more particularly, perhaps, with the former, and Gaelic with the latter—and hence that Kelts, Greeks, and Latins probably derived their origin from a primitive Greco-Kelto-Italic stock—a stock which we may possibly be able to identify with the Pelasgians whose more direct representatives now Von Hahn believed to be the Albanians. Among the chief events of the Classical Period, or half-millennium before Christ, were the Keltic invasions, not only of the countries occupied by their ancient kinsmen in Italy and in Greece, but invasions also of Macedonia, Thrace, and Asia Minor, in which last they established their kingdom of Galatia. It is these historical relations with the Greeks that have, I believe, given rise to the Gaelic 'Tale of the King of Greece.' For the history of the Kelts as a great European Race has been as continuous as that of the Hellenes themselves since the upbreak of the Ancient Civilizations in the Sixth Century B.C. Dating the history of Modern Civilization from that great Epoch, it is found to be divisible into five clearly distinguishable half-millennial Periods. And each of these Periods in the history of European-Asian Civilization, is characterized by a special class of events in the history of the Keltic Race. The first Period is, for it, a Period of Conquests; the second, of Subjections; the third, of Northern Kingdoms; the fourth, of Subversions; and the fifth, of Resurrections. These facts, and particularly the last class of them, do not, I think, verify the somewhat petulant iterations of a certain learned and lucid, but not unprejudiced historian, that the great English-speaking is an Anglo-Saxon, or English, and not, as it truly is, an Anglo-Keltic Race.

We, therefore, as such a Race, in aiding the Greeks, aid the representatives of the near, if not nearest, kinsmen of our Keltic ancestors. And it is curious to remark that the most distinguished of English-speaking Philhellenes—the most distinguished of those who have sought to deliver from bondage 'Beauty, the daughter of the King of Greece'—have, almost all, had in their veins a more than usual proportion of that Keltic blood which is common to the whole Britannic Race.

HISTORICAL INTRODUCTION.

> '*The Oracles are dumb:*
> *No voice or hideous hum*
> *Runs through the archéd roof in words deceiving;*
> *Apollo from his shrine*
> *Can no more divine*
> *With hollow shriek the steep of Delphos leaving.*
> *No nightly trance, or breathéd spell*
> *Inspires the pale-eyed priest from the prophetic cell.*'
>
> MILTON : *Ode on the Nativity.*

> '*Though the feet of thine high-priests tread where thy lords and our forefathers trod,*
> *Though these that were Gods are dead, and thou being dead art a God,*
> *Though before thee the throned Cytherean be fallen, and hidden her head,*
> *Yet thy kingdom shall pass, Galilean, thy dead shall go down to thee dead.*'
>
> SWINBURNE : *Hymn to Proserpine.*

THE SURVIVAL OF PAGANISM.

SECTION I.

THE FACT OF THE SURVIVAL OF PAGANISM.

1. IN Plutarch's Dialogue 'On the Cessation of Oracles,'[1] Kleómbrotos, the Lacedæmonian, who had been travelling in Egypt and the Soudan,[2] and who had met, among others, at Delphi, the Grammarian, Demetrius of Tarsus, who had been travelling in Britain, at the opposite end of the Roman world[3]—this Kleómbrotos informs the company that Æmilian, the Rhetorician, had told him a wonderful story touching the mortality of Dæmons. On a voyage made by his father, Epitherses, to Italy, when they were still not far from the Echinádes Islands, the wind fell, and they were drifting in the evening towards the Islands of Paxi. Then, suddenly, as the passengers were drinking after supper, a voice was heard from one of the islands, calling on a certain Thamus so loudly as to fill all with amazement. This Thamus was an Egyptian pilot, known by name to but few on board. Twice the voice called him without response, but the third time he replied; and then the voice said, ' *When thou comest over against Palódes, announce that the great Pan is dead.*' On hearing this, all were terrified, and debated whether it were better to do as ordered, or not to trouble themselves

[1] *De Def. Orac.*, xvii.
[2] Περὶ τὴν Τρωγλοδυτικὴν γῆν.
[3] Τῆς οἰκουμένης.

4 Historical Introduction.

further about the matter. As for Thamus, he decided that if there should be a wind, he would sail past, and say nothing; but if it were a dead calm and smooth sea, he would give his message. When, therefore, they were come over against Palódes, there being neither breath of wind nor ripple of wave, Thamus, looking towards the land from the quarterdeck, proclaimed what he had heard: '*The great Pan is dead.*'[4] Hardly had he said this, when there arose a great and multitudinous cry of lamentation, mingled with amazement.[5] And as this had been heard by many persons, the news of it spread immediately on their arrival in Rome, and Thamus was sent for by the Emperor, Tiberius Cæsar. Such was the story of Æmilian, as reported by Kleómbrotos. As Æmilian was an 'old man' when he told the story, and as his father had flourished under Tiberius, the period of the 'Dialogue' would appear to be about the end of the first century A.C., in the reign of the Emperor Trajan. But as Tiberius died in 37 A.C., having succeeded his stepfather, Augustus, in 14 A.C., the date of this death of Pan has been plausibly assumed to coincide with that of the crucifixion of Christ.

2. Now, as it singularly chanced, one September day in 1880, it was amid the very scene of this romantic legend of the death of Pan—and certainly no more splendid scene could be imagined for such a legend than that vast mountain-girt sea-plain and gleaming land-locked bay identified with Palódes,[6] on the Albanian coast, opposite Corfu—it was in my boat in the bay, and while wandering over the plain of Vutzindró[7] (Βουντζιντρὸν), that an Epirote friend spoke to me of the recently-published ᾽Άσματα τοῦ ᾽Ηπείρου ('Songs of Epeiros'), collected by Dr. Aravandinos, of Ioánnina, and of which, next day, he was good enough to

---

[4] "Οτι ὁ μέγας Πὰν τέθνηκεν.
[5] Μέγαν οὐχ ἑνὸς ἀλλὰ πολλῶν στεναγμὸν, ἅμα θαυμασμῷ μεμεγμένον.
[6] Ptolemy, Plutarch, and the word itself, sufficiently identify Palódes with the muddy bay of Vutzindró.—LEAKE, *Northern Greece*, vol. i., p. 100.
[7] Once, perhaps, the property of Atticus, the friend of Cicero.—*Cicero ad Attic.*, l. iv., ep. 8.

The Survival of Paganism. 5

present me with a copy. Singularly it thus chanced. For this Plutarchian legend is often repeated or alluded to as a fact by mediæval authors, as also by Rabelais, by Spenser, and by Milton; its essential, if not formal, truth has, indeed, become almost an article of Christian faith; and yet the result of the modern study of Folk-lore—and the result more particularly in my own case of the studies occasioned by that conversation on the 'Songs of Epeiros' amid the scenes of this Epirote legend of the death of Pan —has been a conclusion directly contradictory of what has hitherto been the popular Christian belief with respect to the destruction of Paganism. That conclusion may be thus stated. Among the masses of the Greek people Christian Church-beliefs have not only not substituted themselves for, but have hardly even traceably influenced, Pagan Folk-beliefs; further, a comparison of the Folk-songs of the Greeks with the Folk-songs of other nominally Christian peoples shows that this non-penetration of professed Christian beliefs is not peculiar to, but only somewhat more conspicuous among, the Greeks; and hence, finally, we may affirm that, so far as concerned or concerns the masses of the Christian peoples, there was as little of essential as of formal truth in the legend of the mystic voice at Paxi, and of the multitudinous lamentation at Palódes. Or, as one may otherwise express it, the great Pan of Pagan writers is not, nor ever has been, dead; and neither the birth nor the death of the great Pan of Christian writers—'Christ, the very God of all shepherds, which calleth Himself the great and good Shepherd'[8] —neither the birth nor the death of Christ had the effect so fondly fancied by Christians, and so finely described in those famous lines of Milton's—

> 'The lonely mountains o'er,
> And the resounding shore,
> A voice of weeping heard and loud lament;

---

[8] E. K. (Edward Kirke) commenting on the line
 'When great Pan account of Shepherdes shall aske,'
in the *May Eclogue* of SPENSER'S *Shepherd's Calendar*.

From haunted spring and dale,
Edged with poplar pale,
The parting Genius is with sighing sent ;
With flower-inwoven tresses torn
The Nymphs in twilight shade of tangled thickets mourn.'[9]

3. Startled as some readers may be by the conclusion thus expressed, it may be desirable to give, or refer to, some passages confirmatory of it in Christian writers. 'At the outset,' remarks the Rev. Mr. Tozer,[10] 'we may say broadly that the beliefs of the modern Greeks respecting death and the state of the dead, so far as we have the means of judging of them, are absolutely and entirely Pagan. In

[9] *Ode on the Nativity*, s. xx. I venture to think that Professor Masson (*Milton's Poetical Works*, vol. iii., p. 356) is probably mistaken in imagining that

'A voice of weeping heard'

refers to the Massacre of the Innocents at the *birth* of the Christian Pan, and to Matt. ii. 18, and Jer. xxxi. 15; and not rather to the 'great cry of lamentation mingled with amazement' of the Plutarchian legend of the *death* of the Pagan Pan. It is true that 'the mighty Pan' of line 89 must be interpreted to refer to the Christian Pan. But the lines

'The lonely mountains o'er,
And the resounding shore,
A voice of weeping heard and loud lament,'

are not only, the last one, a tolerably close translation of Plutarch, but the first two a singularly graphic description of Palódes, the scene of the death of the Pagan, and no description at all of Bethlehem, the scene of the birth of the Christian Pan.

I may add that, as these lines can be construed only by such strained interpolations as the following :

'The lonely mountains o'er,
And [o'er] the resounding shore,
A voice of weeping [is] heard and loud lament,'

one is tempted to suggest 'hoar' for 'o'er.' This would not only be uncontradicted by any MS., but would be in accordance with Milton's usage in *Allegro*,

'From the side of some hoar hill ;'

and in the third song in *Arcades*,

'On old Lycæus and Cyllene hoar.'

But against such an emendation it is, I fear, a fatal objection that it would involve a change of tense from that of the context.
[10] *Highlands of Turkey*, vol. ii., p. 322.

The Survival of Paganism. 7

the numerous ballads which relate to these subjects there is not a trace of any features derived from Christian sources, while the old classical conceptions are everywhere manifest. It may be said, indeed, that in any country the views on the subject of religion which might be gathered from a collection of popular songs would be of a very questionable description, and would not fairly represent the beliefs of the people. But this objection does not apply to the modern Greek ballads, as they are the simple and straightforward expression of the ideas of an unlettered people on the points to which they refer. Some of the songs are intended for Christian festivals, others are dirges to be sung at funerals, and others relate to subjects akin to these. But in none of them does the belief in a Resurrection or a Future Judgment make itself apparent. That the people at large have no knowledge of those doctrines it is hard to believe; but, at all events, they have not a sufficiently firm hold on their minds to come prominently forward, and they certainly have not succeeded in expelling the old heathen notions. And if most of the figures which we associate with the Inferno of the Greeks, such as Pluto, Persephóné, Hermes, Kérberos, etc., are now wanting, it should be remembered that, in ancient times, the popular conceptions of such a subject were in all probability much simpler than the elaborate scheme which is found in the poets.' Similar conclusions are expressed by other scholars.[11] And Archbishop Whately affirms generally,[12] and with equally good reason, that 'the vulgar in most parts of Christendom are actually serving the Gods of their heathen ancestors. But they do not call them *Gods*, but Fairies or Bogies, and they do not apply the word *worship* to their veneration of them, nor *sacrifice* to their offerings. And this slight change of

---

[11] Compare PASSOW, *Carm. Pop. Præfatio;* FAURIEL, MARCELLUS, and LEGRAND, *Chants populaires de la Grèce;* and the books of THIERSCH, of SANDERS, and of SCHMIDT on the *Volksleben der Neugriechen.*
[12] *Miscellaneous Remains*, p. 274.

name keeps most people in ignorance of a fact that is before their eyes.'[13]

4. There is, however, something of superficiality in the Archbishop's notion of modern Paganism as showing itself only in a veneration of Bogies and Fairies. By characteristics of a far deeper and more general kind must Paganism, and particularly Western Paganism, be defined, if our study of Greek Folk-songs is to have any important historical result. In Western Paganism, whether as it flourished before, or as it has survived since, the destruction of its Sanctuaries, we find, I think, universally three General Characteristics, which may perhaps, be thus respectively distinguished: (i.) a profound feeling of oneness with Nature, and a mythic personalizing of its phenomena, inanimate as well as animate; (ii.) Unconsciousness of Sin in sexual love, that is, not mere lust, and non-belief in a supernatural state of Rewards and Punishments; and (iii.) a profound feeling of Family kinship, and patriotic devotion to the Fatherland. By characteristics of an exactly opposite kind would historical Christianism have to be distinguished. But here I must confine myself to pointing out some of the illustrations of these Pagan characteristics which the reader will find in the following Folk-songs.

5. First, then, as to the feeling of oneness with Nature, and the personalizing of its phenomena. The impressions produced by natural phenomena lead to their being personalized in two different ways—a direct way, and an indirect. Personalizing in the direct way, the Sun is represented as pityingly addressing a sad and lonely Deer;[14] or as angry with the Moon and Stars.[15] The Dawn is spoken of as a man whom alone a widow's daughter desires as husband.[16] The Moon weeps in sympathy with the sorrowing Virgin;[17] and is prayed to by a

[13] Compare, for instance, for the Teutonic Race, GRIMM'S *Deutsche Mythologie;* DASENT, *Popular Tales from the Norse;* and HENDERSON, *Folk-lore of the Northern Counties;*—and for the Slavonic Race, RALSTON, *Songs of the Russian People* and *Russian Folk-tales;* DOZON, *Poésies populaires Serbes,* and *Chansons populaires Bulgaresa;* NAAKE, *Slavonic Fairy-tales;* and CHODZKO, *Contes Slaves.*

[14] *Trans.,* p. 85.   [15] *Ib.* p. 112.   [16] *Ib.* p. 141.   [17] *Ib.* p. 101.

child going to a night-school,[18] in the bad times of unchecked Turkish oppression. The Stars are brimming with tears;[19] and the words used in speaking of the setting of the Morning-star, as likewise of the Sun—βασιλεύω and βασίλευμα—denote also reigning as a king.[20] One boastfully speaks of himself as the son of the Lightning, and of his wife as the daughter of the Thunder.[21] Mountains are asked questions and respond.[22] Proudly Olympus disputes with Kíssavos, and boasts of his glories; or, falling in love with his fellow mountain, now called by the feminine name of Ossa, they become the parents of the Klepht Vlachava;[23] whose head, when he is slain, his faithful dog carries to his mother Ossa, and buries in the snows of her bosom. Into Rivers lovers would fain transform themselves, and so consciously embrace their mistresses and rid themselves of the poison of passion.[24] Things inanimate of all kinds are represented as living— discovering the kiss of lovers;[25] asking questions of, and making requests to a saint;[26] or fascinated by a siren;[27] her pillow and couch sympathetically respond to the complaint of a forsaken wife;[28] a bridge is rent in twain and a stream ceases to flow on hearing the sad lament of a widow;[29] and a ship stops sailing, horrified at the groan of a prisoner.[30] Trees, and especially the Cypress,[31] Apple,[32] and Rose-tree;[33] and Fruits— Lemons,[34] and Apples;[35]—and Flowers—Basil and Carnation—are all endowed with human feeling and with speech; nay, by the blooming and withering of a Rose-tree and a Carnation,[36] a mother knows of the health, and finally of the death, of her son, a klepht on the mountains. It is Birds—Eagles,[37] Partridges[38] and Crows,[39] Cuckoos,[40] Blackbirds[41] and Nightingales[42]—who sing the dirges of the slain, or give warning to the living of death or betrayal; 'that he may have a gossip with Birds' (νἄχω μὲ τὰ πουλιὰ κουζέντα), the dying klepht begs that he may

---

[18] *Trans.* p. 202. [19] *Ib.* p. 101. [20] *Ib.* p. 79. [21] *Ib.* p. 80. [22] *Ib.* p. 93.
[23] *Ib.* p. 228. [24] *Ib.* p. 92. [25] *Ib.* p. 142. [26] *Ib.* p. 96. [27] *Ib.* p. 74.
[28] *Ib.* p. 176. [29] *Ib.* p. 125. [30] *Ib.* p. 203. [31] *Ib.* p. 91. [32] *Ib.* p. 92.
[33] *Ib.* p. 154. [34] *Ib.* p. 137. [35] *Ib.* p. 137. [36] *Ib.* p. 243. [37] *Ib.* p. 241.
[38] *Ib.* p. 214. [39] *Ib.* p. 254. [40] *Ib.* p. 253. [41] *Ib.* p. 253. [42] *Ib.* p. 199.

be carried up to a mountain-ridge;[43] a Bird, πουλί, bewails her hard fate in colloquy with a king's daughter;[44] a Partridge reproves an erring Bulgarian girl;[45] and an Owl heralds the approach of Vampires.[46] Finally, among Beasts, a Deer complains to the Sun of the cruel hunter who has killed her child and her husband;[47] a Horse understands the entreaties of his mistress, and wins a wager for his master;[48] and a Wolf, on being questioned by a shepherd, complains of having been illtreated by his dogs, when he was about to regale himself on a lamb.[49]

6. But besides this primitive and eternal poetry of the direct personalizing of Nature, animate and inanimate, there is also, in these Folk-songs, what may be called an indirect personalizing of Nature in the creation of Beings mythically representative both of universal and of special aspects of Nature—in the creation, in a word, of Gods and Demi-gods. The Fates (Μοῖραι) and Chance (Ριζικόν) still hold the same place as of old, as Powers above and behind all Gods.[50] But the most remarkable of all the mythical Beings mentioned in our Folk-songs are, perhaps, οἱ τρεῖς Στοιχειὰ τοῦ Κοσμοῦ—the three Elements (or Spirits) of the Universe.[51] 'I strongly suspect,' says the Rev. Mr. Tozer,[52] 'that here the underlying idea is that of the Holy Trinity.' And another writer, in alluding to these Stoicheia, speaks of them as 'the three Earth-Spirits, whoever they may be.' The song, however, in which they are mentioned belongs to Saloníca; Thessaloníca was famous for its worship of the Samothracian Kábeiri; and the Kabeirian God of Thessaloníca was adored as one of a Trinity of which the youngest had been put to death by the others.[53] I venture to think

[43] *Trans.* p. 256.   [44] *Ib.* p. 89.   [45] *Ib.* p. 154.   [46] *Ib.* p. 130.
[47] *Ib.* p. 85.   [48] *Ib.* p. 86.   [49] *Ib.* p. 87.   [50] *Ib.* p. 111.
[51] *Ib.* p. 75.   [52] *Highlands of Turkey*, vol. ii., p. 317, n.
[53] See Lactantius, Julius Firmicus Maternus, and Clement of Alexandria, as cited by Lenormant in DAREMBERG'S *Dictionnaire des Antiquités, Cabiri*, p. 769 *and fig.* This Christ-like personage appears as a young man on the coins of Thessalonica. And the story of his death, with the figures of the other members of the Kabeirian Trinity, is represented on the metallic mirrors of Etruria, which, in the second half of the fourth, and in the third century B.C., appears to have been strongly

that, in bringing these facts together, I have identified these Τρεῖς Στοιχεῖα τοῦ Κόσμου of Salonica with the Kabeirian Trinity of the Thessalonians. Next among the mythical personages of our Songs may be named Elioyénneté and Hántseri,[54] of whom the lay is an evident Sun-and-Moon myth, or Endymion-and-Seléné story. And next among the greater Gods of modern Greek Folk-life, and so holding a place similar to that of the God of the Underworld in the ancient Mythologies, is Charon. A Charon we find also among the ancient Etruscans,[55] and both names appear to have been derived from the Egyptian Horus;[56] though the emblems of Charon are those of a Kabeirian God. But it was not till the sixth century B.C. that there was sustained and general intercourse between Greece and Egypt.[57] Hence, it was not probably till about this date that Charon took his place in the imagination of the Greeks; hence, not till about the same time that the notion of the Devil got separated from that of God in the Hebrew Mythology.[58] And the reason of Charon being thus adopted as a Greek God or Demi-god, may be found partly in the fact that Hades could now be restricted to signifying a place, and not, as hitherto, both a place and a person.[59] But, in the old Aryan Mythologies,

---

affected by an influence proceeding from Macedonia and the Isles of the Thracian Sea. See GERHARD, *Ueber die Metallspiegel der Etrusker*, in his *Gesam. Akad. Abhandl.*, vol. ii.

[54] *Trans.* p. 69.   [55] See DENNIS, *Etruria*, vol. ii., pp. 182—191·3.
[56] See WILKINSON, *Ancient Egyptians*, vol. v., p. 433.
[57] This was in consequence of the establishment, by Psammetichus, of Greek mercenaries, Ionians and Karians, on the Pelusiac or eastern branch of the Nile, at a place called Stratopeda, or the Camps (HERODOTUS, ii. 154), and of the permission given by the same Pharaoh for the settlement of Greek merchants at Navkratis on the right bank of the Kanopic Nile. See GROTE, *History of Greece*, vol. ii., pp. 496-97, with respect to the apparently conflicting statements on this point of Herodotus and Strabo. But this introduction of Charon into the Greek Pantheon was but one of the lesser consequences of that opening of the Nile by Psammetichus of which the greater results made an epoch in Hellenic thought.
[58] Compare 1 *Kings* xxii.—iv. with 1 *Chron.* xxi.; and see ROSKOFF, *Geschichte des Teufels*, b. I., ss. 199-2126, REVILLE, *Histoire du Diable*, and GOLDZIEHER, *Mythology among the Hebrews*.
[59] *Trans.* pp. 116, 129.

there were a vast number of minor mythical Beings below the Universal Trinity of Heaven, Earth, and Hell, the Creator, the Preserver, and the Destroyer. Similarly, in the Neo-hellenic Mythology, below the modern representatives of these Greater Gods, there are a great number of minor poetic creations more or less obviously expressive of the impressions made by special natural phenomena. Among these, the following will be found in the Translations given below—Stoicheia[60] of Mountains, Rivers, and Wells; Nereides[61] of Rivers; Lamias[62] of the Ocean; the Tragoudistria,[63] or Siren; the Drakos[64] and Dra-

---

[60] *Trans.* p. 76, 78. Στοιχεῖον appears to be derived from στείχω, *to go*, especially, *to go after one another in line or order.* Hence, στοιχεῖον, may have originally signified that which moves. From this it would readily come to mean, as in present popular usage, 'the principle of life or spiritual power which lies concealed in every natural object, animate or inanimate.' Later, in Platonic and subsequent philosophic usage, στοιχεῖα means 'elements.' Plato's στοιχεῖα were ideas. Those of Empedocles were forms of matter, and he endeavoured to show that there were but four. In another usage of the word, the signs of the Zodiac were called στοιχεῖα, and the term seems to be used generally for the 'Heavenly Powers.' Such Biblical critics as, for instance, BAUR (*Christenthum*, s. 49) and HILGENFIELD (*Galaterbrief*, s. 66), are of opinion that it is certainly in this sense that St. Paul uses the phrase τὰ στοιχεῖα τοῦ κοσμοῦ, and that he attributes to these Genii, or Spirits of the Universe, a distinct personality. Compare *Gal.* iv. 3, etc.; *Col.* ii. 8, 20; and *Ephes.* vi. 12. The Revised Version, however, still retains the old translation of 'elements' or 'rudiments,' and so misses completely the true meaning of these passages. See GELDART, *Modern Greek*, pp. 201—5; and *The Gospel according to St. Paul*, pp. 25—5.

[61] *Ib.* p. 125. The Greek Nereids are unlike our Northern Fairies (see MAURY, *Fées du Moyen Age*) in being almost universally malevolent, and not diminutive, but full-grown women. They are, however, called καλαῖς κυράδες, or 'Good Ladies.' But we use a similar flattery when we exclaim 'Good God!' on anything happening particularly bad.

[62] *Ib.* p. 75. The Lamia of the Greek Islands seems to be connected with whirlwinds and waterspouts. The Lamia of PHILOSTRATUS (*De Vita Apollonii*) is a serpent in the shape of a woman. Different as they are, each of these Lamias is a mythical representation of a fact of human experience, and both convey the idea of serpentine motion. The Lamia of Keats is taken from the story of Philostratus, as told by BURTON, *Anatomy of Melancholy*, p. iii., s. ii.

[63] *Ib.* p. 74.

[64] *Ib.* p. 79. 'The Dragon of popular Mythology,' says Mr. Baring Gould, 'is no other than the thunderstorm rising at the horizon, rush-

The Survival of Paganism. 13

kissa;[65] the Panoukla,[66] or Plague; and Theria,[67] or Monsters. And in yet another class must be named such creations as Digenes,[68] and the Enchanted Deer—a Christianized version, apparently, of the story of Agamemnon and the Sacred Hind of Artemis; Máyissas,[69] or Witches, sometimes of a thousand years old; and most terrible, though not the last of all,[70] Vampires,[71] or Animated Corpses.

7. So far as to the first characteristic of the following Folk-songs. Now, as to that unconsciousness of Sin in sexual love, and nonbelief in a supernatural state of Rewards and Punishments, which we next remark. For striking illustrations of the former characteristic, I may refer the reader more particularly to the *Vow to St. George*, and to *Yánnakos, or the Assassinated Husband*, and to the *Erotic* and *Humouristic* Songs generally.[72] Indeed, in the two songs particularized, there seems to be no consciousness of sin, even in such infamous incidental crimes as rape and murder. In the *Vow to St. George*, the Saint is represented as bribed by a Christian maiden

---

ing with expanded, winnowing black pennons across the sky, darting out its forked fiery tongue, and belching fire.'—*Werewolves*, pp. 172, *and flg.* There may also, however, be in the notion some reminiscence of the monsters of the primeval world. See the author's *At a Highland Hut, Fraser's Magazine*, October, 1874.

[65] *Trans.* p. 79. [66] *Ib.* p. 204. [67] *Ib.* p. 78. [68] *Ib.* p. 83.
[69] *Ib.* pp. 80, 81. AFANASIEF, *On the Poetic Views of the Old Slavonians*, interprets Witches also—very questionably however, I think—as originally Nature-myths. See RALSTON, *Russian Folk-tales*.

[70] Though not mentioned in the following Folk-songs, there are such other frightful creations of the popular fancy, as the Empusa, Mormo, Gorgo and Gello, etc. See B. SCHMIDT, *Volksleben*.

[71] Vampire-tales flourish most luxuriantly among races of Slavonic descent, and it is from Slavs that the Greeks have borrowed both the name, and certain views and customs with respect to Vampires. But the Vampire bears a thoroughly Hellenic designation in the Islands—at Crete and Rhodes being called καταχανᾶς; in Cyprus, σαρκωμένος; and in Tinos, ἀναικαθούμενος. And a number of passages may be quoted from classic authors to prove that in Ancient Greece spectres were frequently represented as delighting in blood. See B. SCHMIDT, *Volksleben der Neugriechen*, ss. 168—171; and RALSTON, *Russian Folk-tales*, p. 319. See also PASHLEY, *Travels in Crete*. Trans. 126, 129.

[72] *Trans.* pp. 184 *and flg.*

to hide her from a pursuing Turkish lover, and as discovering her place of concealment on being more largely bribed by the Turk. In *Yánnakos*, a lover prays to God Himself that he may find a husband 'in bed, in his shirt, and ungirt with his sword,' and 'as he had prayed, so he found Yánnakos.' And in the *Humouristic Songs*, we find either the incontinence of monks and nuns satirically treated as a matter of course; or the consequences of attempted continence are satirized in language that cannot be reproduced[73]—yet quite justly, as the experiences of my sojourn on the Holy Mountain proved.[74] As for unbelief in a supernatural state of Rewards and Punishments, every one of the pieces in the section I have named *Charonic* may be cited in evidence. To die is simply to be carried off from home and friends, and all the joys of ὁ ἀπάνω κόσμος, the Upper World, by the remorseless Charon. The Earth, which is sometimes spoken of as the Mother of Charon, is also identified with him: and hence, in the dialect of Epeiros, one says for 'he died' either τόν ἔφαγεν ἡ Γῆς, or τόν ἔφαγεν ὁ Χάρος—'The Earth,' or 'Charon ate him.' The abode to which Charon bears off the souls of mortals, when he does not 'eat' them, is sometimes represented as an Underground Region to which there is a descent by stairs;[75] and sometimes it is spoken of, with significant allegory, as a Tent, either green or red outside, but always black within.[76] As for the Dead, they are represented, in general, as Shades as pale and mournful as in

[73] As, for instance, in the last half dozen lines of *Yanni*, ARAVANDINOS, 367. See also OIKONOMIDES, B. 8, 10, 11, etc.
[74] I allude more particularly to the Confessions with which I was favoured by a monk with whom I had opportunities of becoming rather intimate. The poor wretch had had the doctrine of Hell so ground into him, that he really believed he would be eternally damned for his intrigues with country wenches, when managing the farms of his convent in the island of Thasos, and on the mainland. He could not, however, see any real sin in what seemed to him still so natural; and he consoled himself with the reflection that his future torments would be as nothing compared with those of his brethren who preferred more cultured, indeed, but unnatural, objects of passion.
[75] *Trans.* p. 117.   [76] *Ib.* p. 116, 118.

The Survival of Paganism. 15

Homer; and, as also in Homer, it is only the most atrocious criminals who are, after death, affected by punishment for deeds done in the body—this, however, not as a Tantalus or a Sisyphus, but by being transformed into Vampires. In the *Myriológia*, or Dirges, the mourners in no single instance console themselves with the hope or belief that the beloved dead are in a state of bliss. The dead son can comfort his mother only by directing her to a hill where she will find herbs of forgetfulness.[77] And a wife can but say of her husband that he 'has taken the Black Earth for a second wife, and a Tombstone for a mother-in-law.'[78] Even among the Songs specially distinguished as Θρησ-κευτικά—Religious, or Christian—a visitor to the Other World finds Good and Bad, or rather Poor and Rich, all in one place, the only difference in their condition being that the Poor are in the warm sunshine, and the Rich in the chilly shade.[79]

8. The third characteristic of the Songs, I have defined as a profound feeling of Family kinship and patriotic devotion to the Fatherland. In illustration of the former I may refer generally to the Exile Songs, and to the *Myriológia* or Dirges; and also to such incidents, for example, as that of the Brothers' rescue of their Sister from Charon; and such requests by a dying man as that his Mother may be told not that he is dead, but only that he is 'married in a far country.' As to devotion to the Fatherland, the whole class of Historical Songs may be cited in evidence. The ballad of the *Capture of Constantinople*[80] ends with the assured prophecy that, after long years, the Panaghía and the Icons shall dwell again in Ayia Sophia, the Holy Basilicon of the Divine Wisdom, founded by Constantine, and rebuilt by Justinian. Never, through centuries of oppression, has the hope expressed in this prophecy been extinguished. Generation after generation, mothers have sent their sons to battle against the Turks; and to mothers less heroic, sons have cried, 'Mother, I tell thee, I cannot serve the Turk— I cannot, it is beyond endurance.'[81] Again and again, times

[77] *Trans*. p. 125. [78] *Ib*. p. 125. [79] *Ib*. p. 109.
[80] *Ib*. p. 200. [81] *Ib*. p. 243.

innumerable, there has arisen from patriot ranks the Homeric shout :[82]

Λεξίντες, κάμετε καρδιά, σὰ Χριστιανοὶ φανῆτε /
Τοὺς Τούρκους να παστρέψωμε.
'Heroes, take heart, show yourselves Greeks !'[83]
And we'll clear out the Turks.'[84]

Nor has this been sworn only, but in great part done. And ἡ δούλη "Ελλας—'Enslaved Greece'—is now restricted to those Northern and still Turk-ruled provinces whence come these Songs.

9. Such, then, as evidenced by our Greek Folk-songs, are the facts of the survival of Western Paganism in every one of its essential characteristics; and I may add that nowhere, perhaps, will the reader be more struck with the absence of distinctively Christian sentiment than in the 'Odes' for the Feasts of the Christian Church.[85] Recognising these facts, we ask with a new interest what the origin was of that legend of the death of Pan which was not improbably told to Plutarch himself, as well as to the personages of his 'Dialogue,' at Delphi,[86] and which has been seized on with such avidity by Christian writers, as at least a mystical type of, if not a direct testimony to, the overthrowal of Paganism. This question can hardly, I think, be dismissed with the observation that, of the passengers who heard the mysterious voice, 'many were drinking after supper,'[87] though it may be noted that the story was told by a professional Rhetorician. Most fictions have a kernel of fact.[88] And, riding one day along the sandy beach near Nicopolis—the city built to commemorate that battle of Actium which was not only a battle

[82] Ὦ φίλοι, ἀνέρες ἐστὲ καὶ ἄλκιμον ἦτορ ἕλεσθε, *Il.* v. 529.
[83] Literally ' Christians ;' but see note, *Trans.* p. 242.
[84] *Trans.* pp. 240, 242 *and fig.*   [85] *Ib.* pp. 94 *and fig.*
[86] Plutarch seems, from what he himself says (Περὶ τοῦ 'Ει ἐν Δελφοῖς), to have been at Delphi during the Emperor Nero's visit, in 66 A.C.
[87] πολλοὺς δὲ καὶ πίνειν ἔτι δεδειπνηκότας.
[88] Wild as it is, even the great British cycle of Arthurian fiction has been shown by MR. SKENE, (*Four Ancient Books of Wales,*) and myself, (*Arthurian Localities,*) to have a clear kernel, not only of historic fact and provable time and place, but of still living local tradition.

The Survival of Paganism.

between Augustus and Antony, but a war between the East and the West, and a victory, though but a political victory, of Europe over Asia—riding along this historic beach one day, and observing that the island of Paxi was within clear view of the city where, according to the apocryphal Epistle to Titus, Paul ' determined to winter '[89] —Paul who gave a religious victory to Asia over Europe —there occurred to me what I may offer as a possible answer to this question as to the origin of the legend of the death of Pan.

10. Might it not possibly owe its origin to the enthusiastic imagination of some convert from Paganism, a presbyter of the Primitive, if not Pauline Church of the City of Victory; but an Epirote versed in all his country's legends, and particularly with those which had just been used by Virgil, and which consecrated to every Roman the environs of Palódes[90]—might it not possibly owe its origin to the poetic fancy of an ecstatic meditation on the very sea-beach along which I was journeying, outside the walls of the Pagan, and now long-ruined city?[91] For what was originally but a fable, making a fine peroration to an edifying discourse, would naturally get reported as a fact that had actually occurred. Or—still more probably, perhaps—might not voyagers actually have heard some enthusiastic convert to Christianity on a still evening, calling out from the beach of Paxi, 'Ἀπάγγειλον—Spread the tidings that the great Pan is dead!' Whether either or neither of these two suppositions be accepted, I venture to think that it is, at least, important, with reference to the origin of this story of the death of Pan, to note, not only the Pagan consecration of the scenes of it, but—what has not, so far as I am aware, hitherto been noted in this

[89] See for a discussion of the question as to the wintering of Paul at Nicopolis, RENAN, *St. Paul, Introd.*, pp. xxxvii.—xlvii.
[90] See *below*, p. 25.
[91] In the beginning of the fifth century Nicopolis was plundered by the Goths. It was still, however, in the sixth century, the capital of Epeiros. But during the Feudal Period it lost its importance, and Preveza, at the end of the promontory, was built out of its ruins.

connection—the proximity of the Apostolic Church of Nicopolis. Nor is it, perhaps, less important to note, along with this proximity of localities, a synchronism of dates. The date of the reporting of this story of the death of Pan is the date also of the Apocalyptic literature, of which the great masterpiece is the 'Revelation of St. John the Divine.' Probably, also, as we have seen,[92] or at least possibly, it was when he was at Delphi with the Emperor Nero, in 66, that Plutarch himself heard the legend which, in his 'Dialogue,' is said to have been reported at Delphi. And the synchronism just noted becomes especially significant when we reflect on what Nero was to that last of the Hebrew prophets, the Seer of Patmos, when writing his Ἀποκάλυψις at Christmas, 68-9.[93] Though ignominiously slain in June, 68, Nero was by some believed to have taken refuge with the 'Kings of the East,' the Kings of Parthia and of Armenia; by others to be resuscitated in the false Nero who established himself in the island of Cythnos, near that of Patmos. And Nero was, to the Hebrew Seer, at once the seven-headed Beast, and that one more particularly of its heads[94] which was 'as though it had been smitten unto death, and his death-stroke was healed'[95]—the Beast the numeric value of the letters of whose name, Νέρων Καῖσαρ, transcribed in Hebrew, is 'Six hundred and sixty and six.'[96]

11. Such was the time, whatever may have been the circumstances, of the origin of this Apocalyptic legend of the death of Pan. But the announcement of the Proselyte of Nicopolis—if so we may call the originator of the legend—is now known by all scholars to have been as visionary as was the revelation of the Seer of Patmos. None, however, even of those writers who have most clearly pointed out the survival of Paganism in contemporary or recent Folk-belief, have, so far as I can recall,

[92] *Above*, p. 16, note 86.
[93] See RENAN, *L'Antichrist*, chaps. xiii.—xvii.
[94] Rev. xvii. 11.
[95] *Ibid.* xiii. 3.   [96] *Ibid.* 18.

The Survival of Paganism.

seriously attempted to account for this survival. But, unsatisfied with merely establishing the fact, we shall here endeavour to ascertain the cause, of the survival of the Aryan Paganism of the West. For the discovery of this cause cannot but have an important bearing on our whole conception of Progress, and on our theory more particularly of the origin, and hence nature and history, of Christianity. But before proceeding to investigate the cause, I must say something more of the fact. This I shall do in pointing out the relations of the scenes of the modern Pagan Folk-songs to the sites of the ancient Pagan Sanctuaries. For thus, more powerfully, perhaps, than in any other way, I may bring home the fact that, though the sacred Oaks lie prostrate, chopped, and charred, all about them there has never ceased to flourish a green and lusty Copse; that, prostrate as may be the Gods of the poets, never to the Deities of the people have their sacrifices failed; that never

'From haunted spring and dale,
Edged with poplar pale,'

never have the Nymphs 'with flower-inwoven tresses' really departed;[97] nay, that even the greater Olympian Gods are transformed only, and deformed,[98] in Greek Christianity, rather than dead — ruined though their Sanctuaries are; and that every glorious peak or promon-

[97] As the Rev. Mr. Tozer mildly puts it, 'When Milton, in describing the overthrow of Paganism [wrote those lines], he fixed on one of the most essential elements in Greek mythology, but at the same time had hardly realized, perhaps, *how permanent and ineradicable this belief was.*'—*Highlands of Turkey*, vol. ii., p. 315.

[98] Compare the Christian portraits of Father Jehovah with the Classic statues of Father Zevs; the Christian portraits of Christ with the Classic statues of Apollo; the Christian portraits of the virgin Mary with the Classic statues of the virgin Athená. Christian art generally portrays its Gods in paintings; Classic art, in statues. But a statue of the Trinity—an old and a young man with a small bird between them—adorns the Graben at Vienna—a statue profoundly instructive for those who would understand why it was that the believers in an unfigured Allah contemned and conquered their Christian adversaries, expelled them from Asia, and enchained them in Europe.

tory, consecrated of old to almighty Zevs, is sacred now to the Omnipotent (Παντοκράτωρ) ; or of old, to the Sungod, "Ηλιος, Apollo, now to St. Elias ("Αγιος Ελίας); or to the virgin Athená (Παρθένος), now to the virgin Mary (Παναγία).[99]

SECTION II.

PAGAN SANCTUARIES AND FOLK-SONG SCENES.

CROSSING the lake of Ioánnina, and climbing to a shepherd-village on the steep side of Metzikéli—an outwork of Pindus, towering some three or four thousand feet above the level of the lake, itself a thousand feet above the level of the sea—we gain a platform from which we see a great part, and can conveniently begin the description, of the first of those Turkish provinces of Greece to which the following Folk-songs belong. On the November morning on which I actually made this ascent, setting out on a shooting expedition with the French Consul, lake and mountain were alike covered with a thick mist that made our crossing of the lake a long and somewhat anxious voyage. But suddenly, as we approached the village on the first ridge of the mountain, the sun arose in unclouded glory on the summits of Pindus, coming over the Thessalian plains from Mount Olympus. Before the all-conquering God the mist vanished from the hollow of the lake ; traces only of its discomfiture were left in disjointed wreaths, some lying reluctant still on the hillsides, but most floating swiftly away ; and all South Albania, or Epeiros, lay clear before us, from the Pindus to the Ionian Sea. I look for the localities of the "Ασματα τοῦ 'Ηπείρου, the 'Songs of Epeiros.' And presently it strikes me that the localities both of the origin and of the scenes of these modern

[99] See POLÍTES, Νεοἑλλήνικη Μυθολογία ; and compare the books of THIERSCH, of SANDERS, and of B. SCHMIDT, on the *Volksleben der Neugriechen.*

The Survival of Paganism. 21

Songs are identical with the site and environs of the ancient Oracle of Dodona, and Sanctuaries of Zevs, Dióné, and Hades. A similar observation we shall make when looking for the localities of the Songs of Thessaly, and of the Songs of Macedonia. We shall find, in a word, that the modern centres of the still characteristically Pagan Folk-songs of Northern, or 'Enslaved,' Greece are none other than the ruin-covered sites of the ancient Sanctuaries of Dodona, of Olympus, and of Samothrace. And thus, everywhere in Northern Greece, in describing the country of the ancient Sanctuaries, I shall describe the scenes of the modern Songs.

SUB-SECTION I.—ALBANIA.

1. Easily, in the clear air, we descry, from where we now stand, the rocky bridle-path over those hills of the Souliots on the opposite side of the valley, which takes one, in a couple of hours' ride from Ioánnina, to the Glen of Dodona,[1] 'of the hard winters,'[2] yet 'the beloved of Zevs.'[3] Some time before standing here on Metzikéli, I had had a week of exploration and adventure in those mountains. Arrived at the summit of the ridge of the bridle-path, we were fitly warned by a clump of fine oaks that we were about to descend to the Sanctuary of that Dodonean Ζεὺς πατήρ, Father Zevs, to whom the oak was sacred, not only because of the strength of its timber, but the nourishment of its fruit.[4] A long, steep, and winding

---

[1] The true site of Dodona seems now to have been proved beyond dispute by the results of the diggings of M. KARAPANOS, as set forth in his *Dodone et ses Ruines*. But it is instructive still to read Colonel LEAKE'S arguments in support of his conjectural site of the city of Dodona on the hill of Kastritza, and of the temple of Dodona on the rocky peninsula of Ioánnina, the former to the side of, and the latter facing Metzikéli, which he identifies with Tomaros, pointing out that the name is still preserved in the adjacent village, called Tomarokhória (*Northern Greece*, vol. iv., pp. 168—201). Compare also POUQUEVILLE, *Voyage de la Grèce*.
[2] Δωδώνην δυσχείμερον. *Il.* v. 255. Δωδωνῆς μεδέων δυσχειμέρου. *Il.* xvi. 234.
[3] Τῇδε Ζεὺς ἐφίλησε. HESIOD, ap. Schol. in Soph. *Trachin*, 1169.
[4] See DE GUBERNATIS, *Mythologie des Plantes*, t. ii., pp. 68—9.

descent brings us down to a retired glen. We ride up to walls of great stones, nicely fitted to each other, but uncemented; and of which the few courses that are still standing form a quadrangular space on an eminence jutting out from the hills. We dismount, and climbing along the walls, presently take in the whole scene, and find it worthy of its fame. East and west runs the glen; low are the hills to the north, whence we have come; but over them rise, in the distance, the summits of Pindus. To the south, to our right, therefore, as we look eastward down the glen, towers up the great mass of Tomaros—now called Olytsika—between 4,000 and 5,000 feet above the level of the glen, which is itself some 1,500 feet above the level of the sea. This is the grand feature of the scene. Above the villages on the lower slopes is a fringe of the primeval oak-forest. And above this again a long range of grandly precipitous heights.

2. For the ruined and razed later Temples[5] much, but for the primitive Sanctuary little, restoration is required. It was probably but a grove of oaks of a somewhat grander size on this eminence, with a fountain springing up under their giant branches. Richly mosaic'd, indeed, is the floor of this Temple. But its pavement is only of rough stones, covered with lichens and mosses; or of grasses, with wildflowers interspersed. Rich gifts also adorn its altars. But they are only the first flowers of spring, or first-fruits of autumn, or firstlings of the flocks and herds nourished by these. Music agitates or soothes the soul in this Temple. But it is the music only of the wind itself on those sacred vessels of metal which commemorate the origin of new powers over Nature and Man; or the music of rustling leaves and tinkling waters; or the music of thunder-bolts resounding through the re-echoing mountains. And light fills this Temple with joy, and darkness makes it the abode of terror. But its light is only the

[5] A very interesting description of a picture of the temple of Dodona, with its garlanded oak, and golden dove, its choral dances, sacrificing priests, and ministering priestesses, is given by PHILOSTRATUS, *Icon*, l. ii., c. 34, and is cited by LEAKE, *Northern Greece*, vol. iv., p. 199.

Star of our Earthly Day, or the Golden Lamps of the Day of the Universe. The Temple itself is at once Temple and Divinity. And the hymn that its priestesses chant is but a first simple verse of that which every prophet and poet adds to, and renews—but a verse of the eternal hymn of man's worship of the divine ensphering Heaven, and the maternal nourishing Earth.

Ζεὺς ἦν, Ζεὺς ἐστι, Ζεὺς ἐσσεται, ὦ μεγάλη Ζεῦ !
Γᾶ καρποὺς ἀνίει, διο κλήζετε μητέρα Γαῖαν ![6]
Zevs was, Zevs is, Zevs will be, O great Zevs!
Earth bringeth forth fruits, therefore call Earth Mother!

3. But the Sanctuary of Dodona was only one locality in a system of Holy Places which together localize all the chief ideas of the creed of Aryan Paganism. The Glen of Dodona was the Sanctuary of the Pelasgian God of the Upperworld, the Sky-god, the Sun-god, Diespiter, Ζεὺς πατήρ, Diaushpiter.[7] With him was joined Dióne, but a feminine form of Zevs (Ζεὺς, gen. Διός), and the name under which, by the Pelasgians of Dodona, the Earth-mother, Γῆ μήτηρ, Δημήτηρ, was worshipped.[8] And the deep and dark ravines of Souli were the Sanctuary of the God of the Underworld, Hades, "Ἄδης, "Ἀίδης, 'Ἀϊδονεύς,[9] the Dis (gen. Ditis) of the Pelasgians of Italy, and the Vedic Aditi, the Earth considered as the Receptacle of the Dead. And just as, to the north, the strath of Ioánnina is like a forecourt to the Sanctuary of Zevs; so, to the south, the Acherusian Plain, with its rivers of

[6] PAUSANIAS, X. xii. 10.
[7] Ζεῦ ἄνα Δωδωναῖε Πελάσγικε.—Il. xvi. 233.
[8] STRABO, vii. 329. The Dioné of the Pelasgians of Dodona was afterwards identified with the Héré of the Pelasgians of Peloponnesus. Ἡ Ἥρα Διώνη πάρα Δωδωναίος (Schol. Od. iii. 91); and Héré would appear to be derived from the old Greek Ἔρα, the Earth.
[9] The proof of this is to be found, not merely in ancient writers, but in existing facts. Two churches within, and two at Glyky and Paramythia, entrances to, the mountains of Souli, and thus no fewer than four—nearly all—the Souliot churches, are dedicated to Ἀϊδονεύς, under the but slightly changed name of 'Αϊ' Δονᾶτο ('Άγιος Δονᾶτος.) And the legends attaching to Ai' Donato both as a person and as a place—the most remarkable, perhaps, of the latter being preserved in the first of the Folk-songs given below—these legends are all of a distinctively Hades character.

Achéron and Kókytos,[10] was the forecourt of the 'House of Hades.' To this forecourt it was that Odyssevs drew the Ghosts of the Dead athirst for the blood of his sacrifices; and here it was that passed, according to Pausanias,[11] the whole of the wonderful, and often most pathetic, scenes of the Eleventh Book of the *Odysscy*. For ere he could penetrate to the 'House of Hades' itself, 'pale fear gat hold of Odyssevs, lest the high goddess Persephóné should send him the head of Gorgo, that dread monster, from out of Hades.'[12] The intimate connection of all these localities, and the reason of the distinctively systematic character of Aryan Holy Places generally, has not hitherto, I believe, been pointed out. But here I can only indicate the reason in suggesting that it is connected with that characteristic *relativity* of Aryan conceptions which has caused Aryan theology to be always Trinitarian,[13] and so, the antithesis of that Unitarian Semitic theology in which God is represented as the absolute One, Yahveh, or Allah.[14]

4. The Acherusian Plain, of old the country of the Thesprotians, with its capital Pandosia, on an eminence in the middle of the plain, extends to the sea. On a conical rock, swept round by the waves, is the citadel of the famous Parga, from which come so many of our Songs, and which was probably founded, about 1330, by inhabitants of the ancient Toróné (Palæo-Parga) gathering about the sanctuary of the Hyperaghía

---

[10] 'There seems no reason to doubt that the Gurla, or river of Suli, is the *Achéron;* the Vuvo, the *Kókytos* of antiquity, and the great marsh or lake below Kastri, the *Acherusia*. The course of the Achéron through the lake into the *Glykys Limen* accords perfectly with the testimony of Thucydides, Scylax, Livy and Strabo; and the disagreeable water of the Kókytos is mentioned by Pausanias.'—LEAKE, *Northern Greece*, vol. iv., p. 53.
[11] I. xvii. 5.
[12] BUTCHER and LANG, *Odyssey*, p. 191.
[13] As to the distinction between the Aryan Neo-Platonic, and that monstrous hybrid the Semitic Christian Trinity, see *below*, pp. 56—8.
[14] See further with regard to the modes of conception characteristic of the Semitic and Aryan races respectively, *below*, pp. 54—6.

The Survival of Paganism. 25

Virgin. The western side of the plain is bounded by the hilly, and now Muslim-peopled, district extending to, and beyond, the ancient Thýamis and modern Kálamas. This was, of old, the southern frontier of the country of the Chaonians,[15] with Kórkyra (Corfu), imaginatively identified with the Homeric *Scheria* where dwelt the Phœacians,[16] lying off its coast-line. And as the wandering hero of the *Odyssey* lands on the Thesprotian shore, Γλυκὺς λιμὴν (Sweet Harbour, now Port Fanari), the wandering hero of the *Æneid* lands on the Chaonian shore at the Bay of Palódes (Vutzindró), near the ancient city of Βουθρωτὸν (Butrinto).[17] According to Dionysius of Halicarnassus,[18] Æneas, landing at Ambracia, now Arta, journeyed to Dodona, while his son Anchises sailed on with the fleet to Buthrotum, where Æneas rejoined them. But whether journeying up from Buthrotum, as in the epic of Virgil, or down towards Buthrotum from Dodona, as in the legend of Dionysius, the scene of the pathetic interview of Æneas with Andrómaché, the widow of Hector, may with equal reason be placed on the banks of the Thýamis, near the confluence of the stream now called the Kremnitza. And the ruins called Palæa Venetia, and the town of Philiates—which seems to preserve a reminiscence of the name—we may identify with the New Ilion, said to have been founded by Hellenus, and of which the actual existence is attested by Livy, and the Tables of Peutinger.[19]

5. But now—after this round through the mountains of Dodona, down by the Achéron-Gurlá to the sea, and up by the Thýamis-Kálamas, and the New Ilion to Ioánnina again—let me describe what lies at our feet as we stand here on a ridge of Metzikéli. The great strath of Ioánnina was of old the country of the Molossians, and,

[15] Βάρβαροι δὲ Χάονες ἀβασίλευτοι.—THUCYD., ii. 124.
[16] See WELKER, *Kleine Schriften*, ii.; *Die Homerischen Phäaken, und die Inseln der Seligen.*
[17] *Æn.* iii.
[18] *Antiq. Rom.* l. 1, c. 50.
[19] See LEAKE, *Northern Greece*, vol. iv., p. 176 n.

at a still earlier period, the many-peopled, flock-and-herd-covered, harvest-abounding land of Hellopía, described by Hesiod[20]—the original Hellas itself, according to Aristotle[21]—the country of the primitive Selli, Elli, Hellenes, and Greeks.[22] South-eastward, it bends to Arta and the Ambracian Gulf, on one side of which is the ancient Nicopolis and modern Préveza; and on the other, the promontory of Actium; and outside of the gulf is the gleaming Ionian Sea, with its islands of Levcádia, and beyond it, on the far horizon, Kephalonía. The town of Ioánnina probably owes its origin to refugees from Dodona, after its destruction by the Goths, under Totila, in the sixth century (551); and its name it certainly owes to St. John the Baptist, whom its founders chose as their patron. Its bishops sat at the Council of Constantinople in 879; it was taken in 1181 by the Norman Behemond, the bastard of the great Robert Guiscard; and in 1431 it surrendered to the Turks. On the inland slope of a high and rocky promontory is the walled upper quarter of the city; and this magnificently picturesque promontory, crowned formerly by the Castle of the 'Lion of Ioánnina,' Alí Pashá, now bears at its highest edge his Tomb (1822), beside the marble-columned mosque of Arslan Aga. Having ever before my eyes, in the nunnery at Ioánnina where I lodged, the stupendous wall of Metzikéli on the other side of the lake, much had my curiosity been excited to see what was at the back of it—Zagórie,[23] whence come many of our Epirote songs. And at length, having gained the summit of Metzikéli, in our shooting expedition, the French Consul and I looked down on a vast amphitheatre of forested mountains, descending to a bottom at

[20] Ap. Schol. in SOPH. *Trachin.* 1169.
[21] *Meteorol.* i. 14. But according to Homer the name of Hellenes was originally applied to the inhabitants of Southern Thessaly, and the Phiotide (*Il.* ii. 683). Homer himself, as is well known, calls the Greeks Achæans, as these were, in his time, the most numerous of all the Hellenic tribes. (*Il.* ii. 684; ix. 141; *Od.* iii. 251.)
[22] For a discussion of the derivations and meanings of these names, see MAURY, *Religions de la Grèce antique*, t. i., pp. 38, 39, text and notes.
[23] A Slav name, meaning 'Behind the Mountain.'

a profound depth, with a midway zone of scattered villages, and with, apparently, no means of communication with the outer world save over the trackless mountain summits. A northern realization this out-of-the-world world seemed to be of the Happy Valley of Rasselas, Prince of Abyssinia.

SUB-SECTION II.—THESSALY.

1. From the plain of Ioánnina, the land, as we have seen, of Hellopía, and the primitive country of the Hellenes, it is a long day's (more commonly a day and a half's) journey up the hills adjoining Metzikéli; down their long and steep descents; along a succession of glens; through their meandering streams times without number; then again up long winding ascents; and so across the broad mountain-spine of Pindus. Vlach Shepherdesses are among the most prominent figures in the Erotic and Humouristic sections of the following Songs; and a word, at least, may be said, in passing, of the Capital of the scattered communities of the Cis-Danubian Roumanians.[24]

[24] From the third (270) to the thirteenth century (1222) we have no direct historical evidence of the existence, in Roumania, of Roumanians. Worse still—at the former date they are mentioned only as being *removed* from Roumania. Whence had they come, when, at the latter date, we find again, in Roumania, Roumanians? For more than a hundred years now this question as to the origin of the Roumanians has been debated; and among the chief investigators of the problem may be named Thunmann (1774), Sulzer (1781), Engel (1794), Rösler (1871), Pic (1880), and Slavici (1881). According to one theory—that, it must be admitted, of the majority of these German writers—the Roumanians did actually disappear from Roumania, emigrating thence when Aurelian created his Cis-Danubian Dacia (270-75); and immigrating thither only shortly before we have documentary evidence of them again in Roumania (1222). According to the other theory—that, naturally, of the Roumanians themselves —there was never a general immigration from Trans-Danubian Dacia, notwithstanding the orders of Aurelian ; and hence, the origin of the Roumanians in Roumania is to be traced to no other general immigration than that of the *infinitas copias* of colonists *ex toto orbe* under Trajan (106). The Roumanians have in them not improbably some strains, at least, of the blood of the ancient Thracians and Dacians. See *below* (p. 33), with respect to the connections of the Thracians with the Trojans, and possibly with the Teutons.

This is Mézzovo, the surpassingly picturesque Metropolis of the Mountains. It was founded by Vlach shepherds, who, in the sixteenth century, escaping from Turkish tyranny in the plains of Thessaly—no longer a semi-independent Μεγάλη Βλαχία, Great Wallachia—sought here to preserve their freedom. And from Mézzovo it is but two hours—first down a steep descent, and then up a long ascent to the knife-like summit, neck, or 'yoke,'—amazingly narrow, considering that it has been the gate of so many invading hordes and armies[25] passing from Thessaly into Illyria, or from Illyria into Thessaly—the *Zygos* from which, upwards of 5,000 feet above the sea, we look down on the first of the three great divisions of Thessaly, the long and ever-widening glen of the Peneiós, and see afar, over the eastern plain, the summits of Olympus—of old, the human birthplace, and divine home of the Olympian Gods; and, in our days, the chief fortress of Freedom, and cradle of Folk-song in Northern Greece.

2. Through enchanting forest-glades, we ride down the glen of the Peneiós to those wonderful cliffs, Μετέωρα Λίθοι, on which the Metéora Monasteries are perched—those cliffs which form one side of the gate into the plains of Thessaly, and the beauty, yet wonder and terror, of which have, in our Folk-songs, attached to one of them, the mountain-rock of Varlaam (Βουνὸ τοῦ Βαρλάμη), a story of a nine-headed Drakos. I passed the night at the Turkish guard-house of Krea-Vrissi (Cold Fountain), also mentioned in our Songs. And next day, when, after being hauled up 300 feet through the air to the cloisters of the Great Metéoron, I considered the position of these Monasteries, it struck me as a rather remarkable fact that between the ruined and deserted Sanctuaries of Greek Paganism —between Dodona and Olympus, and between Olympus and Samothrace—there should have chanced to be established the chief, though now declining, Sanctuaries of Greek Christianism—between Dodona and Olympus the

---

[25] Among others, that of Cæsar, after his failure against Pompey at Dyrrachium, and before his victory at Pharsalia, 48 B.C.

Mid-air Monasteries of the Metéora Cliffs, and between Olympus and Samothrace the Hermitage Convents of the Holy Mountain. Nor remarkable only seemed this fact, but instructive the relations thus observed. For Historical Monuments are the telephones and phonographs by which communities of men transmit their voices to their fellows across the abysses of Time. These voices, however, need generally to be somehow magnified, so that we may hear them. Nothing magnifies like contrast. Hence, noting the topographical relations of these Metéora Monasteries —between Dodona and Olympus—did make their voices audible. These Mid-air Monasteries are materialized utterances of social despair and diseased aspiration. What else could have urged men to the deadly perils of scaling their inaccessible precipices — the prodigious labours of crowning their untrodden summits with domed and pillared churches, and galleried and cloistered convents? And when we turn for verification of what we seem to have heard to the historical facts of the time, and the circumstances of the building in mid-air and peopling of these Monasteries, we gain fullest assurance that we have not misheard their voices.[26]

3. As we round the eastern horn, 1,000 feet high, of the crescent-shaped range of the precipices on which the Convents are perched, and come to the village of Kala-

---

[26] A manuscript, discovered and translated by M. HEUZEY ('*Les Couvents des Météores,*' *Revue Archéologique*, March, 1864), gives us an invaluable detailed account of the foundation of these Monasteries, and particularly of that of the great Metéoron, in the fourteenth century, and of their history up to the middle of the sixteenth century. Now, in its political anarchy and social misery, the fourteenth century, the century of the foundation of these Monasteries, was to South-eastern Europe what the eighth century had been to North-western Europe. For it was the century of the Latin Kingdoms, Principalities, and Duchies, into which the Greek Empire had been partitioned; the century of the encroaching Slav Empire of Stephen Dushan (1350) on one side; and on the other, of the extending Ottoman Empire of Murad I. (1360), presently to be established at Adrianople (1362) and soon at Thessalonica (1372). And hunted and harried the Greeks also now were by those sea-and-land-robbers—pirates and brigands— the vermin ever bred by political anarchy.

baka,[27] a magnificent view suddenly opens of the vast Plains of Thessaly, through which the Salemvria, or Peneiós, henceforward flows till it reaches the Olympian defile of Tempé. A perfectly flat, unbroken, prairie-like expanse of corn and pasture-land is the Western or Upper Plain of Thessaly; and at the extremity of a ridge that juts into the plain from the Cambunian Hills, that are its northern boundary, one descries the ancient castle and town of Trikka (Τρίκκα), which the Byzantines, changing a name which had ceased to have significance into one that had significance, turned into Trikala, the 'Thrice beautiful.'[28] The Plain of Trikala, or of Upper Thessaly, is separated by a low ridge of hills from the Plain of Lower Thessaly, or of Lárissa, which stands in the middle of the prairie on the flat southern bank of the Peneiós. Historic and song-famed Tirnovo is to the north; historic and song-famed Armyro, Domoko, and Pharsalia, to the south—Pharsalia, the first of the three great battlefields—Pharsalia (48), Philippi (42), and Actium (31)—of the tragic Trilogy of the Roman Civil Wars—the first here in Thessaly, the second in Macedonia, the third in Epeiros. To the east of Pharsalia, and thus in the south-eastern, mountain-encircled corner of Thessaly, was the Phthiotide, the Homeric Hellas, the land of the Achæans, the kingdom of Achilles. As the western boundary of the Thessalian Plains is the range of Pindus, its eastern boundary is the range of Pelion, the chief seat of the Insurrection of 1878, in which Mr. Ogle perished—killed, or murdered.[29] Running down into the Magnesían pro-

[27] Kalabaka was the scene of the besung victory (*Trans.* p. 254) and ignored rout of the Greek Invasion of 1854; under the name of Στάγοι it was the seat of the Bishopric that so long contended with the Metéoron for supremacy over the adjoining hermitages and monasteries; and it was identified by Colonel Leake with Æginion, where the junction was effected between the forces of Julius Cæsar, which had come over the Zygos Pass, and those of his lieutenant Domitius before the battle of Pharsalia.

[28] Many similar changes might be instanced in England.

[29] Whether killed or murdered was a question debated still with extraordinary passion, when I was at Volo at Christmas, 1880—81. Some time before his death I had made the acquaintance of Mr. Ogle at the Sclavonic Athens, Ragusa.

montory, the Pelion range encloses the Pagasæn Gulf, whence Jason sailed; and into which once more will a 'Golden Fleece' be brought to Volo, the ancient Iolcos, and future 'Liverpool of Greece.' The northern and southern boundaries of the Thessalian Plains are the two great mountain-ribs, as it were, of that mountain-backbone of Greece, the range of Pindus. It is the southern mountain-range that, in the Western Plain, is the more beautiful; the northern, in the Eastern Plain. The former are the mountains of Othrys, and those of Agrapha, so often mentioned in our Klephtic Songs; and the beauty and grandeur of their mistily blue and serrated wall is, in Upper Thessaly, a perpetual enchantment. But in Lower Thessaly it is the northern range that alone attracts our eye; for that, here, is the 'Shining One,' the sublime Olympus,[30] not an enchantment only, but a religion.

4. Olympus belongs equally to two modern Provinces, to two primitive Peoples, and to two orders of Gods. Its vast range extends from the defile of Tempé, which separates it from the maritime range of Ossa and Pélion, to the defile of the Sarandáporos, which separates it from the inland range of the Cambunian Hills. Its southwestern and landward side belongs to Thessaly, its north-eastern and seaward side to Macedonia. On the Lower Olympus, towards the defile of Tempé, I spent a week with a boar-hunting party; on the Higher Olympus, towards the defile of the Sarandáporos, on both its landward and seaward sides, and in the adjoining hills, I spent six weeks with a brigand-hunting expedition. Most strikingly dissimilar I found the aspects of Olympus on its Thessalian and Macedonian, its landward and seaward sides— the home-fields each, of old, of a different race of Men— the temple-precincts each of a different order of Gods. On its Thessalian side, and especially towards the Sarandáporos, Olympus rises in mighty lines, steep and bare, from an arid and desolate plain. On its Macedonian side, and especially towards Tempé, Olympus, towering over a

[30] Ὄλυμπος appears to be derived from λάμπω. See CURTIUS, *Grundzüge der Griechischen Etymologie*, b. i., s. 231.

glorious sea-plain, rises clothed with oak and pine forests. South of the abysmal rent that severs it in two is the forest of Kallipeucté, through which the legions of the Consul Philip forced their way, and turned the position of Persevs, King of Macedonia, on the Pierian Plain; and north of that sublimely severing ravine is the Pierian Forest, defiling through which, by the pass of Petra, the young Scipio again turned the position of Persevs, who then, retiring before the united Roman forces, suffered at Pydna a defeat which incorporated Macedonia in the Roman Empire.[31] Such are some of the historical memories of the Olympian Forests. But, like a Zevs, with lower limbs only clothed, Olympus shows a breast of which the naked heights hold perennial snows in their crevices, and a brow diademed with marble[32] peaks that gleam in the empyrean 10,000 feet[33] above the sea.

5. Such is the mountain, or rather the mountain-range —the unconquered home of Freedom, and cradle of Folksong in Northern Greece. But, as I have said, Olympus was, of old, the seat of two Races of Men and the sanctuary of two Orders of Gods. These two Races were on its south-western, inland, or Thessalian side, the Pelasgian Perhæbians; and on its north-eastern, maritime, and Macedonian side, the Thracian Pierians. Thracians and Pelasgians—these are the two Races we constantly encounter at the origin of Hellenic history. What part had they respectively in the formation and education of the Hellenic tribes, very mixed as these certainly were in the sources both of their blood and of their culture? Can the two great modern Races of Western Europe—the Teutons and the Kelts—be connected with either of these two great primitive Races of Aryan Europe? May the Teuton, for instance, believe that the ancient Pierians of

[31] The topographical details of this famous campaign, as given by Livy (xliv.), have been admirably worked out by M. HEUZEY, *Mont Olympe*, pp. 50 *and flg.*

[32] Frequently in our Folk-songs the mountains of Northern Greece are characterized as μάρμαροβουνά.

[33] The exact height of Olympus, according to the Admiralty charts, is 9,754 feet.

The Survival of Paganism. 33

the eastern side of Olympus[34]—and the Kelt, that the ancient Perhæbians of the western side[35]—were ancestors, or kinsmen of ancestors? And may Teuton and Kelt thus reverence Olympus, not as the birth-land only of the Gods of the Greeks, but as the birth-land of the Gods given to the Greeks by the ancestors of Teuton and of Kelt? These are questions which can here be only suggested for consideration. I can here only further point out that, on the Pelasgian side of Olympus, there was a Sanctuary of Zevs at a more ancient Dodona;[36] a stream flowing from the gorge of the Sarandáporos, to which an infernal origin was attributed; and, at Æáné, a Sanctuary of Hades;[37] and that, on the Thracian side of Olympus, there were the Sanctuaries of quite another order of Gods—the Sanctuaries of Apollo and the Muses, and the Tomb of Orphevs.[38] The divine Republic of the

[34] DR. KARL BLIND, in a note he has kindly favoured me with, says that the earliest reference, so far as he knows, to the Teutonic kinship of the Thracians, is that by JORNANDES in the sixth century; after which comes a poem by FISCHART, the German scholar and satirist of the sixteenth century, who claims Orphevs for the Germanic connection. Next came VOSS (end of last and beginning of this century), in the Dedication to his translation of the *Iliad* and *Odyssey*. WIRTH, in his *Geschichte der Deutschen* (1846), elaborately argues for this kinship. The same view was upheld by WACKERNAGEL, and by JACOB GRIMM in his *Geschichte der Deutschen Sprache* (1848). Professor SCHŒTENSACK published a special treatise on the subject, *Die Thraker als Stammväter der Gothen* (1861). And DR. OSKAR MONTELIUS, in a treatise published in the *Nordiske Tidskrift* (1884), endeavours to show that Germanic populations dwelt in the Danubian countries in the sixth century B.C. But the Trojans were certainly of Thracian origin, and hence. DR. BLIND'S special contribution to the controversy has lain in his attempt to prove the Germanic connection of the Trojans. See his note in SCHLIEMANN'S *Troja* (1884); the correspondence, in the *Academy* of Jan. and Feb., 1884; and his article in the Leipzig *Magazin*.

[35] In reference to this hypothesis of a connection between the Kelts and the Pelasgians, it would be desirable that the linguistic relations of the two great Keltic dialects, Gaelic and Kymric, to Latin, Greek, and Albanian, were more fully investigated.

[36] Called Bodóné in the ancient Æolic dialect of the Perhæbians. Its site, according to M. HEUZEY (*Mont Olympe*, p. 62), was probably near that of the monastery of the Holy Trinity.

[37] *Il.* ii. 753. Compare LUCAN, *Phars.* vi. 375.

[38] It is a great pyramidal mound, up which one may ride, in the

Olympian Gods arose, in fact, from the armed Peace of the Olympian Races; and as we find a temple of Zevs on the Thracian side at Dium,[39] we find a temple of Apollo on the Pelasgian side at Pythion.[40]

SUB-SECTION III.—MACEDONIA.

1. The two opposite sides of Pindus—Metzikéli and Zygos—were the stations from which we began our survey of Epeiros and Thessaly respectively; and now, from the heights of the Castle of the Seven Towers,[41] the citadel of Saloníca, we shall begin our survey of Macedonia —of the sites of its Sanctuaries and the scenes of its Folk-songs. The chief feature of the landscape is ὁ θεῖος Ὄλυμπος, the divine Olympus, that magnificently closes in the bay of Saloníca—the inner reach of the gulf—and makes it like a vast land-locked lake. Olympus, as has been said, belongs geographically equally to Thessaly and to Macedonia; but, pictorially, it is incomparably grander as seen from the capital of Macedonia, than as seen from the capital of Thessaly. I have, indeed, seen nothing yet to be compared with Olympus as seen from Saloníca. Far overlapping the promontory, now called Karaburnou, which bounds the bay of Saloníca on the east, and where Æneas founded Æneia,[42] the line of the Olympian range begins with the sudden cleft which marks the defile of Tempé between Ossa and the root of Olympus. From the summit of the cleft the line gradually and slightly declines, forming the ridge of the Lower

---

sea-plain under Olympus. According to PAUSANIAS the monument was a column with a marble urn on the top of it (*Beot.*, 300).

[39] Its probable site, according to HEUZEY, is occupied now by a church dedicated to Ἅγιος Παρασκευή, St. Friday; and I only succeeded in bringing away a Christian inscription.

[40] Colonel LEAKE (*Northern Greece*, vol. iii., p. 341), says that he had 'not been able to ascertain the existence of any remains' at Pythium; but, in the midst of our brigand-hunting, I was fortunate enough to get two or three hours to explore this West-Olympian Sanctuary of Apollo.

[41] In Greek, Ἑπταπύργιον; in Turkish, *Yedi-Kouléler-Kalessi*.

[42] DIONYS. HAL., *Antiq. Rom.*, l. i., c. 50.

Olympus; and from the end of this lower range there rises —to the height, as has been said, of 10,000 feet—the grand outline of the many-peaked Higher Olympus. At the seaward foot of the mountain lies the Pierian plain, the original home of the Muses—

Μοῦσαι 'Ολυμπιάδες κοῦραι Διὸς αἰγιόχοιο ;[43]

the daughters of Zevs and Mnemósyné—of the resplendent Sky and Memory. (How profoundly true is this as a parentage of the Arts—a mythic statement of the causes of Poesy in every one of its forms!) And away to the right is the long broken line of the Cambunian Hills—fine, but without the grandeur of the Ossa and Pelion range on the left. But it is not the grandeur of its form so much as the amazing and most poetic variety of its aspects that makes Olympus so truly a mountain of the Gods. Sometimes it appears in the ordinary light of a naked mountain-mass. More frequently, however, it clothes itself in all sorts of ethereal garbs. Now its summits are hid in clouds, while its sides and bases are clear; now its sides and bases are shrouded in mist, while its summits are divinely bright; now its peaks, or even its whole mass, is glittering in the many-folded silver mantle of its snows; now it is touched with the unspeakably magical lights of sunrise or of sunset, or with the ineffable beauty of the everlasting poem of Endymion and Seléné; and now it is the splendid and majestic seat of the Sky-god's darting of his lightnings and hurling of his thunderbolts.

2. Such are the views of Olympus that greet and gratify eye and soul at Salonica. For nearly a year this ancient and still populous and many-nationed city—of which the name was changed from Thermæ to that of Thessaloníké in honour of the sister of Alexander the Great—was my headquarters; but never did I return from one of my various expeditions, of many weeks each, without being delighted anew with the divine and ever-varying beauty of Olympus. From Salonica and its

[43] HESIOD, *Theog.* 25.

suburb, Kallameriá, come many of our Songs. Steeply the city rises from its wave-washed quay, or more accurately, from the *Via Ægnatia*, the old Roman road from the Adriatic to the Ægean, which here, traversing Saloníca in its whole length, forms its main street. At the eastern end of the street, and at the Kallameriá gate of the city, sits, with his primitive sort of lute, an old blind Homer, a rhapsodist of these Folk-songs, and generally surrounded by a little crowd of listeners. At this gate the walls have been in part demolished, in consequence of a sudden and short fit of Turkish 'improvements,' which exposed and destroyed many sculptured sarcophagi. Save, however, at this eastern gate, and on the side towards the sea, Saloníca is still surrounded by towered and picturesque mediæval walls, of which the substructures are of Hellenic, and even Pelasgian antiquity. Only a passing allusion can here be made to the almost unparalleled number of great historic events witnessed by these walls—always apparently retaining the same general lines, however variously reconstructed—historic scenes extending back to the Persian occupation under Xerxes (480 B.C.). At the sea-end of the eastern walls is the Venetian fort, and Turkish prison, known as the Bloody Tower. And leaving it, the road along the sea-shore takes one, in twenty minutes, to the charming marine suburb, with its appropriate Greek name, Kallameriá, 'Fairquarters,' but over-towered by the Slav-named Mount Chortiatch—a conjunction of names singularly significant of the relations of races now in Macedonia.[44]

3. To the west—to our right, as we stand on the Citadel-heights—lies the great seaward plain of the Vardar; the river which was celebrated by Homer as 'the fairest stream that flows in all the earth,'[45] and of which the Homeric and Classical name, "Αξιος, Axius = Axe or Esk, is one of the multitude of names that testify to an early

[44] Sometimes, however, the name of an inland town or village is Greek, while the population is Bulgarian, as in the case of Neochóri, some four miles from Saloníca.
[45] *Il*. ii. 850.

The Survival of Paganism.

Keltic occupation of Macedonia and Thrace. The term Macedonia I here use with the wide meaning given to it by later usage. But originally, Macedonia was but the country west of the Axius, and up to that mountain-range of Scardus which is a continuation of the great chain of Pindus. Here, in great upland plains, surrounded by wild and rocky mountains, and in that particularly of Pelagónià, now Monastír, 1,500 feet above the sea, was the Cradle of the Macedonian Monarchy.[47] Extending seaward, its capital was established at Edessa — now, because of its *waters*, called *Vodhena* by the Slavs—with the upland plain of Emáthia behind it, and under, and before it, the sea-plain in which the new capital of Pella was founded by Philip, the father of Alexander the Great. A semicircular sweep of hills bounds this plain to the south ; and the Bérrhœa (Vérria) of St. Paul is among the towns built on their declivities. A stalagmitic cavern at the foot of the hills between Vérria and Niaousta—the ancient *Kition*—with a fountain near it, and with a glorious view over the broad plain to Pella, may be identified, by a passage in Pliny,[48] with the cave to which Aristotle often retired with his young pupil, Alexander. It is called *Palæo-Sotíros*, having been made into a sort of church. Its memories, I venture to say, make it worthy of a nobler consecration. Behind these hills, with this most august and sacred cave in their northern face, is the valley of the Haliacmon. And at Æané we enter the region, already described, of the Holy Places of Mount Olympus.

4. Facing the Olympus range, and forming the eastern side of the gulf of Salonica, is the Chalcidic Peninsula,

[46] In Thrace these names are particularly numerous : Sadoc, Sparadoc, Medoc, Amadoc, Olorus, Lutarius, Leonorius, Cormontorius, Lomnorius, Luarius, Cavarus, Bithocus or Bituitus. See RENAN, *St. Paul*, p. 136 and n.; and HEUZEY, *Miss. de Mac.*, pp. 149 *and fig.* The origin of many of these names, however, may date only from the later Keltic Kingdoms established by the Gauls in their eastern migration after the death of Alexander the Great.

[47] See DELACOULONCHE, *Mém. sur le Berceau de la Puissance macedonienne, Arch. des Missions*, 1 Serie, t. viii., 1858.

[48] *Hist. Nat.* xxxi. 20. See the Memoir of M. DELACOULONCHE, just cited (p. 704).

with its three long finger-like promontories. Of these, the westernmost is the promontory of Cassandra, of which the villages were destroyed, and their inhabitants put to the sword, in consequence of their having naturally, but too rashly, declared in favour of the Greek Revolution of 1821. The easternmost promontory is the ridge, some forty miles long, and four or five broad, of the "Ἅγιον "Ὄρος, the Holy Mountain, cut across at its root by the Canal of Xerxes, and ending in the sublime marble peak that rises precipitously from the sea to the height of between 6,000 and 7,000 feet—the peak of the Thukydidean 'Ἀκτή, the Herodotean "Ἄθως, the Homeric peak on which Héré rested on her flight from Olympus to Lemnos.[49] But different are its associations now. Not a living creature of Eve's unholy sex—save inevitable insects, particularly of the carnivorous tribes — is allowed to set foot on Holy Athos. For since the sixth century, Athos has been the great pilgrim-visited Sanctuary of Greek, or Eastern Christendom—indeed, the first Convents here are said to have been founded by the Empress Helena, the mother of Constantine the Great, in the beginning of the fourth century. During the so-called 'Middle Ages,'[50] there were founded on the Holy Mountain a score of Monasteries. Nowhere in the world is there a set of buildings to be compared with them in the number of their remarkable characteristics—the picturesque grandeur of their sites; the antiquity of their older walls, which average, I suppose, some 800 years; the princely spaciousness of their quadrangles, with gorgeously frescoed churches in their midst; the priceless treasures of these churches, and of the convent-libraries; and, above all, the yet breathing Christian Mediæval life of their inhabitants. These Monasteries, however, as communities numbering some of them, even still, 300 monks or more, are but on

[49] Possibly the legend may have some connection with the traditional occupation of this promontory of Athos by the Pelasgian creators and worshippers of Héré. See *above*, p. 23, and n. 8.
[50] See *below*, p. 47, n. 7.

a lower grade of ascetic sainthood. Besides the score of Monasteries, there are a great number of Sketes, 'Ασκη- τήρια, or Σκήτια, connected with the Convents, as the Halls at Oxford with the Colleges. The largest collection of these ascetic households is in umbrageous and gloriously picturesque ravines, fitly dedicated of old to Nereids and to Nymphs. But there is a higher degree still of sainthood. In the corries, on the crags, and in the caves, the most inaccessible all round the seaward face of Athos— one of the caves to which I climbed could be made utterly inaccessible by the removal of a narrow plank—live, in solitary seclusion, an uncounted number of pre-eminently saintly hermits. And across the sea these miserable wretches look unashamed on the divine home of the Olympian Gods.

5. On the other side of Holy Athos one sees, rising sheer some 6,000 feet out of the eastern sea, the Island-Sanctuary of still elder Gods, the Gods of Samothrace. But between us and it is the island of Thasos, an ancient seat of Phœnician Civilization; in the corner of the mainland, the sacred birthplace of Aristotle, Στάγειρος, now Isvor;[51] and on the coast opposite Thasos, Abdera also of philosophic fame. I chance to be the only Englishman who has visited and explored Samothrace; but here I need only briefly recall what I have elsewhere fully described, or pointed out[52]—the supreme beauty and sublimity of this volcanic, and often earthquake-rent island-mountain; the antiquity of its deluge-traditions, and of its consecration as a Sanctuary of the Gods of the Underworld; the association and identification of the Kábeiri with these Gods of Samothrace—the Kábeiri who, as I have endeavoured to show, were originally the divinized discoverers of, and workers in iron, and hence institutors of the Iron Age—

δαήμονες ἰσχαρεῶνος
* * * * * *
Θρηϊκίης δὲ Σάμοιο πυρισθενέες πολιῆται.

---

[51] Described in a letter of mine to the *Times*, 21*st* April, 1881.
[52] *Contemporary Review*, May, 1882.

Historical Introduction.

> Expert at the Forge
> * * * * *
> Fire-powerful inhabitants of Thracian Samos ;[53]

the significance of the site of the Temple-city of Samothrace, and grandeur of its ruins, dating from the earliest age of the Pelasgian immigration to the noblest period of Greek art; and the renown of the Mysteries of the Kábeiri which brought to Samothrace pilgrims the most celebrated—here, that Prince of Macedonia and Princess of Epeiros, who were the parents of Alexander the Great, first fell in love with each other[54]—and which made it, at length, the one common Sanctuary of the Greco-Roman world. But what it is here chiefly important for us to note is the extraordinary continuity, to this day, in Macedonia, of Hellenic custom, sentiment, and thought, in connection with Samothrace. The great Festival of Initiation into the Mysteries of the Kábeiri seems to have been held about the 22nd of the modern Greek July, and the beginning of our August.[55] And at this very season pilgrims still resort to Samothrace from all the neighbouring coasts and islands; camping out in tents and huts in the woods; curing themselves of all manner of diseases in the miraculous hot sulphur-water; returning thanks still to the Gods of the old Greek Pantheon, though under new Christian names; and really keeping still the Feast of the Kábeiri, though calling it that of the 'Twelve Apostles." And still the characteristic Songs of Samothrace are about Gods of the Underworld—about Charon, who is really a Kabeirian God; though, in name, he appears to be connected with the Egyptian Horus.[56] And most curious, perhaps, of all—not only is an ancient round church at Salonica, built by Constantine, and now the mosque of Sultan Osman, said to be on the site of a

---

[53] NONNUS, *Dionys.* xiv. 23, xxix. 193; and see the other authorities quoted in the above-cited article, pp. 847—8.
[54] PLUT., *Alex.* 2.
[55] See CONZE, *Archeologische Untersuchungen auf Samothrake*, b. ii., s. 39.
[56] See *above*, p. 11.

Temple of the Kábeiri—but, in a Folk-song of Saloníca,[57] there appears, as already noted,[58] to be a distinct reminiscence of the Kábeiri themselves in the τρεῖς Στοιχειὰ τοῦ Κοσμοῦ who watch the flocks of a Macedonian shepherd.

When, on the steep side of Metzikéli, our eye searched for the localities of the origin, and of the scenes, of the modern Folk-songs of Epeiros, it found them all in the mountains of the site and environs of the ancient Oracle of Dodona, and Sanctuaries of Zevs, Dióné, and Hades; and similar has been the result of inquiry with reference to the localities of the Folk-songs of Thessaly and of Macedonia. Besides this curious coincidence of the chief scenes of modern Folk-songs in Northern Greece with the chief sites of ancient Sanctuaries in Northern Hellas, we have found that these Pagan Sanctuaries have not only been for ages ruined and deserted, but that their sites have been all overbuilt with Christian churches; nay, more: we have found that now there stands, and has visibly stood for a thousand years, between the ruined and deserted Sanctuaries of Samothrace and Olympus, the Holy Mountain, the great Sanctuary of Greek Christendom, and for half that period, between Olympus and Dodona, the chief offshoot of this Christian Sanctuary, the Convents of the Metéora Cliffs. But the most striking characteristic of the modern Folk-songs of which the scenes are thus identical with the sites of the Ancient Sanctuaries we have found to be their almost unalloyed Paganism. Surely, then, these topographical relations should not only bring home to us that fact of the unbroken continuity of Paganism, in all its essential characteristics, from the Classic to the Modern Period—that fact of the survival of Paganism which was stated in our First Section; but should make, at the same time, visible, as it were, before us, the fact of the domination of Christianity for nearly 2,000 years; and so, should enable us, perhaps, in some degree, not only to recognise, but to

[57] *Trans.* p. 57. [58] *Above*, p. 10.

realize the wonder and interest of this fact of the survival of Paganism—the wonder and interest of the revelation made to us, not only, though perhaps most strikingly, by Greek Folk-lore, but by Aryan Folk-lore generally— the revelation in popular life of a vast and profound layer of untouched Paganism, similar, in its general sentiment, if not in its special beliefs, to the prevalent Paganism of the Higher Culture. And now—the wonder and interest of the Survival of Paganism having, I trust, been sufficiently brought home—I would proceed to what I said, in concluding our First Section, would be our ultimate task, the investigation of the Cause of the Survival of Paganism. Those readers who do not care for such investigations—those readers to whom—slightly to alter the well-known lines—
> A primrose by the river's brim
> A simple primrose is,
> And it is nothing more—

may now conclude their perusal of this Historical Introduction. But those readers to whom facts are of interest only in their relation to ideas—in their relation to those larger facts which are their causes—such readers may, perhaps, be willing to follow me a little further.

SECTION III.

THE CAUSE OF THE SURVIVAL OF PAGANISM.

1. DULY recognise this fact of the general Paganism, to this day, of Folk-belief, as evidenced by its most genuine expressions, and our ordinary histories of Religion, and particularly of Christianity, will be seen to be merely histories of religious thinkers who exercised but a more or less partial, and more or less passing influence on the great mass of the people. We have, at length, recognised that a true history of Polity is something very different from what it was till very recently—a history of political actors—kings, statesmen, and generals. But we have not yet recognised that a true history of Religion is something

The Survival of Paganism. 43

very different from what it is still—a history of prophets, popes, and heresiarchs. Great, however, though the effect of a Religious Revolution may be on Literature and Art, its effect on the essential contents of Folk-belief may be almost *nil*. And the immensely important historical fact revealed by study of the Folk-lore and Folk-life of the Christian Peoples is, that there is such a discrepancy between nominal and actual Belief and Conduct as is—not unparalleled, perhaps—but extraordinarily exceptional in the whole history of mankind. The very basis of the whole system of professed Christian Belief is belief in Hell. Without the support of this infernal crypt, the Christian Church, with its every pillar of doctrine, falls sheer into the chaotic ruin of utter unreason. Yet, as the study of Folk-lore, and every other mode of experimental inquiry, shows, only sporadically and spasmodically have the masses of the so-called Christian peoples really believed in the Christian Hell, or really, therefore, believed in that 'Gospel' of popular and historic Christianity which has no meaning without belief in Hell. And similarly is it with regard to Conduct. Just as the most characteristic of the moral prescriptions of Islam is abstinence from Wine, the most characteristic of the moral prescriptions of Christianity is abstinence from Women, or, at least, strict limitation of sexual relations to but one only of the other sex, and perpetuation of these relations for the lifetime of the two parties. Subordinate to this is every other moral prescription of Christianity. And yet, here again, the study of Folk-lore, and every other mode of experimental inquiry, shows that the most characteristic of the moral prescriptions of Christianity is as little obeyed as is the most indispensable of its dogmatic assumptions believed. Monogamy denotes only the conditions under which the State recognises cohabitation, not by any means—though this appears often to be assumed even by philosophic writers—that there are no sexual relations save under these statutory conditions. With partial exceptions in certain Protestant countries, the domination of the Christian Creed and Christian Code has effected almost as little change in the essential religious beliefs, and actual sexual relations of the Aryan peoples of Europe,[1] as is effected in the social customs of Asiatic peoples by the domination of a new Dynasty. But the history of saluted Dynasties is not the history of Polity; nor is the history of professed Creeds the history of Religion.

2. Not only, however, is there beneath all our professions of Christian Belief and Conduct a widespread *survival* of Paganism in all its essential characteristics—its feeling of oneness with Nature, and mythic personalizing of its phenomena; its unconsciousness of Sin in sexual love, and unbelief in a future state of Rewards and Punishments; and its feeling of Family kinship, and patriotic devotion to the Fatherland—not only is there such a *survival*, but in no way, perhaps, can, at least, the literary side of the Modern Revolution be better characterized than as a *revival* of Paganism. That great literary movement, the origin of which will be for ever associated with the names of Macpherson and of Rousseau,[2] is more vaguely and vulgarly referred to as a 'return to Nature.' But if we duly study the works of the greater poets of the Modern Revolution—and especially of Burns, who, as I have elsewhere endeavoured to show,[3] was 'the first to give, though in fragmentary form, full, forceful, and poetic expression to all the moods of what we distinguish as the

[1] DEMOSTHÉNES, in the following sentence, accurately describes these relations, not only as they were in his own day, but as, notwithstanding the hypocrisies of Christianity, they still are : Τὰς ἑταίρας ἔχομεν ἡδονῆς ἕνεκα, τὰς δὲ παλλακὰς τῆς καθ' ἡμέραν θεραπείας τοῦ σώματος, τὰς δὲ γυναῖκας τοῦ παιδοποιεῖσθαι.

[2] Between 1759 and 1762 ROUSSEAU completed and published the *New Heloise, Social Contract*, and *Emilius;* it was in these very years that MACPHERSON published his *Fragments of Gaelic Poetry*, and *Fingal, an Ancient Epic Poem;* and the Poems of the Badenoch Highlander and Aberdeen Graduate excited a European enthusiasm no less great than that excited by the Romances of his great contemporary of the Genevan Lake and Montmorency Woods.

[3] *Macpherson, Burns, and Scott, in their Relation to the Modern Revolution* (*Fraser's Magazine*, April, 1880).

The Survival of Paganism. 45

Modern Spirit'[4]—we shall find that what is really meant by the vague phrase 'return to Nature,' would be more clearly defined as a revival of Paganism in all its essential characteristics. Notwithstanding, however, a revival, as well as survival, of Paganism in sentiment and in belief; and notwithstanding that the facts of sexual relations are practically unchanged among the European as well as the Indian Aryans; yet overthrown ancient Paganism was in all its institutions and sanctuaries, and with Christianity a new world unquestionably arose. A problem thus presents itself of the highest historical importance—a problem which may be thus stated: How came it that ancient Paganism was overthrown in all its institutions and sanctuaries, and that a new world arose with Christianity; and yet that, notwithstanding the domination of Christianity for nearly 2000 years, Paganism, in all its most essential characteristics, still flourishes in the most genuine expressions of popular sentiment and belief; nor only has thus survived in Folk-lore, but has everywhere, for more than a century now, been manifestly reviving in Literature? Such, stated in detail, is that question which we have now to consider with respect to the Cause of the Survival of Paganism.

3. But with reference more particularly to the first clause of our problem—What were the causes of the overthrow of ancient Paganism?—a preliminary question arises: Did that Era of the birth of Jesus, proposed by the Roman Abbot of the barbaric court of Theodoric, the Ostrogoth, at Ravenna (525)—Dionysius Exiguus, Denis le Petit—really separate the time before from the time after it in any such decisive and general way as has been supposed since the adoption of this Era in the darkest of the dark ages? Professor Freeman, in the Rede Lecture of 1872,[5] implicitly put this Era aside in insisting on a

[4] *Fraser's Magazine*, April, 1880, p. 523.
[5] Published in his *Comparative Politics*, 1873.

46   *Historical Introduction.*

Unity of History in which there is no such thing as 'ancient' and 'modern.' The cause, however, to which Professor Freeman attributes the origin of the distinction which he rejects is a very minor one compared with that which a more philosophic outlook on History would have shown to be the true cause, namely, the supreme importance attributed, and necessarily attributed, by the Christian faith to the Era of that conception at Nazareth, and birth at Bethlehem, fondly imagined to be events in the Incarnation of the Creator of the Universe. And Professor Freeman's notion of the 'Unity of History,' is almost as false as that notion of disunity which he attacks. Because there is no really trenchant division between the Classical Period and that which succeeded it, Professor Freeman insists on our 'casting away *all* distinctions between ancient and modern;' and because the conquests, the laws, and the language of Rome have immensely influenced a certain age of Western development, he insists further on the 'absolute identity of Roman History with Universal History.'[6] But in the spring of the same year (1873), in the autumn of which this Rede Lecture was given to the world in book-form, I published another theory of the 'Unity of History'—a theory worked out under the influence of Comte, of Hegel, and of Hume—the latter not only the true Father of the Scottish School of Philosophy, but the true Founder of the European, as distinguished from the Syrian Philosophy of History; a theory which, so far as it differs from the theories of the thinkers just mentioned, is based, philosophically, on a new generalization of the conception of Law —the Principle of Co-existence—and historically on the discovery of a great European-Asian Revolution which, while it trenchantly divides 'ancient' from 'modern' history, unites, at the same time, the histories of Europe

[6] Professor Freeman's recent article on *Some Neglected Periods of History*, in the *Contemporary Review*, May, 1884, seems to show that his notions of the 'Unity of History' have been neither corrected nor developed since his statement of them a dozen years ago.

The Survival of Paganism. 47

and Asia as at once correlative, and reciprocally influencing developments; a theory which connects this discovered fact of the General Revolution of the Sixth Century B.C. with an Ultimate Law of Thought, more or less clearly, and more or less generally stated by thinkers so different as Scottish Pyschologists, Hegelian Transcendentalists, and Spencerian Evolutionists ; and a theory which, in like manner, connects its profounder historical causes—Economic and Racial Conditions—with the fundamental principles of the New Physio-psychology.[7] Ignored, and —so far as it has been in the power of able Editors and others—suppressed as this theory has as yet been, I venture to think that the results obtained in the course of twenty long years spent in the verification of it justify me in predicting that it will, in the future, be the basis of all scientific histories of Civilization.

4. The monkish Era of the birth, or rather, of the conception[8] of Jesus, does *not* separate the times before from

---

[7] See the *New Philosophy of History* prefixed as an *Introduction* to *In the Morningland*, of which the second edition was published under the title *Isis and Osiris;* see also *The New Theory of History and the Critics of 'Pilgrim-Memories,'* and *New Principles of a History of Civilization*, prefixed to the third edition of *Pilgrim-Memories*. Besides these general statements of my Theory of European-Asian Civilization, more special statements of branches of my Theory will be found in *Isis and Osiris, Pilgrim-Memories*, and *Europe and Asia*, and with respect, more particularly, to religious and philosophic development in the two first, and to economic and political development in the last. And already in 1869, in that special study of the Sixth Century A.C., of which some results were given in my Essay on *Arthurian Localities,* those five great half-millennial Periods of European-Asian Civilization, which are constituted by five great Epochs of synchronous revolutionary events—the Sixth Century B.C.; the First Century A.C.; the Sixth Century A.C.; the Eleventh ; and the Sixteenth—these Periods had already, in 1869, been stated ; and a protest had been entered against that darkening of History which arises from lumping together the thousand years from the Sixth to the Sixteenth Century, and confusing under the single name of 'The Middle Ages,' two utterly different half-millennial Periods.

[8] The Era of Dionysius began nine months before the birth of Jesus, and the Incarnation being the great event that determined the Era, Christian Chronologists were much exercised by the knotty question, Whether they should date from the conception or from the birth?

the times after it, as different Ages. The combined results of a vast variety of historical researches show that it is not the century of Christ, but the sixth century before Christ, that truly divides the Ancient from the Modern Civilizations. For the sixth century before Christ was the century of Confucius, in China; of Buddha, in India; of Cyrus the Great and the New Zoroastrianism, in Persia; of the Babylonian Captivity (588—536), the so-called Second Isaiah, and the triumph of Jahvehism, in Judæa; of Psammetichus, its last Pharaoh, and of the worship of Isis and Horus, the divine Mother and Child, rather than of 'Our Father,' Osiris, in Egypt; of Thales, the Father of Philosophy, of Pythagoras and Xenophanes, the Fathers also of religious and ethical Reform, and of Sappho and Alkaios, the first of the new subjective and lyric school of Poetry, in Greece; and finally, in this rapid indication of its greater synchronisms, it was the century of those Political Changes from Monarchies to Republics which were but the outward sign and seal of far profounder Economic Changes both in Greece and at Rome.[9] And of the events of this General Revolution of the Sixth Century B.C., the most profound, but also the most powerful, as historic causes, were these Economic Changes. For they resulted in the destruction of the economic system of Primitive Socialism, and the initiation of that separation of Labour and Capital which distinguishes our present system of Transitional Individualism. And having this result in Europe, these Economic Changes effected, for the first time, a profound differentia-

---

[9] The dates of the birth of Confucius vary only between 550 and 551 B.C. As to the date of Buddha, see the *Academy* of 1st March, 1884, in which Professor Max Müller gives new proofs of the date of his death being 477—8 B.C.; and compare Mr. Müller's discussion of the date of Chandragupta, the basis of Indian Chronology, in his *History of Sanscrit Literature*, pp. 242—300. As to the other synchronisms, see SPIEGEL, *Avesta*, b. i.; EWALD, *Die Propheten des Alten Bundes*, b. ii., and GOLDZIEHER, *Mythology among the Hebrews*; SHARPE, *Egyptian Mythology*; ZELLER, *Presocratic Philosophy, First Period*; GROTE, *History of Greece*, vol. ii., p. 505 n., and F. DE COULANGES, *La Cité antique*.

tion between Asiatic and European Civilization—an economic differentiation which I have been, I believe, the first to point out as the profoundest fact and cause in the history of European-Asian Civilization.[10] We see, then, that, in all the countries of Civilization, from the Hoangho to the Tiber, there occurred movements in this Sixth Century B.C. that definitively broke up the previously existing, and decisively initiated, not only new forms of Civilization, but such new forms of Civilization—such new forms, that is, of economic and political, of religious and moral, and of philosophical and literary development—such new forms as must be distinguished as *genera* marking a new Age, rather than as *species* marking but a new Period. Of course, continuity of development can be clearly traced across this Sixth Century, and that, meagre comparatively as are our records. But so great is the difference between the Civilizations on this, and on the other, side of the Sixth Century B.C., that the men on the other side of that great Epoch—the men of Old India, Old Assyria, Old Judæa, Old Egypt, Old Greece and Rome—must be distinguished as Ancients from Moderns. And so little, in comparison, is the difference between the men on this and on the other side of the Christian Era, up to the Sixth Century B.C., that the name of 'Ancients' in nowise truly belongs to them; and has, indeed, only been given to them under the influence of the false monkish theory of Dionysius the Little. The men of the half-millennium antecedent to the Christian Era were but Moderns of the Classical Period.

5. But, overthrown as ancient Paganism thus began to be in the Sixth Century B.C.; overthrown through the action of Economic Changes that, in Europe, transformed the very constitution of society; overthrown through that

---

[10] See *Europe and Asia* (1879), and particularly pp. 471—4; and *Socialism as a Law of Economic Development*, first delivered as a Lecture to Workmen in April, 1883, and afterwards published in *To-day*, of October of the same year.

portentous succession of Persian, of Greek, and of Roman World-conquests, which filled the whole of the Classical Half-millennium, intermingled at once the blood of Peoples and the rites of Religions, and won for the Aryan Race supremacy over all other Races; overthrown by the aspirations of that vast Moral Revolution indicated by the change from the old Religions of Custom to the new Religions of Conscience preached by the prophets of that Sixth Century—Confucius, Buddha, Zoroaster,[11] the Second Isaiah, and Pythagoras—that vast Moral Revolution indicated hardly less by the change from the objective epic poetry of Homer and Hesiod to the subjective lyric poetry of Alkaios and Sappho; and overthrown by those great results of the common use of demotic and alphabetic, instead of hieratic and hieroglyphic, writing[12] —the emergence of Philosophy from the swaddling-bands of Theology, and the escape of Literature from the colleges of Priests—how came it that ancient Paganism, by so many consilient causes overthrown, was not extirpated? In order clearly to answer such a question, the causes of the overthrow of, at least, Western Paganism, must be more closely considered, and more specifically defined. In other words, we must consider and define the forces that gave Christianity its triumph. Now, from the point of view of the great General Revolution of the Sixth Century B.C., Christianity appears as but the Western result of 500 years of the working of the forces of a Revolution which initiated a new Age in the general development of Humanity. This Revolution, in every sphere of it, whether economic and political, or moral and religious, or philosophical and literary, is marked by the same general characteristic of a new development of the Individual, and of Conscience, a new development of

[11] The date of Zoroaster is still unsettled; but whether he belonged to the Sixth Century B.C., or to a period long anterior, the doctrines associated with his name had now their chief vogue and influence.
[12] As to the date of the substitution of demotic for hieratic writing, see GOODWIN, *Hieratic Papyri, Cambridge Essays*, 1858.

Inwardness and Subjectivity. And hence that development of Conscience and of Subjectivity which, though the central characteristic, is the hitherto unexplained element of Christianity, is explained by referring it to an antecedent and more general Revolution thus characterized; and by showing that the new development of the Individual and of Subjectivity characteristic of that antecedent Revolution is in accordance with, and is a verification of a Law of Mental Development which has its analogue in the Law of Physical Evolution.[13] But only a general explanation is thus given of the origin of Christianity. The causes of its triumph must be more specifically defined. Note then, that a new Species does not arise isolatedly, but as one of innumerable other variations. Nor is the survivor that establishes itself as a new Species the best or the most beautiful, but only that best adapted to the conditions of the environment; and hence, that richest in elements capable of nourishment, rather than liable to destruction, by the environment. Thus it was with Christianity. It was the Species, not the best, nor the most beautiful, but the best adapted to conditions of ignorance, anarchy, and barbarism. For of all the innumerable Sects, the rivals or distanced forerunners of Christianity,[14] of all the Sects, Stoic, and Epicurean, Neo-Platonic, Hermetic, and Theosophic—the products of that wonderful intellectual chemistry which had in Alexandria its chief laboratory,[15] at the beginning of what we now call the Christian Era— Christianity alone succeeded in combining the five ele-

---

[13] This Law of Mental Development I have thus stated: *Thought in its Historic Development, advances, under Terrestrial Conditions, from the conception of One-sided Causation, through the Differentiation of Subjective and Objective, to the conception of Reciprocal Causation.*
[14] ' Ce titre leur convient, quoique plusieurs soient contemporaines de l'ère chrétienne, d'autres un peu postérieures ; car l'évènement d'une religion ne date que du jour où elle est accepté par les peuples, comme le règne d'un prétendant date de sa victoire.'— MENARD, *Hermes Trismegiste, Introd.*, pp. x., xi.
[15] ' Cette étonnante chimie intellectuelle qui avait établi son principal laboratoire à Alexandrie.'—*Ibid.*, p. x.

ments of contemporary sentiment and thought, not the most rational, but the most powerful.

6. These elements were, first of all, the myth of the dying and re-born God. Shattered as was belief in all the various Gods to whom this myth was attached, the belief in incarnation was still as prevalent, the myth of a God-man dying and rising again as enchanting, and the death-songs of Linus, of Adónis, and of Manéros as pathetically affecting as ever. And attached to a new personage, who had actually exercised a commanding personal influence, and died on the cross of the Sun-gods, the central myth of Paganism could not but have a new vogue and triumph. Secondly, in its doctrine of Immortality, and in its Eschatology, its doctrine of the end of the world, damnation, and glory, Christianity gave a new form to doctrines no less prevalent than the myth of the God-man, though far less deeply rooted in the Aryan world. Thirdly, in preaching the new-old doctrines of Christianity, the great Ephesian, the author of the Fourth Gospel, and Paul of Tarsus, not only took up all that was noblest in the moral sentiment of the time, but gave it unsurpassed expression. Paul made the Christ-legend of the Galilæans a means of convincing of sin and powerfully persuading to righteousness. And the story of the Galilæan fishermen was told by the unknown Ephesian with a simplicity, ineffable tenderness, and sublimity that make it—even more truly than the story told by Thukydídes—a κτῆμα ἐς ἀεί, a 'possession for ever.' Fourthly, uniting the moral sentiment characteristic of the time with the monotheism that had not only been taught in the Mysteries, but publicly preached since the Sixth Century B.C., God was proclaimed as a Father, and this—which would appear to be especially due to Jesus—in a far closer and more personal sense than when the same name had been given of old to Ζεὺς πατήρ, Father Zevs. Finally—and this was the special and triumphant distinction of the new Sect that was to become a new Religion—not only were these various

sentiments and ideas common to all the Aryan peoples thus reproduced in Christianity, but—as I have elsewhere shown[16] in considering the Christian Revolution 'in its intellectual aspect,' discussing the cause of the uncompromising hostility between Neo-Platonism and Christianity, and demonstrating the antagonism of the fundamental conceptions of the Neo-Platonic and the Christian Trinity —these various sentiments and ideas were united with the notion of an External and Personal, as distinguished from an Immanent and Impersonal God, and hence with the notion of Creation as opposed to Emanation, and of Miracle as opposed to Law. But from this notion, as developed in Christianity, there resulted the most direct antagonism to every one of the essential characteristics of Paganism : there resulted a demonizing rather than divinizing of Nature ;[17] an ascetic as distinguished from a natural conception of Purity—a conception, that is, of Purity as consisting, not in the predominance of affection over passion, but in abstinence from sexual relations ; an insistance on superstitions of future Reward and Punishment denounced by every noble Pagan,[18] and uncredited even by boys 'save not yet washed for coin ;'[19] and a sinking of the Citizen in the Saint. And hence it is in examining the nature and origin of the Christian God-idea that we may, at length, discover what the Cause was of the Survival of Paganism.

[16] *Isis and Osiris*, chap. i., sec. ii., *The Development of the Notion of Miracle*.

[17] It is just its exceptional character, as I have elsewhere noted, that has made so famous the charming letter of Basil the Great (b. 326, d. 379) to his friend Gregory of Nazianzen, describing his mountain-hermitage in the Armenian forest overlooking the plain through which flows the rapid Iris. See BASILEI M., *Epist.* xiv., p. 93, and ccxxiii., p. 339. Only in Gregory of Nyssa, the brother of Basil, do we find, among the early Christians, a similarly refined feeling of Nature.

[18] See, for instance, PLUTARCH, *De Superstitione*, iv. ; *Moralia*, t. iv., pp. 197—8. Ed., Dübner.

[19] See JUVENAL, *Sat.* ii. 149—52.
'Esse aliquid Manes et Subterranea Regna,
Et contum et Stygio ranas in gurgite nigras,
Atque una transiere vadum tot millia cumba
Nec pueri credunt, nisi qui nondum ære lavantur.'

7. The Christian idea of a single Interfering Personal God is a distinctively Semitic idea; and it is *because this idea of an Interfering God is a distinctively Semitic idea, obnoxious to the scientific Aryan mind;* it is because of this that Aryan Paganism has survived through all the long domination of Christianity, and is everywhere now reviving. Next to, or rather side by side with, Economic Conditions, stand Racial Conditions, as the most profound of Historical Causes. Nor is anything, perhaps, in Man's history more remarkable than the permanence of the specific characteristics that still distinguish, as they have ever distinguished, the two great Races of the White Species or Variety of Mankind—Semites, and Aryans.[20] Intellectually, Semites—Jews and Arabs—are still, as they have ever been, distinguished by absoluteness, concreteness, personality of conception; Aryans, by relativity, abstractness, impersonality of conception. The evidence of these specific characteristics is to be found, first of all, in their respective languages. With the Semite,' says Professor Sayce,[21] 'the Universe is an undivided whole—not a compound resolvable into its parts. The Semite has never developed a true verb... the Aryan noun, on the contrary, pre-supposes the verb. It is difficult to compare the rich development of the Aryan sentence ... with the bald simplicity of Semitic expression. The Aryan sentence is as well fitted to be the instrument of the measured periods of reasoned rhetoric as the Semitic sentence is of the broken utterances of lyrical emotion.' Next, such evidence is to be found in the contrasted Semitic and Aryan conceptions of God. To the Jews, since, at least, the Sixth Century B.C., and to the Arabs, since, at least, the Sixth Century A.C., and to their respective prophets previously to those epochs of national monotheism, God is a Personal Being, external to the World, an Absolute One, Yahveh, or Allah. To Aryan thinkers, unin-

[20] To another great Race of the White Species the ruling castes of the Ancient Egyptians seem, as I think, probably to have belonged.
[21] *Science of Language*, vol. i., p. 178; and compare RENAN, *Histoire des Langues Semitiques*.

fluenced by Semites, God has ever been either but a name for the Infinite and Unknowable,[22] or has been conceived as the Thought or Power immanent in the World, or System of Things,[23] or as a related Trinity, the Supernatural Persons of which but thinly disguise such natural elements as those necessary for Generation;[24] or such natural objects as Heaven, Earth, and the Underworld;[25] or such natural processes as Creation, Preservation, and Destruction.[26] *Quibus explicatis*, says, in reference to Pagan Theology, Cicero, who had probably been initiated in the Mysteries of Samothrace—*quibus explicatis, ad rationemque revocatis, Rerum magis natura, quam Deorum cognoscitur*.[27] And still further and conclusive evidence of the difference between the fundamental intellectual conceptions of Semites and Aryans is to be found in the fact that those sublime intellectual creations—Science, Jurisprudence, and the Drama—Mankind owe to the Aryan Race alone.[28] For the essential condition of these creations

---

[22] 'Can we define Him, they said, or apprehend Him?' writes Max Müller of the Indian Aryans. 'No,' they replied, 'all we can say of Him is No, no! . . . Whatever we have called Him, that He is not. We cannot comprehend or name Him.'—*Origin and Growth of Religion*, p. 360.

[23] The God of Aristotle, for instance, was a principle of abstract Thought which moves a coeternal world of which He, or It, can neither change nor suspend the immutable Laws.

[24] See PAYNE KNIGHT, *Worship of Priapus*, and *Symbolical Language of Ancient Art and Mythology;* DULAURE, *Histoire des differens Cultes;* and INMAN, *Ancient Faiths*, and *Pagan and Christian Symbolism*.

[25] As in the Trinity of Dodona. See *above*, p. 23.

[26] As in the Brahmanic Trinity. [27] *De Nat. Deor.*, i. 42.

[28] Most of the great names of so-called 'Arabian' Science are names of Aryans writing in Arabic, the general language of Literature, in the true Mediæval Period (500—1000) in the East, as Latin was in the West. And 'cette science,' says M. Renan, 'cette science et philosophie Arabes n'etaient qu'une mesquine traduction de la science et de la philosophie grecques.'—*De la Part des Peuples Semitique*, pp. 17, 18. Compare the same author's *Averroes* (Ibn. Roschd.), p. 88 *flg*. The contributions made to Philosophy and Science by persons of Semitic blood, yet not only speaking and writing, but thinking in Aryan languages, cannot be taken as evidence of native Semitic capacity for Philosophy and Science. But even if such Semitic contributions to Philosophy and Science are considered, it will be found that they are

is relativity of conception, and what flows from that, the notion of God as immanent in, rather than external to the Universe, and hence the notion of Emanation rather than Creation, of reciprocal Action, rather than arbitrary Will, and of Law rather than Miracle.[29]

8. But profoundly different as are thus the characteristic intellectual conceptions of Semitic and of Aryan men, Economic and Political Conditions may be powerful enough to induce in an intellectually higher, the ideas of an intellectually lower, Race.[30] This is not the place to point out the Economic and Political Conditions that induced in Aryans the lower intellectual ideas of Semites, and submerged, for a thousand years, the splendid conquests of the Classical Period of Aryan Science. I must here confine myself to indicating the further proof of the Non-Aryan character of the notion of an External Interfering God, and hence, Creation and Miracle, which is afforded by the facts of the revolt of the Aryan mind against this Semitic notion wherever it has been imposed on Aryans. Of this revolt the first proof is

---

not so much creative as elaborative ; not enunciating new ideas, but working out ideas already enunciated by Aryan thinkers.

[29] And that these antithetic notions characterize Semite and Aryan respectively, was the opinion also of St. Paul (1 Cor. i. 22). 'The Jews,' he says, 'require a sign, and the Greeks seek after wisdom.'

[30] This will, I believe, be found to be one of the most important principles of a Scientific Mythology, and especially important in the explanation of the origin of that most variously constituted, perhaps of all Mythologies, the Greek. That Greeks as Greeks, or indeed, that Aryans as Aryans, were ever savages, is, I venture to think, a contradiction in terms. For the abstractness and the inflections characteristic of Aryan, and particularly of Greek, speech directly negative a natural savagery—a savagery the result of deficient brain-development. But Economic Conditions may so lower and degrade men of the highest Races as to make possible the adoption, or even creation, of myths monstrous even as those not only possibly but necessarily originating in the brains of lower Races. And hence, in studying the varied web of Greek Folk-mythology, I would regard those myths which have their analogies among the lowest savages, as records certainly of enslavement to masters, either of their own, or of another Race, and as records probably also of mixture, in their economic or political enslavement, with cerebrally lower Races.

The Survival of Paganism.

to be found in the long, desperate, and, at length, despairing struggle of the Neo-Platonists against Christianity. For the secret of this struggle—as, following M. Jules Simon,[31] I have elsewhere shown with some fulness[32]—the secret of the bitter and unvanquishable antagonism of the Neo-Platonists to Christianism is to be found, not in any difference of moral spirit and aspiration, but in a profound difference of intellectual conception—a difference revealed especially in the investigation of the but superficially similar Neo-Platonic and Christian doctrines of the Trinity. They are, in fact, two rival philosophies,[33] of which the latter is more particularly characterized by the entirely new meaning it gave to $\Theta a\upsilon\mu a$, and *Miraculum*, which, as yet, meant only a 'Wonder,'[34] and not, as after the triumph of Christianity, a Supernatural Event, or act of an External God.[35] For the Neo-Platonic and Christian Trinities are not merely contrasted in the relations of their Hypostases or Persons to each other, but—what is of far more importance—in the relations of these Triune Hypostases, or Persons, to Nature, or the Universe. In the Neo-Platonic Theory, the Universe itself is a system of Hypostases, more or less divine, all *emanating* from God by a necessary expansion, and returning to Him by a concentration equally necessary. In the Christian Theory, the World has neither proceeded

---

[31] *Histoire de l'Ecole d'Alexandrie*, t. ii., pp. 308—41. Thomas Taylor, in the *Introduction* to his Translation of the *Parmenides* of Plato (1793), sees that there is a difference between the Neo-Platonic and the Christian Trinity, and calls the latter 'a dire perversion of the highest procession from the First of Causes' (p. 185). But he has no clear, if any, notion of what the difference really is.

[32] *Isis and Osiris*, chap. i., *The Christian Revolution in its Intellectual Aspect*.

[33] 'En comparant la Trinité chrétienne avec celle d'Alexandrie, M. Jules Simon ne compare donc rien moins que deux philosophies rivales.'—SAISSET, *Revue des Deux Mondes*, t. vii., p. 808.

[34] And this is all it still means in the Greek Folk-songs. See, for instance, *The Miracle of St. George, Trans.*, p. 107.

[35] Hence Professor Huxley's definition of a 'Miracle' is historically untrue, and his criticism of Hume's definition has but a superficial plausibility. See his *Hume*, pp. 130, *flg.*

from, nor has it been engendered, but *created*, by God, who is conceived as outside and independent of the world, which may be annihilated by a *fiat* as arbitrary as that by which it was created. The relation of the Universe to God is thus, in the Neo-Platonic theory, reconcilable at least with the conceptions of Science. For if the theory of an Emanating Trinity is but a dream, the notion of Emanation is the pregnant germ of the conception of Law, and a prophecy of verifiable theories of Evolution, Development, and Progress. On the other hand, the Christian conception of the relation of the Universe to God is a direct negation of the most fundamental conceptions of Science. For the notion of Creation is but the supremest form of the notion of Miracle, and a prophecy of the intellectual exercitations alone compatible therewith—barren disputes of Monks, and logomachies of Schoolmen. But masculine Reason was overpowered by feminine Emotion. *Vicisti Galilæe!* And every forecast of Greek Philosophy as to the consequences of the triumph of this Galilæan Religion was only too fatally fulfilled. As foreseen and predicted by the Neo-Platonists, the triumph of Christianity closed the Schools of Philosophy, and strangled Science; brought with it a view of Nature and Humanity which necessarily led to fanatical asceticism, and hateful intolerance; and by giving to Morality the supernatural sanctions of Heaven and Hell, gave a new force and consecration to that base supernaturalism of the vulgar Ethics for which Greek Philosophy had begun, at least, to substitute the natural sanctions of the Individual Conscience and the Common Good.

9. Yet, though vanquished, not in vain had the Neo-Platonists fought. Not only before, but for a thousand years after, the closing of the Schools of Alexandria and of Athens (529), Neo-Platonism, with its notion of Emanation, and germ, at least, of the conception of Law, urged and enabled all Christians of greater intellectual capacity to modify, at least, the Semitic anthropomorphism of their Creed. Great was this influence of Neo-Platonism on the

Greek Fathers; and particularly on St. Clement, Origen, and Gregory of Nyssa; but little, on the Latin Fathers, save the greatest, St. Augustine;[36] who, however, knew the Neo-Platonists only in Latin translations. Yet before the closing of the Schools of Athens, a Christian contemporary of the last Athenian philosophers wrote those treatises, which go under the name of Dionysius the Areopagite, and which were destined, not only to transmit to the West the Neo-Platonic tradition and influence, but to carry it on till the rise of Modern Philosophy with Descartes and Bacon. For it chanced that the works of Dionysius, with the Commentary of St. Maximus the Martyr, were presented by the Emperor of the East, Michael the Stammerer, to the Emperor of the West, Lewis the Debonnair, and were translated by that greatest thinker of the Keltic Race, John Scot (Erigena).[37] As in the political world, Charles the Great, so, in the intellectual world, John Scot, at the court of the great Emperor' grandson, Charles the Bald, towers above all contemporaries, not only of his century, but of the whole Mediæval Period (500—1000). And in Scot we see at once the influence of Neo-Platonism, and the revolt of Aryan thought against the Semitism of Christianity, in such ideas as these: Ignorance—or, as we now phrase it, 'agnosticism'—in Theology is to Scot the sign of true wisdom; Creation is not an arbitrary Miracle, but a necessary Emanation, and not accidental, therefore, but coeternal with God; the Universe is a series of God-manifestations, or *Theophanies*, of which the Trinity itself is one; Death is but a metamorphosis; and all Creation returns, at length, to its primordial unity without losing anything save its

---

[36] Both the fact and the character of the Neo-Platonic influence on St. Augustine is evident in such fine and profound passages as, for instance, these : 'Verius enim cogitatur Deus quam dicitur, et verius est quam cogitatur' (*De Trin.*, vii. 7). Or, again, 'Amemus non inveniendo invenire, potius quam inveniendo non invenire te, Domine' (*Confess.*).

[37] See GUIZOT, *Hist. de la Civil. en France*, t. i. ; and ST. RÉNÉ TAILLANDIER, *Scot Erigene*.

miseries and imperfections.[38] But, true to its Semitic origin, Orthodox Theology, even in the Greek Church of the East, has always repelled whatever tended to weaken the notion of a Personal Cause, free and intelligent, which by an act of its will has created, and can similarly annihilate. Still more severe has been the Latin Church of the West. And Scot, therefore, had the honour of having his works condemned in his lifetime by the Councils of Valence (855) and Langres (859). But in the next, or Feudal Half-Milennium (1000—1500) Scot's Translation of the Areopagite's *Theologia Mystica* became the text-book of all the great Mystics. The God, however, of the French Mystics— Hugh and Richard, abbots of St. Victor, Bonaventura, Gerson, and Thomas-à-Kempis—was still of the orthodox and Semitic type[39]—a personal and living God separate from the world. But the God of the German Mystics— Eckart, Tauler, Suso, and Ruysbrock—was more characteristically Aryan—an abstract impersonal principle, truly infinite, and therefore unknowable.

10. Nor only is it thus, in the revolt of the Aryan mind against the Semitic Yahveh-notion of Christianism, that my theory of the cause of the survival of Aryan Paganism may be verified. It may be verified also in the similar revolt against the Semitic Allah-notion of Islamism. But here I can do no more than point to the profound modification of Islamism among the Aryans of India, of Persia, of Anatolia, and of Albania, and more particularly to the Creeds of the Sufis, and of the Dervishes generally, and especially those of the Bektashí Order, to which al-

---

[38] Compare such passages, for instance, as these from the *De Divis. Natur.*: 'Deus per metaphoram amor dicitur, dum sit plus quam amor, unumquemque superat amorem' (i. 70, p. 73). 'Nam et creatura in Deo est subsistens, et Deus in creatura mirabili et ineffabili modo creatur' (iii. 17, p. 238). 'Nullum miraculum in hoc mundo contra Naturam Deum fecisse legimus' (v. 23, p. 469).

[39] May this possibly have been owing to that large admixture of Semitic blood in certain parts of the French population, which M. Renan has recently endeavoured to show grounds for affirming?

The Survival of Paganism. 61

most the whole nation of the Tosk Albanians belong.[40] Yet even this twofold revolt of the Aryan mind against the Semitic Creeds imposed upon it, does not exhaust the means of historically verifying my theory of the cause of the survival of Aryan Paganism. It may be verified also by the historic result of the attempt to reason as an Aryan, yet believe as a Semite. The presupposition of Scholasticism—the origin of which, by the way, we may locally associate with Canterbury and its archbishop, Anselm (1093)—the presupposition of Scholasticism was the rationality of the dogma. Hence St. Anselm's *Credo ut intelligam*—'I believe in order to understand.' But the attempt to understand ended with the impossibility of believing. For it ended with the fatal affirmation that a thing might be at once dogmatically true and rationally false. By the end of the Fifteenth Century the Aristotelian Pomponatius boldly applied this conclusion, not only to the dogma of the immortality of the soul, but to all the greater problems of Philosophy. And the Sixteenth Century[41] is characterized not only by that virtual overthrowal of Semitic Christianity as an intellectual system which was the logical result of Scholastic disputation; but by a rebirth of Science and Philosophy, due to the new force given to the struggling Reason of the West by reconnection with Classical Aryan thought undominated as yet by Semitism. It is true that the very century that saw the rise of a

---

[40] See DOZY, *Histoire de l'Islamism;* GARCIN DE TASSY, *Philosophie et Religion chez les Persans;* DE GOBINEAU, *Religion et Philosophie dans l'Asie Centrale;* THOLUCK, *Sufismus;* and *Bluthensammlung aus der Morgenlandischen Mystik;* PALMER, *Oriental Mysticism;* BROWN, *The Dervishes,* etc.

[41] Between the Sixteenth Century, the beginning of the Modern, and the Sixth Century B.C., the beginning of the Classical Period, many remarkable analogies might be pointed out. Suffice it, however, here to note that, as in the Sixth Century B.C. there came into common use demotic and alphabetic instead of hieratic and hieroglyphic writing; so, in the Sixteenth Century, writing was superseded by printing. And similar were the intellectually enfranchising results of the new practical art that distinguishes each of these Centuries respectively.

Science and Philosophy by which thinkers were more and more emancipated from the domination of the Semitic notions of Creation and Miracle, this very century saw, in another direction, a new domination given, in Western Europe, at least, to these Semitic notions as anti-social as they are anti-scientific. Yet this very fact might be cited in proof of the necessity of Special Economic Conditions to induce in Aryans belief in the God of Semites. It would, however, be here out of place even to attempt to indicate the Economic Conditions that, in the Sixteenth Century, at once created the industrial Middle Classes, and made successful among them that Western Reformation, and Evangelicalism which more closely than ever enchained in Jewish superstitions. It must suffice to remark that, just as the political Barbarism of the West caused the Latin Fathers to be far more dominated by Semitism than the Greek Fathers; so, the economic Individualism of the West has caused the West European Peoples to be, since the Reformation, far more dominated by Semitism than the East European Peoples and particularly the Greeks. And very interesting, I think it is, to note that, just as the Greek Fathers were less Semitic in their Theology than the Latin Fathers; so, the Greek People are more Pagan now in their Folk-songs than any of the Western Peoples.

11. But *was wirklich ist, das ist vernunftlich*.[42] And the large view given of the history of Civilization by that General Theory[43] from which the thesis of the present Essay is a deduction, should enable us to see, not only the Cause of the Survival of Aryan Paganism in such a fact as the irreconcilably antithetic character of the Semitic notion at the core of the conquering Religion—but should enable us to see also the reason, the utility, the justification of the temporary conquest effected by this Semitic notion— this notion of an interfering Personal God, and hence

---

[42] By no means, however, do I accept with Hegel the converse of this maxim : *Was vernunftlich ist, das ist wirklich*.
[43] See *above*, p. 46.

Creation and Miracle. The moral sentiment and enthusiasm—the Love, in the highest sense of the term—which, as the result of the great Revolution of the Sixth Century B.C., was the chief characteristic of Christianity, was far in advance of any development yet generally given, in the West, to the notion of Law. This highly developed moral sentiment, therefore, could find adequate support only in a personal conception of Deity, and a mythology of Miracle. But ideas are worked clearly out only in conflict with their antitheses. It is to the long struggle, therefore, of the Aryan mind in Europe with the Semitic notion of Miracle that we must attribute that supreme development of the idea of Law which, in the Neo-platonic notion of Emanation, existed only in germ—that supreme development of the idea which enables us now variously to define it as Conservation of Energy, Correlation of Forces, Co-existence, Reciprocal Action, Mutual Determination.[44] Reciprocal Action, however, or Mutual Determination, is but the intellectual conception, and technical expression of that highest moral ideal—Love. Adequate, therefore, at length, to the development of the moral ideal, Love, is the development of the intellectual ideal, Law. When this is seen, there can no longer be, for Aryans, a moral necessity for belief in that Semitic Personal God, the very notion of whom is the negation of the idea of Law. Hence, Atheism. But it is an Atheism that means denial only of the Semitic God, and particularly of the God of the Jews. It is an Atheism that is but a return to the God of our Aryan forefathers; a return to that impersonal conception of the Infinite and Eternal,[45] through which alone we can

[44] The extreme difference of the conditions of the struggle, in the East, between Aryan thought and imposed Semitism, as well as the very much later date of the beginning of that struggle—in Persia, the Seventh Century (Saad Ibn Abu Wakkus, 636—41), and in India, the Eleventh (Mahmud of Ghuzni, 1001—24) or rather the Twelfth Century (Mohammed of Ghore, 1193—1206)—sufficiently explain the fact that, as the result of that struggle, there was no development there, as in the West, of the scientific conception of Law.

[45] See *above*, p. 55, n. 20.

fully enter on our inheritance of the matchless treasures of classical Aryan thought; a return to that impersonal God, to whom, through the bonds of imposed Semitism, at least half the greatest theologians of the Christian Church,[46] and all the Aryan theologians of Islam,[47] have struggled; a return to that impersonal conception of the Infinite and Eternal which renders unnecessary the contemptible fallacies and degrading hypocrisies of the vain attempt to reconcile the Semitic notion of an Interfering Personal God with the Aryan conception of a Living and Ordered Kosmos, the Aryan conception, in a word, of Law; a return to that worldview of our Aryan forefathers in which GOD is the sacred name, not of a fictitious Divinity independent of Nature, but of the divine facts of Nature itself, and of that supremest fact of all, the CO-EXISTING INFINITE.

[46] See *above*, pp. 60—2.
[47] *Ibid*, p. 62, n. 37.

NOTE BY THE TRANSLATOR.

MR. STUART GLENNIE, who originally suggested these Translations, has directed the selection of the Folk-songs with the aim of giving as complete a view as possible of all the various phases of Greek Folk-life. As illustrating, therefore, all the nine Sections of his Classification of Greek Folk-songs—a classification based on general principles which he may hereafter have an opportunity of illustrating and defending—this Collection of Translations may, I believe, fairly claim to stand quite alone in its completeness. The Songs belong, however, exclusively to the provinces of Albania, Thessaly, and Macedonia; and they may thus have an additional interest as expressions of the Folk-life of 'Enslaved Greece.' The Originals will, therefore, be found chiefly in ARAVANDINOS' *Songs of Epeiros* (Άσματα τοῦ 'Ηπείρου, 1880), and ŒCONOMIDES' *Songs of Olympus* (Τραγούδια τοῦ 'Ολύμπου, 1881). But in order to the comprehensiveness aimed at, translations are also given from KIND'S *Songs of New Greece* (Τραγώδια τῆς νέας Ἑλλάδος, 1833); PASSOW's *Romaic Songs* (Τραγούδια Ρωμαίκα, 1860); VALAORÍTI's *Memorial Songs* (Μνημόσυνα Ἄσματα, 1861); and various other Sources.

My Translations have, in every case, been made directly from the Greek texts, and without reference to other translations, even in the few cases, among the Songs here given, in which such translations exist. Mr. Stuart Glennie having urged the most exact reproduction possible, the Songs

4*

have been, almost without exception, rendered line for line, and the peculiarities of the metre and rhythm have been closely followed. And whatever may still be the imperfection of these Translations, in every Song I have been indebted to Mr. Glennie for emendations which have made the rendering more literal, the metre more correct, and the versification more vigorous.

I must also gratefully acknowledge my obligations to Mr. Theodore Ralli—a member of the well-known Chiot family, mentioned in Song (for instance, *below*, p. 167) as well as in History—to whose kindness I am indebted, not only for the interest he has taken in the book throughout, but also for the true rendering of many obscure and difficult words and phrases. Nor must I forget the kind encouragement given by Professor Blackie, to whom some specimens of these Translations were submitted two years ago by his former pupil, Mr. Stuart Glennie. As the veteran Scottish Professor was the first scholar in this country who drew attention to the identity of Modern with Ancient Greek, we trust that he will regard this work as a fruit, and, perhaps, as no unworthy fruit, of his endeavour to promote the study of Greek, not as a dead, but as a living Language. And we hope that such study will have not only speculative and scientific, but practical and political results in exciting sympathy, and gaining aid, for that reconstitution of Hellas which is still unachieved, and the fulfilment yet of Shelley's prophetic vision in the first year of the War of Independence (1821)—

> 'Another Athens shall arise,
> And to remoter time
> Bequeath, like sunset to the skies,
> The splendour of its prime;
> And leave, if naught so bright may live,
> All Earth can take, or Heaven can give.'

L. M. J. G.

GREEK FOLK-SONGS.

Quin etiam antiquitatum investigatores haud pauca in his popularibus carminibus reperient satis digna, quae respiciant, velut quod Charontem, fluminum arborumque numina, Parcam adhuc Graecis pro daemonibus venerari mos est. Sed multo magis miraberis quod caeci Rhapsodi vicos peragrantes quales ante triginta fere saecula Ulixis fata et Achilles certamina canebant, etiamnunc festis diebus populum epicis carminibus delectare solent.'—PASSOW.

'*Le plus grand poète de la Grèce contemporaine, c'est le peuple grec lui-même, avec cet innombrable essaim de rapsodes qu'il engendre sans cesse, et qui s'en vont, en quelque sorte sans interruption, depuis le vieil Homère, le premier et l'inimitable, mendiant comme lui, chantant, improvisant, enrichissant chaque jour le trésor de cette poésie dont ils sont les fidèles dépositaires, en même temps que les vulgarisateurs.*'—YÉMÉNIZ.

CLASS I.
MYTHOLOGICAL FOLK-SONGS.

SECTION I.—IDYLLIC.

THE SUNBORN AND HANTSERI.

Η ΗΛΙΟΓΕΝΝΗΤΗ ΚΑΙ Ο ΧΑΝΤΣΕΡΗΣ.

Aï-Donáto (Soulí).[1]

'Ο Χαντσερῆς ἐκίνησε, πῆγε νὰ κυνηγήση
κ' ἐγύρισε 'ς τὸ σπίτι του δίχως καρδιὰ καὶ κρίσι.
κ. τ. λ.

(*Aravandinos*, 446.)

YOUNG Hántseri fared gaily forth, for he was going hunting,
But homeward he returned again, without his heart and witless.
'My mother, at my heart's a pain; and in my head, my mother;
A trembling's taken hold of me; I'll die before the evening!'
'My son, you've at your heart no pain, nor in your head, my Hánts'ri;
You've only seen Elióyenni, and she your eyes has dazzled.

[1] See *Introd.*, p. 11, and p. 23, n. 9.

I'll send the scribes to her for you, and I will send the bishops,
That they may write the dowry down, and gentlemen I'll send her.'
They went, and there they stood and knocked, knocked at her lordly portal.
Elióyenni sat in her hall, five hundred slaves around her,
Some dressed in garments of the blue, and others of the yellow;
In blue, in azure blue they sat, you'd call them noble maidens.
She asked the envoys who they were, and what it was they wanted.
'We're come from Hántseri, to say, he for his wife would take you.'
'His little body I'd not have for horseblock in my courtyard,
For men to mount their horses from, and mules around it tether;
Nor do I want his little eyes to watch and ward my castle.'
When word is brought to Hántseri, it sorely, sorely grieves him.
He loads a mule with golden coin, and to a Witch he hies him.
And when she sees his countenance with grief and sickness written,
Then searchingly she questions him, she questions him and asks him:
'Say, have the brigands robbed thee now, thy cornfields and thy castle?
Or has thy brother slain thy love, and killed thy best belovéd?'
'I've neither lost my castle, dame; nor have I yet a brother;
But I have seen Elióyenni, and I for her am dying.'

'Now go, and take thee Frankish clothes, and dress in
    woman's garments,
And hie thee, hie thee then to her, and knock thou at
    her portal.'
'Who art thou who art knocking with my portal's rings
    of iron?'
''Tis I. I am thy cousin, come to thee from Aï-Donáto.
My mother dear has sent me here, that I may learn to
    broider.'
'And welcome art thou, cousin mine, who comest from
    Aï-Donáto.'
Then lovingly she kisses her, and locks in tight embraces,
And tenderly she takes her hand and leads her to the daïs,
And sits her down to teach her guest how she the gold
    should broider;
A kindling flame within she feels, she feels a flame un-
    wonted.
And when the broidering is done she gives to her the
    spindle.
'O what bad customs you have here, you people in this
    village;
The day long at the broidery, the evening at the spindle!'
The day was done and evening fell, fast coming was the
    darkness,
And Hántseri still was not seen, with musk so sweetly
    scented,
With hounds around him in the field, and scouring all
    the meadows.
'The night has come, Elióyenni, and fast the shades are
    falling;
The cuckoos wend them to their nests, and to their beds
    the reapers;
And I, poor homeless nestling, where shall I go for my
    slumber?'

'O hush thee, hush thee, cousin mine, and sleep thou with my servants.'
'The daughter of a king am I, I am of royal lineage;
So low am I descended now that I must sleep with servants?'
'O hush thee, hush thee, cousin mine, and we will sleep together.'
When they had slept, those two had slept, and when the Sun had risen
Two bowshots high above the hills, and glittered on the hoar-frost,
Then Hántseri his bed forsook, and hastened to his mother.
'O mother, deck the windows now, throw all the doors wide open;
Elióyenni is coming here, and she will be your daughter.'
'Go, go, my son, do thou be still, I will make all things ready;
All that is needed I'll prepare, and will await her coming.'
And when the maiden understood and knew that her heart's burning
Was what none else but Hántseri, he only could extinguish,
Then wildly she began to rave, and madly she discoursèd:
'O friends and servants all of mine, and damsels of my mother,
O light for me the tapers red, and light for me green candles,
For Hántseri is coming soon, and for his wife he'll take me.'
Then forth fares Elióyenni, to Hántseri she's going,
Within his famous garden ground, within Aïdona's castle;
Bareheaded, naked, too, she goes, sad sight, *sigouremént*.[1]
Upon the road, as on she goes, to enter in the castle,

---

[1] *Sicuramente*. Another of the Italian words in this Song is *porta* (portal).

She meets a woman who's a Witch, a thousand-year-old woman;
Who thus accosts and asks of her, and in these words she asks her:
'Who has at even seen the Sun, who has seen Stars at noontide?
Who has seen Elióyenni, a traveller on the highway,
Bareheaded, go, and naked, too, sad sight, *sigoureméné?*
Go, maiden, go, and do thou knock at Hántseri's high portal.'
'Where hast thou seen young Hántseri, O Witch, that thou shouldst know him?'
'Who knoweth not the Sun in heaven, nor knows the Moon at even,
He only knows not Hántseri that is of Aï-Donáto.
Go, go, my girl, knock at his door, at that same door stand knocking.'
Then went up Elióyenni, and at his door knocked loudly,
And all the windows saw she closed, and she began to call there:
'O ope to me, thou Witch's son, O thou of Witch's lineage,
Who with thy spells hast causéd me to wander on the highways!
If this is of thy spells the work, then let me die this moment;
But if this be the work of God, then I will go back homewards.'
Then wakes from slumber Hántseri; he cries, then forth he rushes.
He finds the windows all are shut, and fastened all the portals,
He finds, too, Elióyenni; dead at his gate she's lying.
He draws then out a golden knife, which in his breast he buries;

And by fair Elióyenni he lays him down expiring.
The youth a lowly reed becomes, a cypress-tree the maiden;
And when soft blows the southern wind, they bend and kiss each other.
And as the wayfarers pass by the fields of Aï-Donáto,
They cross themselves full piously, and sing this lamentation:
'See them, the two, so few of days, who passed away so quickly,
When living they had never kissed, but, dead, they kiss each other!'

THE SIREN AND THE SEAMEN.

Η ΤΡΑΓΟΥΔΙΣΤΡΙΑ.

Μιὰ κόρη ν ἐτραγούδαιν ἀπ' ὥρηο παρεθύρι,
τῆς πῆρ' ἀγέρας τὴ λαλιά, κάτου γιαλὸ τὴν πῆγε.
          κ. τ. λ.
(*Aravandinos,* 457.)

A MAID was singing as she sat, within a splendid window,
Her song was on the breezes borne, borne down unto the ocean.
As many ships as heard her lay, moored, and made fast their anchors.
A tartan from the Frankish land that was of Love the frigate,
Furled not her sails by breezes filled, nor yet along was sailing.
Then to his men the captain called, astern where he was standing:
'Ho, sailors! furl the sails at once, and climb ye up the rigging,

That to this charmer we may list, list how she's sweetly singing,
Hear what's the melody to which she her sweet song is singing.'
But so sweet was the melody, so passing sweet her warbling,
The skipper turned him once again, and to the shore it drew him,
And to the masts the mariners kept hanging in the rigging.

THE SHEPHERD AND THE LAMIA.[1]

Ο ΒΟΣΚΟΣ ΚΑΙ Η ΛΑΜΙΑ.

Kallameriá, Salonica.

Πέντε χιλιάδες πρόβατα, δέκα χιλιάδες γίδια,
Τὰ φύλαγαν τρεῖς ἀδελφοὶ κ' οἱ τρεῖς στοιχειὰ τοῦ κόσμου.
κ. τ. λ.

(*Passow*, 524.)

FIVE thousand sheep were in the flock, and there were goats ten thousand,
They tended were by brothers three, and by the three World-spirits.
And one goes out to win a kiss, the second goes a-wooing,
And Yanni, youngest of them all, alone they leave behind them,
To watch and tend the flock of sheep, and lead the goats to pasture.
To Yanni then his mother says, and wisely thus she warns him:
'If you would earn a blessing now from me and from your father,
Stand never 'neath a lonely tree, nor rest beneath a poplar,

[1] See *Introd.*, p. 12, n. 62.

Nor ever on the water's edge make with thy pipe sweet music,
Or there will come the Lamia out, the Lamia of the Ocean.'
But Yanni would not her obey, nor do his mother's bidding;
He stood beneath a lonely tree, he rested 'neath a poplar,
And down upon the water's edge made with his pipe sweet music.
Then from the sea the Lamia came, the Lamia of the Ocean.
'O play to me, my Yanni, play, play with thy pipe sweet music;
If I should weary of the dance, thou for thy wife shalt take me;
If thou shouldst weary of thy pipe, I'll take away thy sheep-cotes.'
And all day long three days he piped, three days and nights he whistled;
And Yanni was quite wearied out, and sorely worn with piping.
She took from him his flocks of sheep, of all his goats she robbed him;
And forth he went to work for hire, and labour for a master.

THE STOICHEION AND THE WIDOW'S SON.

ΤΟ ΣΤΟΙΧΕΙΟ ΚΑΙ Ο ΥΙΟΣ ΤΗΣ ΧΗΡΑΣ.

Στοιχειὸ ξεφανερώθηκε καὶ τρώει τς ἀντρειωμένους,
τοὺς ἔφαγε, τοὺς ἔσωσε, κανεὶς δὲν εἶχε μείνει.

χ. τ. λ.

(*Aravandinos*, 451.)

THERE came forth once a Stoicheiòn devouring all the warriors;

All were devoured and swept away, there was not one
    remaining;
The Widow's Son alone remains, alone of all the
    warriors.
His spear and sword he takes in hand, and forth he goes
    a-hunting,
And hills and mountains o'er he runs, o'er peaks and
    mountain-passes;
No game has risen on the wing, no game is roused in
    covert.
But as the Sun begins to dip, and nears his kingly
    splendour,
He finds a lovely damsel lone, a fair-haired, black-eyed
    maiden.
He stops and thus accosts the maid, he stands and thus
    he asks her:
'My girl, whose daughter may'st thou be? O say, who
    was thy mother?'
'A mother bore me like to thine, a mother like thine bore
    me.'
'What ails thee, maiden? thou art sad, what ails thee that
    thou sighest?'
'Where yonder thou that fig-tree seest, there at its root a
    well lies;
Within I've dropped my splendid ring, the ring of my
    betrothal.
The man who shall go down the well, and find and
    bring it to me,
Him will I wed, and him alone, and he shall be my consort.'
Then quick the youth stripped off his clothes, and down
    the well descended.
'O pull me up, girl! pull me up, for I can find no ring here!'
'Now thou art in, my Widow's Son, there shalt thou stay
    forever!'

THE STOICHEION AND YANNI.

ΤΟ ΣΤΟΙΧΕΙΟ ΚΑΙ Ο ΓΙΑΝΝΗΣ.

'Ο Γιάννης πούχεν έννηά γυιούς καί τούς έννηά μεγάλους,
μιᾷ μέρᾳ ν ἐβουλήθηκαν νὰ πᾶν νὰ κυνηγήσουν.

κ. τ. λ.

(*Aravandinos*, 452.)

NINE stalwart sons could Yanni boast, and they were nine tall brothers,
And they did all agree one day that they would go a-hunting.
When word of it to Yanni came, he ran to give his orders.
'You everywhere may hunt,' he said, 'roam hither, and roam thither,
But to Varlámi's[1] hill alone there must ye never venture;
For there an evil Monster lives, with nine heads on his body.'
But unto him they would not list, but would go to Varlámi;
And out to them the Monster came, with nine heads on his body,
And he snatched up the brothers nine, snatched up, and them did swallow.
When Yanni heard their dismal fate, then grieved was he right sorely;
His spear into his hand he took, and his good sword he girded,
And to Varlámi's hill he ran, and quickly he ascended.
'Come out, Stoicheió! come, Monster, out! and let us eat each other.'
'O welcome my good supper now, and welcome my good breakfast!'
Then Yanni on the Monster ran, with sword in hand uplifted;

[1] The site now of one of the Metéora Monasteries.

Nine strokes he dealt upon the heads, the nine heads of
  his body,
And aimed another at his paunch, and set free all his
  children;
And bore them home at eventide, all living, to their
  mother.

YANNI AND THE DRAKOS.

Ο ΓΙΑΝΝΗΣ ΚΑΙ Ο ΔΡΑΚΟΝΤΑΣ.

Thessaly.

Ποιὸς ἦταν ποῦ πέρασι τὴν νύχτα τραγουδῶντα;
Ξυπνάει τ' ἀηδόνι' ἀπ' ταῖς φωλιαῖς καὶ τὰ στοιχειὰ 'π τοὺς βράχους,
κ. τ. λ.

(*Passow*, 509.)

WHO was it that was passing by at night-time and was
  singing?
From nests arousing nightingales, and from the rocks
  Stoicheia,
And waking, too, a Drakissa in Drakos' arms enfolded?
The Drakos waxes very wroth and calls out in his fury:
'Who was it that was singing there, for I am going to eat
  him?'
'O leave me, Drakos, let me go, O leave me five days
  longer!
For Sunday is my wedding-day, my wedding-feast on
  Monday,
And home I must conduct my bride upon the morn of
  Tuesday!'
The Sun had darkened, darkened quite, the Moon
  herself had hidden,
And now the Morning Star so pure, was going to his
  setting.
'O welcome here my dinner comes, and welcome here
  my supper!'

Thy dinner—it may be of stones, stones may'st thou
  have for supper;
For I'm the Lightning's son, and she is daughter of the
  Thunder!'
'Yannáki, go, good luck to thee, and take thy good-
  wife with thee!'

THE WITCH OF THE WELL.

Η ΜΑΓΙΣΣΑ.

Τέσσαρες καὶ πέντ' ἦταν, ἐννέα ἀδερροί[1]
Τὸν πόλεμον ἀκοῦσαν κι' ἀρματωθήκασι.
κ. τ. λ.

(*Passow*, 523.)

O THEY were four, five brothers, nine brothers in a band,
Who heard of battle raging, and took their swords in hand.
As on the road they journeyed, and on their way did ride,
With thirst were they tormented, but soon a Well espied,
That wide was fifty fathoms, a hundred fathoms deep.
They cast lots who should venture down that Well's side
  so steep;
And as they cast the lot there, on Constantine it fell:
'Let me go down, my brothers—O brothers, tie me well!'
They tied the rope around him, they let him down amain;
But when they would withdraw him, he came not up again.
They tugged, they strained, in vain 'twas, the cord was
  snapped in twain.
'O leave me now, my brothers, leave me and go ye home.
When our good mother asks you what has of me become,
Do not you go and tell her, tell not our mother mild,
I've ta'en a Witch's daughter, and wed a Witch's child.
The clothes she's making for me, tell her to sell them now,
And back to my betrothéd, give ye her marriage-vow.'

---

[1] P is frequently substituted for Λ in the Greek *patois* of the provinces of Northern Greece. See *Preface*, p. xxix., and *Trans.*, p. 115.

THE WITCH MOTHER-IN-LAW.

Η ΜΑΓΙΣΣΑ.

Διαβάταις κι' ἂν διαβῆτι ἀπ' τὸν τόπο μου,
Μηλιά 'χο ϛτὴν αὐλή μου, καὶ κονί↓ιτι.
κ. τ. λ.

(*Passow*, 520.)

O WAYFARERS who're passing, who from my birthplace come,
I've apples in my courtyard, come shake the apple-tree;
Then go and take my greetings unto my mother dear,
And give them to my dearest, my grieving little wife,
And my unhappy children, and all the neighbours round.
O go and tell my dearest, O tell my dear Lenió,
Still if she will to wait me, or marry if she will;
Or if she come to find me, then mourning let her wear.
For I, alas, am married, in Anatolia wed;
A little wife I've taken, a Witch for mother-in-law,
Who all the ships bewitches, so they no more can sail;
And me she has enchanted, that I no more return.
My horse if I should saddle, unsaddled 'tis again;
My sword if I gird round me, it is again ungirt;
I write a word to send thee, and 'tis again unwrit.'

THE BRIDGE OF ARTA.

Η ΓΕΦΥΡΑ ΤΗΣ ΑΡΤΑΣ.

Σαραντατέντι μάστορες κ' ἑξήντα λαβουρέντες
Πύργον ἐθιμιλιώναν τσῆς Ἄρτας τὸ διοφῦρί.
κ. τ. λ.

(*Passow*, 512.)

GOOD five-and-forty masons stout, and labourers full sixty,
Did build the piers of Arta's bridge, and dig out the foundations;

All day they built with all their might, by night the wall down tumbled.
The masons wept, they sorely wept, and made great lamentation,
But all the labourers rejoiced—they were on daily wages.
One Sunday, 'twas an Easter Day, an Easter Day and Feast-day,
The master-mason laid him down to take a little slumber;
And in his sleep he had a dream, a vision in his slumber:
'If you slay not a human life, the walls can ne'er be founded.
No noble may it be, nor serf, nor any 'neath the heavens;
But e'en the master-mason's wife, his wife must be the victim!'
He called to him a labourer, one who would do his bidding:
'Go thou, and to thy lady say, go say thou to thy mistress,
Tell her to dress, and busk herself, and put on all her jewels;
Let her put on her silver gauds, and don her silken garments.
Go swiftly now, and swiftly come, and swiftly bear my orders.'
He went, his mistress soon he found, she sewing was and singing.
'Good morrow to thee, lady mine! good morrow to my mistress!
The master-mason's sent to thee to say: Put on thy jewels;
Put on thy silver gauds and chains, and wear thy silken garments;
Come, let us the foundations lay, and build the bridge of Arta.'
She dressed herself, she busked herself, and put on all her jewels;

She put on all her silver gauds, and donned her silken garments;
And she went forth and found them where they on the stones were sitting.
'Good morrow, lady mine, to thee! good morrow to thee, mistress!
I've lost my first ring from my hand, the ring of my betrothal:
For this I bid thee hither come that thou should'st find it for me.'
But when she went to seek the ring, went down to the foundations,
One man upon her mortar threw, lime heaped on her another;
The master-mason struck her, too, he struck her with his mallet.
'O we were once three sisters dear, and all the three were murdered;
Within a church the first was killed, in convent walls the second;
The third, the best of all, was slain when Arta's bridge was building.
Then, as my hands are trembling now, so may thy columns tremble;
And as my poor heart trembles now, may thy foundations tremble!'

THE ENCHANTED DEER.[1]

ΤΟ ΣΤΟΙΧΕΙΩΜΕΝΟ ΕΛΑΦΙ.

Τρίτη γεννήθ' ὁ Διγενής καὶ τρίτη θὰ πεθάνη.
Πιάνει, καλεῖ τοὺς φίλους του κι' ὅλους τοὺς ἀντρειωμένους·
       κ. τ. λ.

(*Passow*, 516.)

ON Tuesday Dígenés was born, and he must die on Tuesday.

[1] See *Introd.*, p. 13.

He to invite his friends begins, and bids, too, all the
    heroes ;
Minas will come and Mavralís, and Dráko's son is
    coming,
And Tremantáheilos will come, who shakes the earth
    and kosmos.[1]
They go together and they find him lying on the meadow.
'Where hast thou been, O Dígenés, that thou art now
    a-dying?'
'O eat, my friends, eat, eat and drink, for I am going to
    leave you;
On Alamána's mountains high, and o'er Arabia's meadows,
Where once not e'en ten men came out, nor even five
    were passing,
They come by fifties—hundreds now, and pass by with
    their weapons.
And I, unhappy man, came out, came out on foot and
    arméd.
Three hundred bears my hand has slain, and sixty lions
    conquered;
But I th' Enchanted Deer pursued, pursued and sorely
    wounded,
That wears upon his horns a cross, a star upon his fore-
    head;
And bears between his antlers proud, between his horns
    the Virgin.
That crime has filled my measure full, and now I am
    a-dying.
Here in this upper world I've lived, I've lived years full
    three hundred,
And none of all the heroes bold e'er daunted or dis-
    mayed me.

[1] Compare *Il.* xiii. 18. 'And the high hills trembled, and the woodland, beneath the immortal footsteps of Pôseidon.'

The Enchanted Deer.

But now I have a hero seen, unshod, on foot, and arméd,
One who in richest garb was drest, and from his eyes flashed lightnings.
I with my eyes did him behold, and sore my heart was wounded ;
That stricken Deer's my fatal crime, and now I am a-dying.'

THE SUN AND THE DEER.
Olympus.

Τρίχουν τὰ 'λάφια 'ςτὰ βουνά, τρίχουν τὰ 'λαφομούσχια,
Καὶ μιὰ 'λαφίνα ταπεινὴ, δὲν πάει μαζῆ μὲ τ'ἄλλα.
χ. τ. λ.

(*Oikonomides, E. 5.*)

THE Deer are racing o'er the hills, their Fawns around them frisking;
One humble Deer walks all alone, nor with the herd is going.
She saunters only in the shade, and to the left reposes,
And where she bubbling water finds, mixed with her tears she drinks it.
The Sun has seen her from on high, and standing still he asks her:
' O humble Deer, what is thy grief, thou go'st not with the others,
But only saunter'st in the shade, and to the left reposest ?'
' My Sun, as thou hast questioned me, thus even will I answer:
For twelve long years I barren lived, without a fawn and barren;
But after the twelve years were passed, a Fawn had me for mother.
I gave it suck, I tended it till it had lived two summers ;

Then the inhuman hunter came, and shot my Fawn and killed it.
Curst mayest thou, O hunter, be,[1] both thou and all thy treasures,
By whom I now am twice bereaved, of dearest child and husband.'

THE BLACK RACER.

TO ΣΤΟΙΧΠΜΑ.

'Ο Κοσταντῆς κι' ὁ βασιλιὰς ἀντάμα τρῶν καὶ πίνουν,
κι' ἀθηβολὴν εὑρηκανε ποιός ἔχει κάλλιο μαῦρο.
κ. τ. λ.

(*Passow*, 515.)

THE king and Constantine did eat, they ate and drank together,
When rose the question twixt them twain—whose was the best black racer?
The king he stakes him golden coins, for he has wealth in plenty;
And Constantine so poor is he that he his head must wager.
But when the wife of Constantine, his well-belovéd heard it,
Down to the horse's stall she went, and filled with oats his manger.
'The king's black horse if thou canst pass, and win the race, my Black One,
Thy daily rations I'll increase to five-and-forty handfuls;
I'll give these gauds that on me hang, and into horse-shoes change them;
I'll give my golden earrings too, nails for thy shoes I'll make them.'
They ran for forty miles apace, abreast they ran together;

[1] All our misfortunes after gaining the summit of Olympos (*below*, p. 93, n. 1) were attributed to the fawn of a gazelle having been hit by a wild volley poured into a herd on the highest ridge of the mountain.

When they had run the forty-fourth, and neared the five-and-fortieth,
He stopped his course, and him bethought of what his lady'd told him.
Like lightning-flash he came in front, came from behind like thunder,
And 'tween his rival and himself he left ten miles of country.
'O stay, O stay, for I'm the king, and shame me not 'bove measure ;
The wager that we two have laid I'll pay to thee twice over !'

THE SHEPHERD AND THE WOLF.

Ο ΒΛΑΧΟΣ ΚΑΙ Ο ΛΥΚΟΣ.

'Αποκοιμήθ' ὁ πιστικὸς μὲς 'τὸ ῥαβδὶ τ' ἀπάνω·
Καὶ χάνει χίλια πρόβατα καὶ δυὸ χιλιάδες γίδια·

(*Passow*, 503.)

A SHEPHERD laid him down and slept, slept with his crook beside him,
While strayed away a thousand sheep, and wandered goats two thousand.
Then he along a lonely road, a lonely path betook him,
And meeting soon an aged Wolf, he stopped, and thus he asked him :
'O Wolf, say, hast thou seen my sheep? O Wolf, hast thou my goats seen ?'
'Perhaps I am thy shepherd then, and I thy goats am tending ?
There, on that far, far distant hill, away upon the mountain—
There, in the distance, graze the flocks, and goats upon the mountain.

6—2

I went there, too, to eat a lamb, a tender kid to choose me,
When quick the lame dog seized on me, and then the
  mad dog pinned me;
They've broke between them all my ribs, my spine, too,
  they have broken!'

THE SWALLOWS' RETURN.[1]
ΧΕΛΙΔΟΝΙΣΜΑ.
Χελιδόνι ἔρχεται,
Θάλασσαν ἀπέρασε,
κ. τ. λ.
Passow, 305.

SWALLOWS are returning fast,
Over wide seas they have past;
'Neath the eaves they build their nest,
Sing as they from labour rest.

March, O March, thou snowest amain;
February comes with rain;
April, sweetest of the year,
Coming is, and he is near.

Twitter all the birds and sing,
All the little trees do spring;
Hens lay eggs, and O, good luck,
Already they begin to cluck.

Flocks and herds, a numerous train,
To hilly pastures mount again;
Goats that skip and leap and play,
Nibbling wayside shrub's green spray.

Beasts and birds and men rejoice,
With one heart and with one voice;
Frosts are gone, and snow-wreaths deep,
Blustering Boreas fallen asleep.

[1] A survival of the χελιδόνισμα of ancient Greece. A similar welcome is given to the birds of passage at St. Kilda. See *Report of the Crofters' Commission*, vol. i., p. 467.

THE BIRD'S COMPLAINT.

ΠΑΡΑΠΟΝΟ ΠΟΥΛΙΟΥ.

Ενα πουλ' ἴκαμι φωλιὰ 'ςτῆς λεϊμονιᾶς τὸ φύλλο,
Φύσισ' ἀνιμοστρόβιλος κ' ἐπῆρι τὴ φωλιὰ του.
κ. τ. λ.

(*Passow*, 497.)

AMONG a lemon-tree's green leaves a bird its nest had woven;
But wildly soon the whirlwind blew, afar the nest it whirled.
With her complaint she flew away, and with her sore heart-burning,
And built herself a nest again, at a well's lip she built it;
The maidens there for water went, and all her work was wasted.
With her complaint she flew away, and with her sore heart-burning,
And now upon a reedy marsh her little nest she built her;
But fierce and wildly Boreas blew, and far and wide he whirled it.
With her complaint she flew away, and with her sore heart-burning,
And 'mong the almond-leaves she sat, she sat and sad lamented.
Then from a castle-window high a king's fair daughter heard her.
'Would, birdie, I'd thy beauty bright, and would I had thy warbling!
And would I had thy gorgeous wing, thy song of passing sweetness!'
'Why would'st thou have my beauty bright, why would'st thou have my warbling?

Why would'st thou have my gorgeous wing, my song of passing sweetness,
Who eat'st each day the daintiest fare, while I eat pebbles only;
Who drinkest of the finest wines, I water from the courtyard ;
Who liest on the softest couch, on sheets with broidered borders ;
While me my hard fate only gives the fields and snow to lie on ?
Thou wait'st the coming of the youth for frolic and for dalliance,
While I can but the sportsman wait, the sportsman who would shoot me ;
Who'd shoot and roast me at his fire, and sit and sup upon me.
O lady, stay thou in thy place, I've naught that thou shouldst envy ;
For every heart its sorrow knows, nor may another know it.'

THE FIRST OF MAY.[1]

Ω. ΔΗ ΕΙΣ ΤΗΝ ΠΡΩΤΗΝ ΤΟΥ ΜΑΙΟΥ.

'Εμπῆκε ὁ Μάης, εμπῆκε ὁ Μάης, εμπῆκε ὁ Μάης ὁ μῆνας,
ὁ Μάης μὲ τὰ τριαντάφυλλα, 'Απρίλης μὲ τὰ ρόδα.

κ. τ. λ.

(*Aravandinos,* 440.)

O MAY has come, the month of May, the month of May is with us,
May, with her thirty-petalled flowers, and April with his roses.
Thou, April, art in roses drest ; and May, thou month most cherished,

[1] Sung by children at the doors of houses.

The First of May.

Thou floodest all the gladsome world again with bloom
    and blossom;
And me thou twinest tenderly in the embrace of beauty.
Go, tell the maiden that I love, go, give the maiden
    warning,
That I am coming with a kiss before the rain or snow falls;
Before the Danube shall come down, and draw the rivers
    to him.
When it is raining I go forth, and when the shower ceases,
And when the still small rain falls down, then springs
    the sweet carnation.
O open us your little purse, your purse with pearls
    embroidered!
If it has groats in, give them us; and if but pence, yet
    give them,
And if sweet wine within you find, give us that we may
    drink it.

THE SOLDIER AND THE CYPRESS TREE.
O ΛΕΒΕΝΤΗΣ.
Zagorie.
'Ενας λέβεντος κ' ένας καλὸς στρατιώτης,
κάστρο γύρευε, χωριὸ νὰ πάῃ νὰ μείνῃ.
                            κ. τ. λ.
(*Aravandinos*, 414.)

THERE was a youth, he was a valiant soldier,
Who sought a tower, a town wherein to sojourn:
The road he found, and found he too the footpath;
Tower found he none, nor town wherein to sojourn.
He found a tree, the tree they call the Cypress:
'Welcome me, tree! welcome me now, O Cypress!
For I have strayed away from field of battle,
And now my eyes in sleep would fain be closing.'
' Lo here my boughs, upon them hang thy weapons;
Lo here my roots, thy steed to them now tether;
Here lay thee down, rest here, and slumber sweetly.'

THE APPLE TREE AND THE WIDOW'S SON.

Η ΜΗΛΗΑ ΚΑΙ Ο ΥΙΟΣ ΤΗΣ ΧΗΡΑΣ.

Zagora.

Μπρὲ μηλιά, γλυκομηλιά,
δάνεισέ μας τ' ἄνθια σου,
    κ. τ. λ.

(*Aravandinos,* 232.)

'APPLE-TREE, sweet apple-tree,
Lend us now, I say, your flowers,
From your boughs rain leaves in showers!'
'I my flowers do not lend,
Nor my leaves from branches send.
With my arms, and all full-drest,
To the dance I'll with the rest.
More than one I'll wrestling throw,
Three times nine my strength shall know.
On my side the Widow's Son,
That far-famed, illustrious one;
Whosoe'er belies my hand,
And against me dares to stand.'

THE RIVER AND THE LOVER.

Ο ΠΟΤΑΜΟΣ.

Ioannina.

Ποταμέ, σύντα γιομίζεις
κι' ἀρχινᾷς νὰ κυματίζῃς,
    κ. τ. λ.

(*Aravandinos,* 398.)

RIVER, as thou sudden gushest,
And in crested wavelets rushest,
Bear me on thy waters dancing,
On thy whirling eddies glancing;
Let the fair ones come a-washing,
Let the black-eyed come a-bleaching;

Let me here my old love find,
Who to suff'ring me consigned ;
Then I'll wash her body small,
Till come from me the poison all.

OLYMPOS AND KISSAVOS (OSSA).
Litochori.

'Ο "Ολυμπος κι' ὁ Κίσσαβος τὰ δυὸ βουνὰ μαλώναν,
Γυρίζ' ὁ γέρο "Ολυμπος καὶ λέγει τοῦ Κισσάβου.

(*Oral Version.*[1])   κ. τ. λ.

OLYMPOS old and Kissavos, the mountains great, disputed ;
Olympos turns him round, and says to Kissavos says he,
' You
With me you dare to wrangle, you, Turk-trodden
    Kissavos, you !
With me, Olympos old renowned, renowned e'en to the
    City ?
I seventy mountain-summits have, and two-and-sixty
    fountains ;
To every bush an Armatole, to every branch a Klephtë.
And perched upon my highest peak there sits a mighty
    eagle ;
A mirror, in his talon grasped, he holds on high exalted,
And in it he his charms admires, and on his beauty gazes !'

[1] After weeks of Brigand-hunting, we were ascending Olympus from the Pass of Petra, in the glorious sun-filled atmosphere of an August morning ; and when near the probable site of the more ancient Pelasgian Sanctuary of the Olympian Dodona, my servant Demosthénes burst out with this Song, the last lines of which, however, he but imperfectly remembered. By the treachery of our guides, in league probably with the Brigands, the detachment of twenty infantry and two troopers, under a Yuz-bashi, got dispersed, and we narrowly escaped capture during the night which was spent on the mountain. But some two or three days later, our hostess at the village of Litochóri, above the Plain of the Muses, completed my servant's version of the Song. And there and then, with the help of Demosthénes, as much friend as servant, I made the translation here given. The three last lines seem to me a splendidly bold poetic way of saying that there is a magnificent view from the ' highest peak' of Olympos.

SECTION II.—CHRISTIAN.

FOR THE FEAST OF THE CHRIST-BIRTHS.[1]

ΕΙΣ ΤΗΝ ΕΟΡΤΗΝ ΤΩΝ ΧΡΙΣΤΟΥΓΕΝΝΩΝ.

Parga.

Χριστὸς γεννᾶται σήμερον ἐν Βηθλεὲμ τῇ πόλει,
οἱ οὐρανοὶ ἀγάλλονται, χαίρει ἡ κτίσις ὅλη.
κ. τ. λ.

(*Aravandinos*, 151.)

THIS day in Bethlehem's famous town is Christ our Saviour born;
The heavens rejoice and earth is glad upon this happy morn.
In stable lowly He's brought forth, laid in a horse's stall,
The King and the Creator; and the choir of Angels all
Sing to the Holy Trinity, 'Praise be to Highest God,
That over all the earth shall now be spread the faith abroad.'
From out of Persia Magi three were coming on their way,
Led by a shining star that failed them not by night or day;
And on to Bethlehem they go, and ask, with anxious mind,
Where Christ is born; for Him they seek, and Him they fain would find.
When of the Christ-child's birth he heard, then troubled was the King;
Possessed with rage, he said, they must to him the Magi bring.

---

[1] Having been unable to get any more satisfactory explanation of this plural, I would suggest that it may be a survival of the old conception of the Sun-Gods as reborn every year.

For the Feast of the Christ-Births.

The Magi came; he asked of them where Christ to seek
  they'd go?
'In Bethlehem, in Bethlehem, the Scripture saith, we
  know.'
Saith he: 'Go ye and find Him me, go ye and find this
  Lord;
And when ye Him have worshipped there, then come and
  bring me word.'
For he himself would also go to worship and to pray,
With the most wicked treachery intending him to slay.
The Magi went with hastening feet, and when they saw
  the Star
Descend upon a lowly cave, they hurried from afar,
And, entering in the cave, they saw the Virgin Mother
  mild;
Within her arms and on her breast she held the holy Child.
They lowly bend and worship Him, to Him their gifts
  they bring,
The gold and frankincense and myrrh, and praise to God
  they sing.
When they had worshippéd the Christ, they turned them
  back again,
To carry to King Herod word their search had not been
  vain.
An angel out from heaven came down, he said they must
  not go;
Another road he bade them take, another path did show.
The Magi came not. Herod saw his orders had been
  vain.
He said: 'In Bethlehem's town shall not a single child
  remain.'
And fourteen thousand, in one day, they fourteen
  thousand killed;
With lamentation, tears, and woe, was every mother filled.

SAINT BASIL, OR THE NEW YEAR.

Ο ΑΓΙΟΣ ΒΑΣΙΛΗΣ.

Ἅγιος Βασίλης ἔρχεται ἀπὸ τὴν Καισαρείαν,
Βαστᾷ λιβάνι καὶ κερὶ, χαρτὶ καὶ καλαμάρι.
κ. τ. λ.

(*Passow*, 296.)

SAINT BASIL, see, is coming out, from Cesaræa coming;
He carries incense in his hand, and candle, ink, and paper.
The ink upon the paper writes, the paper likewise asks him:
'Whence, Basil, comest thou, O whence, and whither art thou wending?'
'I've from my mother come away, and now to school I'm going.'
'O sit and eat, and sit and drink, and sit and sing thou for us!'
''Tis only letters that I learn, of singing I know nothing.'
'O then your letters well you know, say us your Alpha, Beta!'
He leant him there upon his staff, to say his Alpha, Beta,
And though the staff was dry and dead, it put forth buds and branches;[1]
And from the branches forth there gushed and flowed out freshest fountains,
And all the birds came flying down to wash and preen their plumage;
And with them came his sire to bathe, his aged, aged father.
'For thee, my father, it were meet, to seat thee on a carpet,
And counting out with thy right hand, and with thy left hand lending.
More meet by far 'twould be for thee wert thou on horseback seated,

[1] See note, p. 123.

And see that thou touch not the ground when passing
    through the river.
More meet by far 'twould be for thee to pass o'er in a
    vessel,
And that the cordage of the ship should all with gold be
    covered.
Much have I spoken of my sire, now let me praise my
    mother;
A lady with a marble neck, a crown upon her forehead,
In Basil's chamber they have limned, and thus thy
    portrait painted.
Thou hast a son who letters learns, who learns to use his
    pencil,
And may God's blessing rest on him, and may he wear
    the cassock.
Thou hast a lovely daughter too, a maid without a
    blemish;
She's neither in the city seen, nor e'en in Cesaræa.'

THE FEAST OF THE LIGHTS, OR EPIPHANY.

Ω.ΔΗ ΕΙΣ ΤΗΝ ΕΟΡΤΗΝ ΤΩΝ ΦΩΤΩΝ

Ioannina (John the Baptist Town).

'Εβγᾶτε γιὰ νὰ μάθετε τὸ θαῦμα ὁποῦ ἐγείνη,
ποῦ συγκατέβηκε ὁ Χριστὸς πολλὰ νὰ ὑπομείνῃ:

κ. τ. λ.

(*Aravandinos*, 153.)

O COME and learn the wonder great, the wonder great
    that happened,
How Christ did condescend for men, and much for them
    did suffer.
And then went down to Jordan's brink, and into Jordan's
    waters,
With the command to be baptized, baptized by John
    the Baptist.

'Come, O My John, come hither now, come and do thou baptize Me,
For in this awful wonder thou may'st serve Me and attend Me.'
'My Lord! O no, I cannot look, cannot look on Thy beauty,
Nor can I gaze upon the Dove that o'er Thy head is hov'ring.
My Lord! O no, I cannot touch Thee from above descended,
For the wide earth and all the heavens submit them to Thy orders.'
'Come, O My John, come unto Me, and linger thou no longer;
To this great mystery we perform thou shalt become the sponsor.'
Then John baptized his Lord forthwith, that might be cleansed and purgéd
The sin that Adam first had sinned, and that it might be cancelled ;
And to confound the Enemy, to foil the thrice accurséd
Beguiler of mankind, that he in hell may dwell for ever.

VAIA, OR PALM SUNDAY.[1]

BAIA.

Καλ' ἡμέρα σας, καλὴ χρονιά σας
Καλῶς (σὰς) ηὕραμεν τὴν ἀφεντιά σας.

χ. τ. λ.

(*Passow*, 304 *a*.)

GOOD day! and may a glad year for you shine,
And glad are we to meet you, masters mine;

---
[1] Sung by children at house-doors.

Vaia, or Palm Sunday.

The nightingales are singing in the trees,
The swallows spread their wings upon the breeze.

O bring me balsams, lemon-trees now bring,
And plant them in the gardens now 'tis spring;
The gardens of these lordly houses gay,
Which breathe forth sweetest scents by night and day.

Laz'rus has come, the eve of Passion Week,
Come, too, has he, the Virgin's Son so meek;
And March, rejoicing, him goes forth to meet,
He worships, lowly bending at his feet.

It seems but yesterday that Laz'rus slept,
Lying within the cave while sisters wept;
Grieve ye, and sorrow with the sorrowful,
Show pity, mercy to the merciful.

And raise for me my brother from the grave,
My brother dead, whom yet my heart doth crave.
And many other things to you I'd say,
My lords and ladies, on this day;

Long may you live, and fruitful may you be,
In coming years!

ODE TO THE SEVEN PASSIONS.
Ω, ΔΗ ΕΙΣ ΤΑ ΣΕΠΤΑ ΠΑΘΗ.
Parga.

Καλό είναι τ' Άγιος ό Θεός, καλό είναι νά τό λένε,
όπου το λίγει σώνεται, όπου τ' άκούει άγιάζει.
x. τ. λ.

(*Aravandinos*, 157.)

O GOOD is He, our holy God, and good it is to say it;
And whoso says it, he shall live, and he who hears is sainted;
And he who lists and understands, in paradise shall enter.
Away in far Jerusalem, upon the tomb of Jesus,

Erst not a tree was seen to grow, and now a tree is growing:
For Christ our Saviour is that tree, its branches the Apostles;
Its green leaves are the Martyrs meek, its spreading roots the Prophets,
Who prophesied and said to men what Christ would come to suffer.
My Christ, and Thou hast borne the pain, and borne the suffering grievous,
When martyrized and tortured Thee those curst and sinful Hebrews,
The unbelieving wicked men, a thousand times accursèd!
Unto the Smith they hurried them, for three great nails they wanted;
And he, that day, not only three, but five nails for them fashioned.
'O Smith and Master-craftsman, say, what wouldst thou with these five nails?'
'I'll tell you why I made them, sirs, and this request fulfil me:
The two you through His feet shall drive, two through His hands you'll fasten;
The fifth and longest of them all you through His heart will thrust me,
That out may flow the blood and gall, yea, flow from out His vitals.'
And when the Panaghía heard, she sank to earth and fainted.
O bring ye meat, and bring ye wine, and light cakes bring ye to her,
That I may show the Comforter to all unhappy mothers,
To all the grieving sisters, and to all the grieving brothers;
They should not go and hang themselves, nor take a knife to slay them.

FOR THE GREAT FRIDAY.

ΤΗΣ ΜΕΓΑΛΗΣ ΠΑΡΑΣΚΕΥΗΣ.

Η Παναγιὰ ἐκάθετο μόνη καὶ μοναχή του,
Τὴν προσευχήν της ἔκαμνε γιὰ τὸ μονογενῆ της.
κ. τ. λ.
(*Kind.*)

THE Panaghía sits alone, alone she sits and lonely;
She prays, and all her prayers are for her only Son
belovéd.
A noise she hears, and tumult loud, and very great
confusion;
And forth she comes outside her door, and from her
street she sallies.
She sees the Heavens darkened o'er, and sees the Stars
all tearful;
She sees the bright Moon in the sky, in tears the
dear Moon swimming;
St. John she sees, who comes to her, he weeps, his
breast he's beating.
And in one hand he holds the hair torn from his head
in anguish,
The other holds a handkerchief that with his tears is
dripping.
' Now tell me, tell me, my St. John, O my St. John, now
tell me,
Hast thou not seen mine only Son, hast thou not seen
thy Teacher?'
' I have no mouth to tell of it, nor lips have I to speak it!
Nor can my breaking heart endure to share with thee
the tidings;
But, as thou askest me of this, so let me even tell thee.
See'st thou that hill, see'st thou that hill, that hill both
broad and lofty?

There have the Hebrews thrust Him forth, thrust Him
all bound and pinioned ;
Laid hands on Him as on a thief, and as a murderer led
Him.'
And when our Lady heard these words she swooned
away and fainted.
They jars of water poured on her, three jars of musk
they emptied,
And afterwards rose-water sweet, until she was recovered.
And when our Lady spake again, these were the words
she uttered :
'Let Martha come, and Mary come, Elizabeth come with
them,
Let them come where He may be found before they
crucify Him,
Before they thrust the nails in Him, before they yet have
slain Him !'
As they were journeying on the road, and on the road
were passing,
Long time our Lady wept, she wept, long time was she
lamenting.
And by a Gipsy smith they passed, a smith who nails was
making.
'Thou dog, thou Gipsy dog,'[1] said she, 'what is it thou
art doing?'
'They're going to crucify a man, and I the nails am
making.
They only ordered three of me, but five I mean to
make them ;
Two for his two knees I design, two for his hands I fashion,
The fifth, the sharpest of the five, within his heart
shall enter.'

[1] Gipsies are generally credited in the East with being ready for any base work. See *below*, p. 231.

'Thou dog, thou Gipsy dog,' said she, 'henceforth make thou no ashes.
If thou henceforth shalt ashes make, the wind shall whirl them from thee.'
And then her way she took again unto the Door of Robbers.
The doors were fast shut every one, they fastened were with boulders;
But from their fear they opened wide, all of themselves they opened,[1]
And entered there our Lady in, with tears and lamentation.
There stood the Hebrews all around, they all around were standing,
One spat on Him, one water threw, and mocked at Him another.
She saw her Son upon the Cross, upon the Cross beheld Him:
'Is there no knife to kill me with, no cord that I may hang me?'
And from her Son the answer came, and from the Cross He answered:
'My Mother, shouldst thou slay thyself, then all the world would slay them.
Have patience, *Mána*; then, like thee, will all the world have patience.'
'Tell me, my Son, O tell to me, say when may I expect Thee?'
'On Easter Day, on Easter Day, the Lord's Day and the Sabbath.
Go, *Mána*, go now, to our door, return among our neighbours,

[1] Compare *Il.* v. 749.
'Self-moving groaned upon their hinges the gates of heaven.'
Also *Paradise Lost*, v. 251.
   'The gate self-opening wide,
 On golden hinges turning.'

Spread in the midst a table low, within our dwelling spread it,
With mothers let the children eat, and children with their mothers,
And there let all the goodwives eat, they with their worthy husbands ;
Let all who love us there sit down, all who for us feel sorrow.'

THE RESURRECTION.
Ο ΑΝΑΣΤΑΣΙΣ.[1]

Χριστὸς ἀνέστη ἐκ νεκρῶν,
θανάτῳ θάνατον πατήσας,
Καὶ τοῖς ἐν τοῖς μνήμασι ζωὴν χαρισάμενος.

THE Christ has risen from the Dead,
By death He death hath trampled on,
To those laid in the Graves Life having given.

THE MIRACLE OF ST. GEORGE.
ΤΟ ΘΑΥΜΑ ΤΟΥ ΑΓΙΟΥ ΓΕΩΡΓΙΟΥ.

Ακούστε τὸ τί γίνηκε σὲ τόπο ξακουσμένο !
'Εκ' ηταν κ' ἐφώλειαζε θεριὸ καταραμένο,
κ. τ. λ.

(*Aravandinos*, 159.)

O LIST and hear what once befel within a famous land !
A Monster foul had made his lair, and taken up his stand;
And gave they him not men to eat at morn and eve enow
To take the water from the Well no one would he allow.
For that they cast lots every one, he who the lot should draw,
Must to the Monster send his child, a gift for his foul maw.

---

[1] During Easter, the usual salutation is Χριστὸς ἀνέστη ! ('Christ has risen !') to which the reply is 'Αληθῶς ἀνέστι ! ('Truly he has risen ')—a salutation which greatly impressed me when it was exchanged between passing strangers on the road.

The Miracle of St. George.

Then fell the lot upon the King, fell on his daughter fair,
And to be eaten she must go, that maid of beauty rare.
And then, with tears and loud lament, the King cries out:
'O stay!
Take all my life away from me, but leave my child, I pray!'
But with one voice the people say, and with one mouth they cry:
'Give us thy daughter, O our King, or thou instead shalt die!'
'O dress, adorn her, to the Well then lead my child forlorn;
That when the Monster eats her, she may not be chewed or torn!'[1]
Away in Cappadocia far, St. George hears, mounts his steed,
On his swift horse he rides apace, he's coming with all speed.
As o'er the road they hasten on, and pass with flying feet,
Within a dreary desert place, they Satan chance to meet,
'O great St. George, O great St. George, why such dire haste and speed?
Why do you spur your good swift horse, and forward urge your steed?'
'How, Satan, cursèd Satan, how my name com'st thou to know?
I am a stranger in these parts, my family also.'
And sorely whipping his good horse, he to the Well comes down,
And finds the maiden standing there, like faded apple grown.
'O fly, O fly, thou gallant youth, for fear he should eat thee.

[1] He, no doubt, hoped that the stiffness of the embroidered and silver-ornamented national costume would necessitate her being *bolted.*

That Monster fierce, that Monster fell, by whom I'll
    eaten be!'
'Be thou not troubled, damsel mine, nor yet be thou
    afraid,
But on the name of our bless'd Lord thy thoughts be
    firmly stayed.'
Then he alights and lays him down to take a little sleep,
Until the Monster shall come up from out that Fountain
    deep.
When forth the Monster came the hills did shake and
    were afraid,[1]
And from her fright all deadly pale and bloodless stood
    the maid.
'Awake! arise, O gallant youth, for, see, the water's
    fretting;
The Monster grinds his jaws; his teeth, his teeth for me
    he's whetting!'
He quickly mounts upon his horse, with spear in hand he
    goes,
Soon from the Monster's open mouth a bloody fountain
    flows.
'See, maiden, I've the Monster slain, go back unto thy kin,
That all thy friends and folk may joy, when thee they
    back shall win.'
'O tell, O tell, thou gallant youth, O tell to me thy name,
That I may gifts for thee prepare, and send my lord the
    same.'
'They call me George where I at home in Cappadocia
    live;
But let thy offering be a church, if gifts to me thou'dst
    give.
And set a picture in the midst, a horseman let it bear,
A horseman who a Monster slays, slays with his good
    stout spear.'

[1] See note, p. 84.

THE VOW TO ST. GEORGE.

TO TAΞIMON.

Ἕνα μικρὸ Τουρκόπουλο τοῦ βασιληᾶς ριτζιάλι
μιὰ Ρομηοπούλ' ἀγάπησε, κ' ἐκείνη δὲν τὸν θέλει·
κ. τ. λ.

(*Aravandinos*, 443.)

A LITTLE Turkish youth was he, one of the Sultan's pages,
Who loved, who loved a Romeot maid, but she did not desire him.
Before her does she put the hills, the mountains leaves behind her,
Within the church she gains at last, she kneels and says three prayers:
'Effendi mine, O dear St. George, O save me from the Muslim!
Of candles litras thee I'll bring, and litras bring of incense,
And oil in hides of buffalo I'll bring thee by the skinful!'
There opened then a marble slab, within it hid the maiden.
But see! see there the Turkish youth is drawing near on horseback,
And at the church door he dismounts, and there himself he crosses.
'Effendi mine, O dear St. George, now show to me the maiden;
I'll bring thee candles by the load, and by the load bring incense,
And by the shipful I'll bring oil, I'll bring it by the boatload!'

Now gapes the marble slab again, and there is seen the maiden.
Then lifts she up her voice on high, cries loud as she is able:
'O list, ye mountains and ye hills, ye vilayets and townships,
The Saint for gain has me betrayed, for treasure he's betrayed me!'

PROCESSION FOR RAIN.[1]

Thessaly and Macedonia.

ΠΕΡΠΕΡΙΑ.

Περπεριὰ δροσολογιὰ
Δρόσισε τὴν γειτονιά.
κ. τ. λ.

(*Kind* 76.)

PERPERIÀ, all fresh bedewed,
Freshen all the neighbourhood;
By the woods, on the highway,
As thou goest, to God now pray:
O my God, upon the plain,
Send thou us a still, small rain;
That the fields may fruitful be,
And vines in blossom we may see;
That the grain be full and sound,
And wealthy grow the folks around;
Wheat and barley
Ripen early,

---

[1] In times of prolonged drought it is customary to dress up in flowers a girl, who heads a procession of children to all the wells and springs of the neighbourhood; and at each halting-place she is drenched with water by her companions, who sing this invocation.

Maize and cotton may take root,
Rye and rice and currant shoot;
Gladness in our gardens all,
For the drought may fresh dews fall;
Water, water, by the pail,
Grain in heaps beneath the flail;
Bushels grow from every ear,
Each vine-stem a burden bear.
Out with drought and poverty,
Dew and blessings would we see.

THE VISIT TO PARADISE AND HELL.

Η ΚΟΛΑΣΙΣ.

Παρακαλῶ σε, Παναγιά, καὶ διπλοπροσκυνῶ σε,
νὰ μοῦ χαρίσῃς τὰ κλειδιὰ, κλειδιὰ τοῦ παραδείσου.
κ. τ. λ.

(*Aravandinos*, 160.)

O PANAGHÍA, thee I pray, and twice before thee bend me,
That thou wouldst give to me the keys, in Paradise to enter;
To enter as a living man, to walk there strong and healthy,
And see the rich men how they fare, see how the poor are lodged there.
The poor sit in the sun's glad light, they bask them in the sunbeams,
The rich are wallowing in the pitch, and rolling in the darkness;
And lying there is the Exarch, upon the edge supported,
And looks across towards the poor, and thus he them beseeches:
'O poor, take ye my *aspras*[1] now, and give to me a taper!'

---

[1] The *Aspra*, from ἄσπρος, white, was the smallest silver coin; but the word was used in the plural for money generally, as *pará* (παράδες), the smallest copper coin, now is.

'Here *aspras* are not current coin, and tapers are not purchased.
Exarch, rememberest thou when we in th' other world existed,
Thou gav'st no alms unto the poor, nor helpedst those in sickness?
Exarch, rememberest thou when near thou unto death wert drawing,
Thou wentest not to evensong, nor often unto matins,
Nor yet to holy liturgy, which makes the world to tremble?
Rememberest how, by usury, to fifteen, ten thou changedst,
Didst mingle water with the wine, and with the flour mix ashes?'

SECTION III.—CHARONIC.

THE MOIRAI.

'Από τὸν Ὄλυμπον τὸν κόρυμβον,
τὰ τρία ἄκρα τοῦ Οὐρανοῦ,
κ. τ. λ.

(*Heuzey, p.* 139.)

OH from the summit of Olympus high,
The three extremest heights of Heaven,
Where dwell the Dealers-out of Destinies,[1]
Oh may my own Fate hear me,
And, hearing, come unto me!

CHARON AND HIS MOTHER.
ΧΑΡΟΣ ΚΑΙ Η ΜΕΤΗΡ ΤΟΥ.

Ὁ Χάρος ἰκαλίγωνε ἔξω στὸ φεγγαράκι,
Καὶ ἡ μάννα του τὸν ἔλεγε, κι' ἡ μάννα του τὸν λέγει,
κ. τ. λ.

(*Oikonomides*, Γ. 3.)

OUT in the little moon's white light, his horse was Charon shoeing,
And thus his *mána* said to him, and thus his mother charged him:
'My son, when thou go'st to the chase, when thou go'st forth a-hunting,
Take not the *mánas* who have sons, nor brothers who have sisters,
Take not those who have just been wed, nor those just crowned in marriage.'
'Where I find three will I take two, where I find two, one only,
And if I find one man alone, him, too, will I take with me.'

---
[1] Αἱ Μοῖραι τῶν Μοιρῶν.

CHARON'S WEDDING FEAST FOR HIS SON.

ΧΑΡΟΣ ΚΑΙ ΧΗΡΑΣ ΠΑΙΔΙ.

Βγῆκεν ὁ ἥλιος μαλακός, μαῦρος καὶ πεισμωμένος,
Μήνα μὲ τ' ἄστρα μάλωνε, μήνα μὲ τό φεγγάρι,
κ. τ. λ.

(*Oikonomides*, Γ. 4.)

The Sun has risen clouded o'er, and dark is he and threatening;
Say, is he angry with the Stars, or with the Moon in heaven,
Or angry with the Morning Star that's with the Star of Evening?
He is not angry with the Stars, nor with the Moon in heaven,
Nor angry with the Morning Star that's with the Star of Evening;
But Charon's making merry now, he's keeping his son's wedding;
And boys he slays instead of lambs, and brides for goats he slaughters;
And he has ta'en the widow's son, no other son is left her;
And by his side she weeping goes, walks by his side lamenting:
'O leave him, Charon, leave me him, and I will pay his ransom;
O woe is me, I have but him, beside him I've no other;
I promise gold unto the Earth,[1] piled heaps of pearls I promise,
And Earth shall wear them as a sword, and wear them for tophaiki,
At this glad feast ye celebrate, instead of flowers and violets.'

[1] See *Introd.*, p. 14.

CHARON AND THE SOULS.
ΧΑΡΟΣ ΚΑΙ ΨΥΧΗ.

Γιατ' εἶναι μαῦρα τὰ βουνὰ καὶ στέκουν βουρκωμένα;
Μὴν ἄνεμος τὰ πολεμᾷ, μῆνα βροχὴ τὰ δέρνει;

κ. τ. λ.

(*Oikonomides*, Γ. 2.)

WHY do the mountains darkly lower, and stand brimmed o'er with tear drops?
Is it the wind that fights with them? is it the rain that beats them?
'Tis not the wind that fights with them, nor rain that's on them beating;
But Charon's passing over them, and with the Dead he's passing.
The young men he before him drives, and drags the old behind him,
And ranged upon the saddle sit with him the young and lovely.
The old men beg and pray of him, the young beseech him, kneeling:
' My Charon, stop thou in a town, or near cool fountain tarry,
That water may the old men drink, the young men cast the boulder,
And that the little bairnies all may go the flowers to gather.'
' At no town will I stop to lodge, nor near cool fountain tarry;
The mothers would for water come, and recognise their children;
And know each other man and wife; nor would there be more parting.'

CHARON AND THE YOUNG WIFE.

Ο ΧΑΡΟΣ ΚΑΙ Η ΚΟΡΗ.

Μιὰ λυγερὴ παινέθηκε, πῶς Χάρο δὶ φοβάται,
Γιατ' ἔχει τσοὺς ἐννιὰ 'δερφοὺς, τὸν Κωσταντῖνο γι' ἄντρα.
                                                       χ. τ. λ.

(*Passow*, 413.)

THERE boasted once a cherished one, she had no fear of Charon:
For she had nine tall brothers bold, and Constantine for husband.
And Charon somehow heard of it, some bird the tale had told him,
And he set forth and came to them while seated at their dinner.
'Good greeting to you, árchontes. I greet you, noble ladies.'
' Sir Charon, you are welcome here, Sir Charon, you are welcome.
O sit you down and eat with us, sit down and eat your dinner.'
' 'Tis for no dinner I have come, I came not for your dishes,
I came but for the cherished one, who has no fear of Charon.'
He seized her by her flowing hair, and on her back he threw her;
'Let go thy hold upon my hair, and hold my arm, O Charon;
I'll farewell to my mother say, and farewell to my sisters,
And farewell to my father dear, and farewell to my brothers.
Oh, mother, when comes Constantine, afflict him not, nor grieve him,
But spread his dinner that he dine, and ready make his supper;
For I with Charon must depart, and he no more will see me.'

CHARON AND THE SHEPHERD.

Ο ΒΟΣΚΟΣ ΚΑΙ Ο ΧΑ'ΟΣ.

Samothrace.

Λιβέντης ἰκαταίβαινε τὸ 'να ψηλὸ παγί'ι·
Εἶχε τὸ φέσι του στ'αβὰ καὶ τὰ πετζά του κάτω.[1]

κ. τ. λ.

(*Passow*, 432.)

FROM tow'ring mountain-summit down there strolled a young levénté,
His fez on one side cocked he wore, and loosely hung his gaiters.
And Charon looked at him, he looked, and much was he displeaséd;
And seized him by his flowing hair, and by his right hand held him.
'To take thy soul I'm sent by God, to take thy soul he's sent me.'
'Let go thy hold upon my hair, and hold my hand, O Charon,
And come and let us wrestle on a threshing-floor of marble,
And whoso of the twain is thrown, then his soul be it taken.'
When the levénté grasped his foe, then out the red blood spurted;
But when he was by Charon grasped, with flesh were fed the mountains.
'O Charon, I beseech thee now, take not my soul out from me,

[1] The peculiarity of the Samothracian dialect, as the scholar will remark, even in these two lines, is the elision of ρ. May this possibly be owing to the known survival here to a very late period of the Pelasgian language, which seems to have been connected with the old stem of the Æolic, from which the Dorian and Ionian dialects branched off? Elsewhere λ becomes ρ. (See *Preface*, p. xxix., and *Trans.*, p. 80, note.)

For I have flocks of sheep unshorn, and in the press the
  cheeses;
And I have, too, a lovely wife, not meet to leave a
  widow,
And I have little ones besides, and they should not be
  orphans.'
'Thy flocks of sheep may shear themselves, and press
  themselves the cheeses,
The widows can get on alone, and they can rule the
  children.'
'O Charon, I beseech thee now, take not my soul out
  from me;
Show me where thou thy tent hast pitched, and thee
  to it I'll follow.'
'When on my tent thine eyes shall look, fear will take
  hold upon thee,
For outside it is green of hue, within 'tis blackest darkness;
But open now thy mouth, for I will take thy soul out
  from thee.'

THE JILTED LOVER AND CHARON.

Ο ΓΕΛΑΣΜΕΝΟΣ ΑΓΑΠΗΤΙΚΟΣ.

Στὸν ἅδην ὲὲ νὰ 'πάγω, τὸν Χάρο νὰ ὁμιχτῶ
Νὰ τόνε πιάσω φίλυ, καὶ ἀδερροποιτὸ.
                                    κ. τ. λ.
(*Oikonomides*, B. 37.)

I WILL go down to Hades, with Charon I'll unite,
And for my friend I'll take him, and brotherhood we'll
  plight,
And then perhaps some arrows, some arrows keen he'll
  lend,
That I, against those darlings, a deadly bow may bend,
Who kisses did me promise, all three so sweet and coy,
Then jilted me and cheated, as if I were a boy.

ZAHOS AND CHARON.

Ο ΖΑΧΟΣ ΚΑΙ Ο ΧΑΡΟΣ.

Ζάχος ἐκαβαλίκεψε νὰ πάῃ νὰ βρῇ τὸν ἅδη
Μὲ ἕνα σιδερίχ' ἄλογο, μὲ χρυσωμένη σέλλα.
κ. τ. λ.

(*Passow*, 433.)

As Záhos pricked along the road, in search of Hades going;
The horse he rode was made of iron, and golden was his saddle.
Step after step descended he, and steps again ascended.
Earth saw him, and she shrank with dread; and Charon, fearing, hid him;
And all the Dead who saw him come assembled around and questioned:
'Why, Záhos, hast thou hither come? What, Záhos, is't thou seekest?'
'I'm hither come to see my friends, and then I'll turn me homeward.'
'Thy golden saddle, Záhos, say, hast thou another given,
Who com'st whence there's no return, to regions spider-woven?
Here children are from mothers torn, and mothers from their children.'
Then Charon's courage came again, and by his hair he seized him.
'Let go thy hold upon my hair, and take my hand, O Charon;
And Záhos' valour thou shalt see, and see if he will fear thee.'
Then from his hair he loosed his hold, and by his hand he held him.
And Záhos wrestled sore with him, and three times down he threw him;

But Charon once more courage took, and by his hair he seized him.

' Let go thy hold upon my hair, and take my hand, O Charon !

Again will I stand up with thee, do with me what thou pleasest.'

' Come, let us go and see my Tent that there thou may'st recline thee ;

Outside I hangings have of red, but black the inside hangings.

As for the tent-pegs of my Tent, they are the hands of heroes ;

The knots and ropes around it spread, are maiden's twisted tresses.'

THE RESCUE FROM CHARON.
Η ΑΔΕΛΦΙΚΗ ΑΓΑΠΗ.

Ανάθεμά τον ποῦ τὸ εἰπῆ—" τ'ἀδέρφια δεν πονιοῦνται,"
τ'ἀδέρφια σκίζουν τὰ βουνὰ καὶ δέντρα ξερριζόνουν,
κ. τ. λ.

(Aravandinos, 456.)

ACCURSÉD may he be who said: 'Can Brotherhood know sorrow?'

By Brotherhood the hills are rent, and torn the spreading tree-roots ;

Out in pursuit goes Brotherhood, and triumphs over Charon!

Two Brothers had a Sister dear, through all the world renownéd,

The envy of the neighbourhood, the belle of all the village;

And Charon looks with jealous eye, and for himself he'd take her ;

And to the house he runs and cries, as if he were the master :

' Ho ! open, maiden, let me in, with me to go prepare thee ;

The Rescue from Charon.

For I'm the son of the black Earth, the spider-woven Tombstone!'
' O leave me, Charon, leave me now, to-day take me not with thee,
On Saturday betimes I'll bathe, I'll change my clothes on Sunday,
On Monday morn I'll come to thee, I'll come to thee unbidden.'
But by her hair he seizes her; in terror shrieks the maiden.
See where her Brothers follow them, among the mountain passes,
They fast pursue old Charon till they've snatched from him their Sister!

THE RIVER OF THE DEAD.[1]
Ο ΠΟΤΑΜΟΣ ΤΩΝ ΝΕΚΡΩΝ.

'Απόψε τί μ' επόνεσε τὴ μαύρη ἡ καρδιά μου,
Καὶ ξύπνησα κ'ερώταα την, πάλι ξαναρωτῶ την·
κ. τ. λ.

(*Passow*, 386.)

LAST night so sorely in my breast my woeful heart was aching,
That I awoke and asked of it, and once again I asked it:
'O say, my heart, what is thy pain, why heavily art sighing?
Thou art not keeping the Bairám,[2] a hill thou art not climbing.'

[1] In most of the Thessalian Songs about the 'River of the Dead' it is identified with the great river of Thessaly, the Salembría or Peneiós; and according to Homer, the stream by which the Peneiós is joined near Tempé, and which flows from the gorge of Sarandáporos, has an infernal origin. See *Introd.*, p. 33.
[2] The ordinary phrase among the Greeks of the Turkish Provinces for any national festivity which, being usually accompanied with over-eating, is naturally followed by indigestion.

' O it were better far to climb a hill with leaden burden,
Than see the marvel that I saw, that I saw late last even :
The river swept two brothers down, with kisses intertwinéd ;
And one unto the other said, and one said to the other :
" O tightly, tightly grasp me now, nor, brother, from me sever,
For, if we once should separate, we'd ne'er be reunited." '

DIRGE FOR A FATHER.

ΕΙΣ ΟΙΚΟΓΕΝΕΙΑΡΧΗΝ ΤΑΦΕΝΤΑ.

Γιὰ κάτσετε τριγύρω μου νὰ ἰδοῦμε ποιὸς λείπει !
Μᾶς λείπει ὁ' κάλλιος του σπιτιοῦ, τῆς φαμιλιᾶς ὁ πρῶτος,
κ. τ. λ.

(*Aravandinos*, 428.)

Now sit around me, children mine, and let us see who's absent :
The glory of the house is gone, the family's supporter,
Who to the house a banner was, and in the church a lantern.
The banner's staff is broke in twain, the lantern is extinguished.
Why stand ye, orphan'd children, there, like wayfarers and strangers ?
And from your lips comes forth no wail like nightingale's sad singing ?
Your eyes, why weep they not amain, and stream like flowing rivers ?
Your tears should spread a mere around, should flow a cool fresh fountain,
To bathe the dusty traveller, and give the thirsty water.

DIRGE FOR A HOUSE-MISTRESS.

ΕΙΣ ΟΙΚΟΔΕΣΠΟΙΝΑΝ:

T' εἶν' ὁ ἀχὸς τ' ἀκούεται κ' ἡ ταραχ' ἡ μεγάλη !
μῆνα σὲ γάμο γένεται, μῆνα σὲ πανηγύρι ;

κ. τ. λ.

(*Aravandinos*, 429.)

WHAT is this noise falls on our ears, and what is this loud tumult?
Say, can it for a Wedding be, or can it be a Feast-day?
The Goodwife now is setting forth, to Hades she's departing,
She hangs her keys upon the wall, and sets her house in order,
A yellow taper in her hand. The mourners chant sad dirges;
And all the neighbours gather round, all those whom Death has stricken.
Whoso would now a message send, a letter let him give her;
She who a son mourns unadorned, now let her send his fin'ry;
Whoso a son unarméd mourns, now let her send his weapons;
Write, mothers, to your children dear, and ye, wives, to your husbands,
Your bitter grief, your suffering, and all your weight of sorrow.

DIRGE FOR A SON.

ΕΙΣ ΥΙΟΝ.

'Εσύ, παιδί μ' ἐκίνησες νὰ πᾷς 'ς τὸν κάτου κόσμο,
κί ἀφίνεις τὴ μανούλα σου πικρή, χαροκαμμένη·

κ. τ. λ.

(*Aravandinos*, 432.)

O THOU, my son, departest now unto the Lower Regions,

.And leav'st thy mother sorrowful, heartbroken, and despairing !
Where shall I hide my pain for thee, how shall I throw it from me?
For if I throw it on the road, the passers-by will take it,
And should I hang it on the trees, the little birds would find it.
Where shall I hide my bitter tears, my tears for thy departure ?
If on the black earth they should fall, the grass no more would flourish ;
If they should in the river fall, they would dry up its sources ;
If they should fall upon the sea, the vessels there would founder ;
But if I lock them in my heart, I quickly shall rejoin thee.

DIRGE FOR A DAUGHTER.

ΕΙΣ ΘΥΓΑΤΕΡΑ.

Γιὰ πές μου, πές μου, κόρη μου, πότε νὰ σὲ παντέχω·
νὰ σε παντέχω ξάμηνο, νὰ σε παντέχω χρόνο;

κ. τ. λ.

(*Aravandinos*, 435.)

'O TELL me, tell me, daughter mine, how long shall I await thee ;
Say, six months shall I wait for thee, or in a year expect thee ?
Six months—it is a weary time ; a year—it is unending !'
'My mother, were it but six months, or were it but a twelvemonth,
Then would the evil be but small, the time would fly full quickly.
Now will I tell thee, mother mine, when to expect my coming :

When thou shalt see the ocean dry, and in its place a garden;
When thou shalt see a dead tree sprout, and put forth leaves and branches;[1]
When thou shalt see the raven black, white-feathered like a pigeon.'

DIRGE FOR A SISTER.

ΕΙΣ ΑΔΕΛΦΗΝ.

Δὲν τὤξερ', ἀδερφοῦλά μου, πως τὤχες νὰ πεθάνῃς,
'ς τὴν Πόλ' νὰ στείλ.ω γι' ἄλαγο, 'ς τῆ Βενετιὰ γὶ ἁμάξι.
κ. τ. λ.

(*Aravandinos*, 437.)

I KNEW not, little sister mine, that thou to death wert destined;
To Stamboul I'll for horses send, and for a hearse to Venice,
To Corinth will I send to find, to find and bring me masons,
That they may marble hew for thee, and build a mausoleum.
O masons, build it long and wide, and build it proud and lofty,
That she may stand and gird herself, or she may cross-legged rest her;
And in the wall at her right hand leave her an open window,
That she may see when comes the spring, may see when shines the summer,
When warble all the birds around, the nightingales of springtide.

[1] Compare *Il.* A. 234. 'Verily by this staff that shall no more put forth leaf or twig, seeing it hath for ever left its trunk.'

DIRGE FOR A YOUNG HUSBAND.

ΕΙΣ ΝΕΟΝ ΣΥΖΥΓΟΝ.

Παρακαλῶ σε χάρε μου, καὶ διπλοπροσκενῶ σε,
τὸν νειὸν αὐτὸν ποῦ κάλεσες μὴ τὸν παρακρατήσῃς,
κ. τ. λ.

(*Aravandinos*, 430.)

'O CHARON mine, I beg of thee, and twice I'll bow before thee ;
The youth whom thou hast bid to thee, thou wilt not keep him alway ;
For he a wife has all too young that she be left a widow.
For if she briskly walk they'll say : " She seeks another husband !"
If she walk softly then they'll say: "It is but affectation !"
A little son, too, is his care, a baby in the cradle.'
' No mother dear of his am I, nor yet am I his sister.
The son of the black Earth am I, the spider-woven marble;
And youths I eat, and maids devour, and young men are my quarry.
I eat the bridelings with their coins, the bridegrooms flower-becrownéd ;
And now I've waited forty days, this withered straw to gather,
And on the fortieth day and last shall all his ties be severed.'

THE YOUNG WIDOW.

Η ΝΕΑ ΧΗΡΑ.

Μιὰ κόρη πικροτράγουδει απάνου 'ς τὸ γεφύρι
καὶ το γεφύρι ἐρράγισε καὶ τὸ ποτάμ' ἐστάθη.
κ. τ. λ..

(*Aravandinos*, 473.)

UPON a bridge there sat a girl, a doleful lay she chanted,

Which rent the bridge in twain, and caused the stream to cease its flowing.
The Stoicheión of the stream came out, and sat upon the margin :
' O change, my girl, that melody, and sing another sonnet !'
' How shall I change my melody, and sing another sonnet,
Who have a pain within my heart, for which there is no healing ?
I had my husband lying ill, sore sick upon his mattress ;
He bade me go up to the hills, and healing food to bring him ;
He bade me bring him cheese of deer, and milk of wild goats seek him.
And while I up the mountains went, and to the fields descended,
To set the pen and sheepfold up, and catch a hind to milk her,
My husband married him again, another wife he took him ;
The black Earth for his wife he wed, a Tombstone his wife's mother.'[1]

THE DEAD SON TO HIS MOTHER.

ΕΙΣ ΥΙΟΝ ΑΡΤΙ ΘΑΝΟΝΤΑ.

Πέρα 'ς ἐκεῖνο τὸ βουνό πούναι ψηλὸ καὶ μέγα,
ὁπὤχει ἀντάρα 'ς τήν κορφή, καὶ καταχνιὰ 'ς τὴ ρίζα.
κ. τ. λ.

(*Aravandinos*, 434.)

FAR, far away within that hill, which is both broad and lofty,
Upon whose bosom thick mists roll, and fogs at its foundations ;

---
[1] Compare *Iph. in Aul.*, 461. ' Hades, as it seems, will speedily attend on her nuptials.'

Wild amaranths bud *there* and bloom, two other herbs beside them;
The roedeer eat them, and they die; the brown bears, and they sicken.
There, little mother, thou must mount, those herbs three thou must find thee,
And thou must eat them, mother mine, and so thou may'st forget me.'

THE VAMPIRE.

Ο ΒΟΥΡΚΟΛΑΚΑΣ.

Τσὴ καλομάνας τὸ παιδί, τσὴ χήρας θυγατέρα,
Ποῦ προξενιὰν ἐφέραν μὲς ὀχ τὴ Βαβυλῶνα.
κ. τ. λ..

(*Passow*, 518.)

THERE came to the good mother's child, and to the widow's daughter,
From Babylon a go-between in marriage to demand her.
Her seven brothers all say nay, but Constantine is willing.
'Why should we not wed Areté, my mother, with a stranger?'
'But who will bring her back to me, that I may see my daughter?'
'I, I will bring her back again, and thou shalt see thy daughter;
Twice in the winter shall she come, and three times in the summer.'
When Areté was wedded thence, and married to a stranger,
Then died her seven brothers all, and Constantine was murdered.
The mother sat all sad and lone, a reed upon the prairie;
By night and day she grieved and wept, she wept upon the tombstone,

And tore her hair for Constantine, for her belovéd Costa.
'Arise, arise, O Constantine, arise, and bring her to me,
And keep the promise thou hast made that thou to me
    wouldst bring her—
Twice in the winter she should come, and three times in
    the summer!'
And God has heard her weeping sore, and listened to her
    sorrow :
The tombstone cold a horse becomes, and the black earth
    a saddle ;
The worms are changed to Constantine, who goes to fetch
    his sister.
' A happy meeting, Areté!' 'My Constantine, thou'rt
    welcome.'
' Come, Areté, let us depart—and let us go back home-
    wards.'
' Tell me if 'tis for joy I go, and in my best I'll dress me ;
Or if for evil I must go, I'll go as thou hast found me.'
' Come, Areté, let us depart—come just as I have found
    thee.'
As they were riding on the road, a little bird was
    warbling :
'O God, who art all-powerful, a wonder great Thou
    workest;
That there should walk a living soul, with one that has
    been buried.'
' O listen, listen, Constantine, to what the bird is saying!'
'''Tis but a bird, so let him sing ; a songster, let him
    warble.'
And by the path, as on they rode, again the bird was
    singing :
'O God, who art all-powerful, a wonder great Thou
    workest,
That there should walk a living soul with one that has
    been buried.'

And Areté, who'd heard his song, which rent her heart
in twain, said:
'O listen, listen, Constantine, to what the bird is
saying!'
"'Tis but a bird, so let him sing; a songster, let him
warble.'
And as they went along the road, and near the town
were drawing:
'Go on before, my Areté—go enter in our dwelling;
And I will go and sleep awhile, for I'm o'ercome with
slumber,
And sorely wearied am I too, and tired with my long
journey.'
'Come, Constantine, and let us go together to our
mother.'
'I smell of incense, sister dear; with you I cannot enter.'
Once more within her home arrived, she joyful hails her
mother:
'I'm glad to see thee, *mana* dear!' 'My Areté, thou'rt
welcome.
But whom hast thou come home to see? Wouldst see
thy eight tall brothers?
Ah! they are dead, the seven are dead, and Constantine
is murdered.'
'Why, mother, now, our Constantine has brought me
home to see you!'
Then tightly they embraced and kissed, the mother and
the daughter;
And they were left, those two forlorn, all sad those two
and lifeless;
They hid themselves beneath the earth, the soil all spider-
woven.

THANASE VAGHIA.

ΘΑΝΑΣΗΣ ΒΑΓΙΑΣ. II. 'Ο ΒΡΥΚΟΛΑΚΑΣ.

Πές μου τί στέκεσαι, Θανάση, ὀρθὸς,
Βουβὸς σὰ λείψανο στὰ μάτια ἐμπρός;

κ. τ. λ.

(*Valaoritis*, Μνημόσυνα.)

'O WHY, Thanásé, thus dost thou arise,
Corpse-like and speechless, erect 'fore mine eyes?
O why, Thanásé, at eve dost thou roam,
Find'st thou no sleep e'en in Hades, thy home?

'Over the world many seasons have rolled,
Low since we buried thee under the mould;
Go! for thy presence drives peace from my breast,
Leave me, Thanásé, in quiet to rest!

'Direful on me thy crime's shadow is thrown—
See my condition! Thanásé, begone!
All the world flees from me, none will receive;
Alms to thy widow lone, no one will give.

'Come not so near me! Why frighten and daunt me?
What have I done thus to startle and haunt me?
Livid thy flesh is, and earthy thy smell,
Canst thou not yet turn to dust in thy cell?

'Closer around thee yet gather thy shroud,
Loathly worms crawl on thy face once so proud;
O twice-accurs'd, see'st thou not how they cower,
Ready to spring, and me likewise devour!

'Whence through the wild storm com'st, trembling and shaking,
See'st how the whole earth is rocking and quaking?
Out from thy silent grave how couldst thou flee?
Tell me, whence comest thou, what wouldst thou see?'

'This very night, as I lay in my tomb,
Lonely and silent, 'mid darkness and gloom,
Shrouded, bound, helpless, and turning to clay,
Deep in my grave at the close of Earth's day,

'Cried there above me a dread *kukuvághia*;[1]
Still did he call and say, " Thanásé Vághia !
Rise! for the Dead Men will come thee to wake ;
Rise, for away with them thee they will take!"

'Hearing my name, and the words that he spake,
Made all my rotten bones rattle and shake;
Strove I to hide myself deep in the ground,
By their revengeful eyes not to be found.

'"Out with thee, traitor!" they cry in their ire ;
"Out with thee! thee for our guide we require.
Out with thee! fearful one, not as wolves seek we ;
Show us the way to our long-lost Gardíki!"

'Thus cry the Dead Men as on me they fall,
Thus, as all wrathful, they scream and they call,
Talon and tooth root up rank weeds and tear,
Scatt'ring the black soil, my corpse they lay bare.

'Thus from the quiet Dead me they unbury,
Out of the grave they quick rout me and hurry ;
Laughing and gibing, they wildly deride,
On to Gardíki we run side by side.

'Fly we, and run we, all breathless and fast,
'Neath us the fair Earth we blight and we blast :
Where our black cloud passes on as it flies,
Tremble the cliffs, and from Earth flames arise.

[1] The owl, the herald of the vampire.

Thanásé Vághia.

' Flutter our winding-sheets now far behind,
Flutter like white sails filled out by the wind;
Far on our path, 'neath the light of the moon,
Rotten bones, falling, behind us are strewn.

' 'Fore us went flying the dread *kukuvághia;*
Still did he call and say, " Thánasé Vághia !"
Near to the desolate ruins we drew,
Where this accurséd hand so many slew.

' O what dread witnesses ! fear made me cower.
Deep were the curses on me they did shower !
Bloody the draught was they forced me to drain;
See ! on my lips still the horrible stain !

' Gathering to rend me, upon me they fastened ;
Then was a cry heard, and tow'rds it they hastened :
" Glad we're to find you, O Vízier Alí ;"
Into the courtyard they rush without me !

' On him the Dead Men fall furiously ;
One and all leave me ; then I, fearful, flee,
Breathless I flee from them ; come I to rest
Here with my dear wife, for one night her guest.'

' Now that I've heard thee, Thanásé, begone,
Back to thy grave, though 'tis dreary and lone.'
' Give me for comfort, 'mid darkness and gloom,
Kisses three give me to take to the tomb !'

' When on thy corse oil and wine they did place,
Came I in secret, and kissed thy cold face.'
' Years long and many have passed since that day,
Torment thy kisses hath taken away.'

'Go! for thy wild look my terror increases;
Rotten thy flesh, 'tis all falling in pieces.
Leave me! O, hide those hands! For like to knives
Seem the foul fingers that took those brave lives!'

'Come to me, O my wife! is it not I?
Me, thy Thanásé, in years long gone by?
Do not thou loathe me, and thus from me fly!'
'Go! I'm polluted if thou comest nigh!'

On her he throws himself, seizes and grips.
Close on her mouth press his cold clammy lips;
From her poor bosom, its covering rags,
Tearing in fury, he ruthlessly drags.

Bare he has laid it. His hand forward prest,
Wildly he plunges, and runs o'er her breast.

Turns he to marble, and cold as a snake,
Shivers the Vampire, with fear doth he shake;
Howls like a Wolf, like a leaf trembles he,
Touched have his fingers the All-Holy Tree.

Her Guardian had saved her when helpless she cried,
Vanished the Vampire; like smoke from her side.
Out in the darkness the dread *kukuvághia*
Still was repeating his 'Thánasé Vághia!'

[1] Thánasé Vághia was a Greek lieutenant of the tyrant, Alí Pashá, of Ioannina. When all his other officers had refused to massacre the men of Gardíki, eight hundred in number, entrapped by falsehood and treachery in the courtyard of the Khan of Valieré, Thánasé Vághia offered to begin the butchery. For this deed, according to the Greek superstition, his body, after death, could not decompose, but walked the earth as a Vrykolokas or Vampire, in company with his victims and the Vízier Alí, who had ordered their slaughter.

CLASS II.
AFFECTIONAL FOLK-SONGS.

SECTION I.—EROTIC.

THE FRUIT OF THE APPLE-TREE.

Ο ΚΑΡΠΟΣ ΤΗΣ ΜΗΛΗΑΣ.

'Ο νεὸς μέ τὰ λαγωνικὰ ἐζῆκε 'ς τὸ κυνῆγι
κ' ἐκράτει καὶ 'ς τὸ χέρι του ἕνα μικρὸ γεράκι.
κ. τ. λ.

(*Aravandinos*, 240.)

WITH all his greyhounds fleet around, a youth goes out a-hunting;
A falcon small upon his wrist he bears as forth he sallies.
It frees itself, and flies afar, and in a garden enters;
But quick, his falcon to regain, the hunter follows after.
A maiden fair within he finds, at marble fountain washing;
With whitest pearls she is bedecked, and strings of golden sequins.
'Call off thy dogs, Sir Hunter bold, and tie them to the bushes!

9

I fear they'll bite me, Hunter bold—I fear that they will chase me.'
'My little dogs are better taught, 'tis only hares they worry;
And ne'er to maidens fair as thou do any kind of evil.
O tell me, tell me, maiden mine, what dowry canst thou bring me?
No dowry do I ask of coin, nor dowry of adornment.'
'No dowry dost thou ask of coin, nor dowry of adornment?
Then will I give this apple-tree, all covered o'er with blossom;
All laden, too, with rosy fruit, with fairest, sweetest apples.'
'Thou, maiden, art the apple-tree, and now let fall the apples!'
She broke the strings, and far and wide her pearls and sequins scattered.
'Come, gather, youth! come, gather them, the apples of my fruit-tree;
And gather them again, again, and stoop again and gather!'

THE NEGLECTED OPPORTUNITY.
Zagórie.

Η ΑΠΟΛΕΣΘΕΙΣΑ ΕΥΚΑΙΡΙΑ.

Δικό μ' ἦταν τὸ φταιξιμο,
νὰ χάσω τόσο τρέξιμο.
κ. τ. λ.

(*Aravandinos*, 211.)

MINE was the failing, idiocy,
That lost my running's prize, ah me!
I found thee all alone, I wot;
With kisses sweet I fed thee not;

I gazed on thee unsatisfied,
And thus I sat, by Love tongue-tied.
Thy mother mild, where then was she?
Thy father stern, where then was he?
Thy mother at the church did pray,
Thy sire at Yánnina did stay;
And by thee sat the idiot meek,
Whose downcast eyes the earth did seek.

THE WOOER.
Parga.

Η ΜΝΗΣΤΗΡ.

Παρακαλῶ σε, πέρδικα, καὶ προσκυνῶ σε, κόρη,
νὰ μοῦ δανείσῃς τὰ κλειδιὰ νάμπῶ 'ς τὸ περιβόλι.

κ. τ. λ.

(*Aravandinos*, 212.)

O PARTRIDGE, I entreat of thee, thee I salute, O maiden,
That thou the keys would'st lend to me to enter in the garden;
Carnations sweet, and lemons ripe, that I for thee may gather;
And I a ring of diamonds bright will send thee for a token;
In far Venetia it was wrought, and bought it was at Stámboul,
And for the finger of my bride 'tis by my mother destined.
Thy mother dear I love full well, and I do kiss her hand now;
I'll make of her a mother-in-law, and thou'lt be my sweet consort.

THE LOVER'S DREAM.
Zagórie.

TO ONEIPON TOY ΕΡΑΣΤΟΥ.

'Στὴ ρίζα τοῦ βασιλικοῦ, 'ς τὴ ρίζα τοῦ βαρσάμου,
ἀκούμπησα νὰ κοιμηθῶ, λίγον ὕπνο νὰ πάρω,
κ. τ. λ.
(*Aravandinos*, 213.)

AMID sweet roots of balsam hid, amid green basil's fragrance,
All wearied I lay down to sleep, to take a little slumber;
As on the ground I sleeping lay, there came to me a vision—
My love was being married, and her husband was my rival.
'Twas not enough that she did wed, and did my rival marry,
But me they asked to crown them twain, as groomsman at the wedding.
The golden crowns, too, I prepared, the candlesticks of silver;
The wedding veil I brought to her—it was with pearls inwoven.
My dream, should it be true, and she for husband take another,
All may unto her wedding go, but I will to her shrouding;
All may to her take flocks of sheep, I'll lead a black cat[1] only.

[1] With the hope of bringing ill-luck to the wedding.

THE NUNS.
Grévena.

ΑΙ ΚΑΛΟΓΡΑΙΑΙ.

Ἕνας λιγέντης λέγοντος, ὤμορρο παλληκάρι,
μῆλο κρατεῖ 'ς τὸ χέρι του, λεμόνι 'ς τὴν ποδιά του,
κ. τ. λ.

(*Aravandinos*, 225.)

It is an agile, nimble youth, a handsome pallikári ;
An Apple in his hand he holds, and in his lap a Lemon.
The Apple, bending, kisses he, and thus consults the Lemon :
'O Lemon, little Lemon mine, i' faith I wish to marry.'
'Young man, seek'st thou companionship, a wife art thou now seeking ?
Go to the monastery high, where are the great storehouses,
There wilt thou find a worthy Nun, with three adopted daughters ;[1]
Panághio is the eldest called, and Déspo is the second ;
The third, the youngest of the three, Thanásio the black-eyed,
Who golden coins and fairest pearls the livelong day is sifting.
The siftings bright, both gold and white, she places on her bosom,
That she may make her bosom smell of Summer and of Winter ;
Of Summer with its cooling dews, of Winter with its comfort ;
And of fair Spring the beautiful, with all her flowers and sweetness.'

[1] Ψυχοκόραις, literally 'soul-daughters.' The monks have Ψυχοπαιδιά, 'soul-boys,' many of whom afterwards become Bishops and Archbishops, to whom marriage is forbidden.

THE DESPAIRFUL ONE.
Η ΑΠΕΛΠΙΣΙΑ.

Δὲν σοῦ τὸ εἶπα, σκύλλα κόρη, 'ς τὸ γιαλὸ μὴν κατεβῆς,
τί ὁ γιαλὸς θὰ φουρτουνιάση, κι' ἂν σὲ πάρη θὰ πνιγῆς !
κ. τ. λ.

(*Aravandinos*, 208.)

'HAVE not I bid thee, she-dog's child, not go to ocean down?
For wild and stormy are the waves, and if thou'rt seized, thou'lt drown.'
'If I am seized, and I am launched upon the angry sea,
My body I will make a boat, my arms two oars shall be;
And swimming still, thus will I gain that opposite fair isle,
And there will I my lover find, there we'll the time beguile;
I'd sooner die, in wild waves lost, if such should be my fate,
Than here remain, by day and night, alone and desolate!'

ELENAKI, THE NIGHTINGALE.
Preveza.

ΤΟ ΕΛΕΝΑΚΙ ΚΑΙ ΑΗΔΟΝΑΚΙ.

Τὸ 'Ελενάκι τὸ μικρό, θέλησα νὰ μερέψω
καὶ νὰ τὸ βάλω 'ς τὸ κλουβί, νὰ τὸ μοσχοταΐζω.
κ. τ. λ.

(*Aravandinos*, 224.)

FAIR Elenáki, my wee one, I wished to tame and lead her,
A cage within to prison her, and there with musk to feed her.
From fragrance rank of musk exhaled, and stifling odour shed,
Offended with the cage was she, my nightingale has fled.
The hours I pass in calling her, o'er hills I questioning rove :

'Have you not seen Elenió, my faithless, faithless love?'
'But yesterday we her beheld, the reedy fields among,
And there the wanderer beloved had perched, and sat and sung.'
With fire I all the reeds consume, and all to spoil endeavour,
But Elenáki, my wee one, has fled from me for ever!

THE LAST REQUEST.
Ioánnina.

Η ΤΕΛΕΥΤΑΙΑ ΕΝΤΟΛΗ.

"Οταν θέ—μαῦρά μου μάτια,
ὅταν θέλω ν' ἀπεθάνω,
μιὰ παραγγολὴ θὰ κάνω.

(*Aravandinos*, 219.)

WHEN dark Death, my black-eyed maiden,
When dark Death his grasp shall lay,
On my soul, this boon I'll pray:

That they spread, my black-eyed maiden,
That they spread, in heaven's pure air,
My last couch, and wash me there.

Let her come, my black-eyed maiden,
Let her come and bury me;
Love shall then my sexton be.

Let her see, my black-eyed maiden,
Let her see, and let her know
What it is has laid me low.

Let her say, my black-eyed maiden,
But two words, but two sweet words;
Love's sad dirge these two sweet words.

After that, my black-eyed maiden,
Tears still on me let her shower,
Ere the black Earth me devour.

THE LOVER'S RETURN.

Η ΕΠΑΝΟΔΟΣ ΤΟΥ ΕΡΑΣΤΟΥ.

Δύο χρόνους περπατούσα τὸ γιαλὸ γιαλὸ,
κι' ἄλλους δύο τριγυρεῦσα τὸ βουνὸ βουνὸ.
κ. τ. λ.

(*Aravandinos*, 242.)

A WANDERER o'er the seas two years I've been, I've been;
A wanderer o'er the hills, two more I ween, I ween ;
I leave the distant lands, and now my home is near ;
But ere my friends I seek, I haste to find my dear.
Within a garden, lo ! among the rosy bowers,
She from a crystal vase the coolest water pours.
An apple then I throw, of it she takes no heed ;
I gold and silver throw, and now she's roused indeed.
She raises her dark eyes, and angry is her gaze ;
She opes her rosy lips, and then to me she says :
' Where hast thou, *pousté*[1] vile, and base deceiver, been ?
Nor last year, nor 'fore that, nor yet this winter seen ?'
'In foreign lands I've toiled, with foreigners have wrought;
All I, poor fellow, earned, to thee I've fondly brought.
I've brought a mirror, comb, and knife of silver white :
The mirror in its depths to see thy beauties bright;
The comb, with it to smooth thy golden tresses twined ;
The silver knife to pare the apple's ruddy rind.'

THE WIDOW'S DAUGHTER.

Η ΚΟΡΗ ΤΗΣ ΧΗΡΑΣ.

Μάνα μου, κόρ' ὁποῦ εἶδα 'γὼ 'ς τὸν ποταμὸ νὰ πλένῃ,
εἶχε ἀσημένιον κόπανο καὶ πλάκα μαρμαρένια.
κ. τ. λ.

(*Aravandinos*, 221.)

'MANA, a fair maid I have seen ; she washed beside the river ;

[1] A word originally Persian, but borrowed by Greek and Albanian from Turkish. See DOZON, *Langue Chkype*.

Like silver bright her mallet shone, her slab was whitest
marble.
I gave my gallant steed to her in payment for her kisses;
She hundreds, thousands still can give, and yet again
two thousand;
And I her humble slave would be, a servant in her
courtyard.
Sweep, widow, sweep again and oft, within thy beauteous
courtyard—
Sweep, too, thy doorway, that, through it, in passing and
repassing,
Thy lovely daughter I may see, in musk so softly
nurtured;
All hearts she witches; mine, alas! beneath her spell has
fallen.'
'My only one, my daughter dear, is Sun and Moon in
heaven;
The Dawn alone doth she desire, as spouse to lie beside
her.'

THE PARTRIDGE.

Η ΠΕΡΔΙΚΟΥΛΑ.

'Αγάλι' ἀγάλια περπατῶ σάν τὸ κομμένο φείδι,
νὰ μὴ μ' ἀκούσ' ἡ πέρδικα καὶ πεταχτῆ καὶ φύγη.

χ. τ. λ.

(*Aravandinos*, 222.)

I STEALTHILY and silent tread, as soft as wounded
snake,
So that the partridge hear me not, for then to flight
she'd take.
I come, approach the partridge hid among the thickest
green;
She flutt'ring shakes her wings and plumes her feathers'
silver sheen.

'O say what mother gave thee birth, O thou enslaver
    bright ?'
'For mother I a partridge had, for sire a thrush so gay;
In pigeon's plumage me they dressed and decked in
    bright array.'

THE DISCOVERED KISS.

Parga.

ΟΙ ΕΡΑΣΤΑΙ.

Κόρη, ὅταν εφιλιώμαστε νύχτα ἤταν, ποιὸς μᾶς εἶδε;
Μᾶς εἶδε τῆς νυχτὸς τ'ἀστρί, μᾶς εἶδε τὸ φεγγάρι,
κ. τ. λ.

(*Aravandinos*, 209.)

'My girl, when we each other kissed, the night had
    fall'n; who saw us?'
'The stars of night looked down on us, the moon on us
    was gazing;
She, stooping, whispered to the waves, and to the waves
    she told it;
The ocean told the oar the tale, the oar then told the
    sailor;
And gay and loud the sailor sang, and all the neighbours
    heard it;
So the confessor heard of it, and told it to my mother;
From her my father learnt it soon, and sorely he
    reproached me;
Hard were the angry words he said, and strictly he
    forbade me,
Nor yet without the door to go, nor yet unto the window.
But I will to the window go, to gather my sweet basil,
And I the youth whom I love best will take for my
    companion.'

THE RAKE.
TO ΜΑΡΓΙΟΛΙΚΟ.

Γιὰ ίδέστε τὸ μαργιόλικο καὶ τὸ μαργιολεμένο,
πῶς στρίφει τὸ μουστάκι του σὰν νὰ ἦταν μεθυσμένο·
κ. τ. λ.

(*Aravandinos*, 233.)

' LOOK at this cunning fellow here, so roguish he and sly ;
See how he strokes his long moustache, and leers with
    tipsy eye !'
' I am no cunning fellow, nor a tipsy rogue am I,
My love she has forsaken me, and left me here to sigh.
Bright yellow sequins forty, see, strung on a single
    thread—
They're thine, Maroúsio, if thou'lt make with me one
    night thy bed.'

' With fire be all thy coins consumed, and burnt thy
    sequins all ;
My charms they were not given me within thine arms
    to fall,
Nor are these eyes of mine so sweet, this neck as white
    as snow,
That they with thee and such as thee should ever
    trysting go !'

THE WOMAN-HUNTER.
Ο ΓΥΝΑΙΚΟΘΗΡΑΣ.

Πέρα 'ς τὸν ἄμμο, 'ς τὸ ῥῆμονῆσι,
ἀητὸς 'απέρασε νὰ κυνηγήση.
κ. τ. λ.

(*Aravandinos*, 226.)

DOWN on the beach of an islet lone,
An eagle in search of his prey has flown ;

No stag does he stalk, neither hunts he the hare,
He hunts but the black-eyed, the maidens fair.
' Lips red as rosebuds and sloe-black eyes,
Look from the window and hear my sighs!
Wandering eyes, that are dark as sloes,
How, without me, can ye sleeping close?'
' Braid I am weaving, nor may I stay;
When my task's finished, I'll not say nay.'
Cursed be the braid, and the braider too,
Cursed, who have aught with the braid to do!
I'll send a letter, when in thy hand,
This be assured of, and understand,
That when thou readest it, shouldst thou tear,
Thou, my Light! doom'st me to dark despair!'

THE FORSAKEN ONE.

Parga.

Η ΕΓΚΑΤΑΛΕΙΦΘΕΙΣΑ ΕΡΩΜΕΝΕ.

'Απόψε κρύον ἔκαμε, κρύο καὶ τρεμουντάνα,
κ' ἐχιονιστῆκαν τὰ βουνά, παχνίστηκαν οἱ κάμποι.
κ. τ. λ.

(*Aravandinos*, 228.)

COLD is the wintry night, and cold the mountain-wind is blowing;
The hills are whitened o'er with snow, and all the fields are frozen.
But you, my little gardens lone, do not you freeze and harden,
For I my lover dear have lost, my faithless, faithless lover,
Who swore when we so sweetly kissed that he would love me ever;
And now he has abandoned me, a reed beside the river,

A reed from which the top's been cut, and but the stalk's
   left standing.
At what gay table sits he now, where eating, and where
   drinking?
Whose are the hands pour out to him, the while that
   mine are trembling?
Whose are the eyes that gaze on him, the while that
   mine are weeping?

THE VLACH SHEPHERDESS UNKIND.

ΒΛΑΧΑ, Η ΠΟΙΜΕΝΙΣ.

Διφῶν οἱ κάμποι γιὰ νερά, καὶ τὰ βουνὰ γιὰ χιόνια,
καὶ τὰ γεράκια γιὰ πουλιά, κ' ἐγὼ, βλάχα μ', γιὰ σένα·

κ. τ. λ.

(*Aravandinos*, 235.)

THE fields are thirsting for the rains, and for the snows
   the mountains;
The falcons for the little birds, for thee, my Vlach, I'm
   thirsting.
Thy hand so fair, so soft and white, thy hand so cool
   and snowy,
Three long, long days, three long, long nights, I want it
   for my pillow;
Sweet kisses then I'd feed thee with, I'd feed thee with
   caresses.
But, ah! thou fleest from me, my Vlach, thou fleest, and
   hast undone me!
Up to the branches I will fly, and there I'll sit bewailing;
My weeping great a mere shall make, and flow out a
   cold fountain.
For water will the fair ones come, and come, too, will
   the black-eyed;
And with them my Vlachoúla dear—oft shall I give her
   water.

THE VLACH SHEPHERDESS KIND.

ΟΙ ΒΛΑΧΟΠΟΙΜΕΝΕΣ.

'Ηρθ' ὁ καιρὸς νὰ φύγουμε κ' ἡ ὥρα γιὰ νὰ πᾶμε,
να πᾶμε πέρα σὲ βουνό, σ' ἕνα μαρμαροβοῦνι,
κ. τ. λ.

(*Aravandinos*, 369.)

'THE time has come that we may go, the hour for our departure;
Now let us climb up to the hills, up to the marble mountain;
There will we find a hollow tree, in which we two may enter.'
'My Vlách, where shall we water find to drink when we are thirsty?'
'I have my gourd, thou hast thy gourd, and we can drink together.'
'My Vlácha, bread where shall we find to eat when we are hungry?'
'I have my cake, thou hast thy cake, and bread we'll eat together.'
'My Vlácha, when we feel the cold, what shall we have for covering?'
'My shepherd's cloak, thy shepherd's cloak, will cover us together.'[1]

THE BLACK-EYED ONE.

Η ΜΑΥΡΟΜΜΑΤΑ.

Παίρνουν ν' ἀνθίσουν τὰ κλαριά, κ' ἡ παχνη δὲν τ'ἀφίνει,
θέλα κ' ἐγὼ νὰ σ' ἀρνηθῶ, καὶ δὲ μ' ἀφίν' ὁ πόθος.
κ. τ. λ.

(*Aravandinos*, 234.)

Now would the branches bud and bloom, but hoar-frost holds them prisoned;

---
[1] 'Come under my plaidie, the nicht's gaun to fa';
Come under my plaidie, there's room for us twa.'

The Black-Eyed One.

Now would I sit and spin for thee, but my desire prevents me.
Arise, unto thy mother go, and tell her not to curse me;
I'll make of her a mother-in-law, and she shall be my mother,
Through thee, her second daughter dear, through thee, thou black-eyed maiden.
Thine eyes are like the olive ripe, and like to braid thine eyebrows;
And like a Frankish bow are curved the lashes long that fringe them.
Thy plump, soft hand, so fair and white, thy hand so fair and snowy,
Fain would I make my pillow now upon a marble mountain!
I'd feed thee there with kisses sweet, I'd kiss thine eyes and eyebrows.
Still lower wear thy little fez, thine eyebrows let it cover,
For fear my kisses should appear, for fear they should betray thee,
Lest jealous be the little birds, the nightingale of springtime;
Lest Basil 'gainst thee wrathful be, and wrathful too be Rígas.

THE LOVER.

ΕΡΩΤΙΚΟΝ.

Νὰ μὴ σὲ βλέπω, δὲν βαστῶ,
"Οταν σὲ βλέπω ἀῤῥωστῶ·
χ. τ. λ.

(*Passow*, 532.)

I CANNOT live when absent thou,
Thou present, sickness lays me low;
 'Tis thou my life art stealing,
 'Tis thou who art my healing.

I look on thee, I madly love—
I gaze, my pulses wildly move ;
 My heart doth faint within me,
 No longer reason's in me.

When absent, much I'd say to thee,
Naught can I say when thee I see ;
 My lips refuse their duty,
 My tongue's tied by thy beauty.

I look upon thee, and I burn ;
And when I see thee not, I mourn ;
 Though mad when I behold thee,
 I die if thou withhold thee.

FAIR ONES AND DARK ONES.

ΑΣΠΡΑΙΣ ΚΑΙ ΜΕΛΑΧΡΟΙΝΑΙΣ.

Μπῆκαν ἡ ασπραις 'ς τὸ χορό,
σὰν ἡ βαρκούλαις 'ς τὸ γιαλό.
      κ. τ. λ.

(*Aravandinos*, 378.)

To the dance the fair ones go,
Little boats to sea that row ;
Out come troops of maids brown-eyed,
Oranges in tassels tied ;
Out comes many a black-eyed maiden,
Who's with moles like olives[1] laden ;
Out comes one with eyes of blue,
Waist so slim and fair to view.
Out comes, too, a partridge small,
But with widest skirts of all ;
As she danced and skipped around,
One poor youth cast eyes to ground.

---

[1] Literally, 'covered with olives.' For olives being brown or black when ripe, ἰλαία (or ἰληά), an olive, is the name given to a mole. See next page.

BLUE-EYED AND DARK-EYED ONES.
Zagórie.
ΑΣΠΡΑΙΣ ΚΑΙ ΜΕΛΑΧΡΟΙΝΑΙΣ.

Μπῆκαν ἡ ἄσπραις 'ς τὸ χορό,
βαρυὰ μὲ κάνουν κι' ἀρρωστῶ·
κ. τ. λ.

(*Aravandinos*, 379.)

To the dance the fair ones go,
Sorely lovesick I'm laid low ;
Dark ones come, too, in my sight,
Girls whose waists are slim and slight.
Out, too, come the maids black-eyed—
Curse them ! I for them have died.
Still come those with eyes of blue,
Wearing aprons green of hue ;
Out, too, come the partridge-eyed,
Flower bedecked, and rosy dyed.

THE BLUE-EYED BEAUTY.
Zagórie.
ΓΑΛΑΝΗ, ΠΕΡΗΦΑΝΗ.

'Ανάθεμα ποῦ φύτευε τὸ κλῆμα 'ς τὴν αὐλή σου,
κ' ἐφούντωσεν ἡ πόρτα σου καὶ δὲ μπορῶ νὰ γλέπω.
κ. τ. λ.

(*Aravandinos*, 385.)

MAY he be curs'd who planted there the vine within thy courtyard,
Thy doorway filling with its leaves that I no more can see thee.
Come to thy bowered window now, and from it hang thy tresses ;
Let them a ladder be, and steps, that I may place my feet on,
And I will kiss thee on thy neck, and on thy precious olive.

THE GARDEN.
Parga.

ΤΟ ΠΕΡΙΒΟΛΙ.

Περβόλι μου γραμμένο,
μαργαριταροφραμμένο,
κ. τ. λ.

(*Aravandinos*, 382.)

PICTURELIKE, dear garden ground,
Bordered all with daisies round,
Next the daisies leeks abound,
Marjoram next in rows is found,
In the midst an Apple-tree,[1]
Soon to earth 'twill falling be.
To the fruit a youth approaches,
Him the Apple-tree reproaches:
'Come not, youth, the apples gath'ring ;
See, the leaves are sere and with'ring ;
Counts the master every one,
And for thee, youth, there are none.'

YANNEOTOPOULA.
Ioánnina.

Η ΓΙΑΝΝΗΟΤΟΠΟΥΛΑ.

Μωρὴ Φράγκα, Φραγκοπούλα,
Κι' ὤμορφη Γιαννηοτοπούλα.
κ. τ. λ.

(*Aravandinos*, 392.)

'O THOU Frank, thou Frankopoúla,
Beautiful Yanneotopoúla !
Who has said I do not love thee,
That in worn-out clothes thou'st dressed thee,

---
[1] By the apple-tree and its master an elderly husband is probably meant ; and by the desirable fruit, his wife.

And in soiléd dress remainest?
Busk thee, busk thee, in thy gayest;
Come with me when evening cometh.'
'Why with thee to come dost bid me,
Who art faithless and deceiving?
With thy kisses, and embraces,
One step more and thou wouldst blight me,
Like the dew-drop on the herbage;
Like the wheatear on the meadow,
Wither'd, left alone, and lonely.'

THE LITTLE BIRD.
Zagórie.

TO ΠΟΥΛΑΚΙ.

Τοῦτο τὸ καλοκαιράκι
κυνηγοῦσα ἕνα πουλάκι.
κ. τ. λ.

(*Aravandinos*, 395.)

ALL this summer, this long summer,
One small bird have I been hunting;
Hunting been, and much desiring,
It to catch in vain aspiring;
Snares I set, and birdlime lay—
All my pains are thrown away.
Other method I did choose,
That my bird I might not lose.
I began to sing a lay,
On my violin to play;
Then my songs and violin
Brought my bird my chamber in;
I with my devices all,
Caused her in my arms to fall.

THE CYPRESS.
Ioánnina.

ΤΟ ΚΥΠΑΡΙΣΣΙ.

Φύτεψά 'να κυπαρίσσι
σὲ μιὰ μαρμαρένια βρύση.
κ. τ. λ.

(*Aravandinos*, 397.)

I ONE day a cypress planted
Close beside a marble fountain,
That to wash might come the fair ones,
And the black-eyed with their bleaching.
Came there one, and came another,
Poor, but she with charms was wealthy ;
She illumed the sea and fountain.
' Maiden, where did'st find such radiance ?'
' Chief of Klephtës was my father,
War-chief's daughter was my mother :
From the Sun his charms they'd stolen,
From the Moon they stole her radiance,
They in two shares these divided ;
I, from them, received my portion.'

THE BROKEN PITCHER.
Préveza.

ΤΟ ΣΤΡΑΒΟΠΑΤΗΜΑ.

'Η κόραις ὅλαις εἶν' ἐδῶ
δὲν εἶν' ἐκείνη π' ἀγαπῶ·
κ. τ. λ.

(*Aravandinos*, 396.)

ALL the maidens here I see,
All but her who's dear to me.
Water she has gone to bring ;
I'll go seek her at the spring.

There will I her pitcher crack ;
Empty-handed she'll go back.
Her mother asks when she gets home,
What of her pitcher has become.
'I tripped, my mother, near the well,
And broke my pitcher as I fell.'
'It was no tripping broke your jug,
But likelier far some gallant's hug!'

DISTICHS.

(*Passow*, 103.)

BEFORE thy doorway as I pass, thy ootprint there I know;
I bend, and fill it with the tears that, as I kiss it, flow.

(*Aravandinos*, 214.)

LOVE me as I am loving thee—as I desire, desire me;
The time may come for thy desire when I no more desire thee.

(*Aravandinos*, 234.)

BE curst thou, plane-tree, curst be thou and thy wide branches green,
The pallikars no longer can by Elenió be seen.

THE BULGARIAN GIRL AND THE PARTRIDGE.

Grévena.

Η ΒΟΤΡΓΑΡΑ ΚΑΙ Η ΠΕΡΔΙΚΑ.

Μικρὴ Βούργάρα θέριζε σ' ἕνα κουτὸ κριθάρι,
είχε δρεπάνι δαμασκί, παλαμαριὰ 'σημένια.
κ. τ. λ.

(*Aravandinos*, 281.)

THERE reaped a little Bulgar girl amid a field of barley ;
Her sickle was of damascene, her binds were all of silver.

Right briskly did she reap the grain, but soon her heart
    was aching.
Upon her reaping-hook she leaned, that she might bear
    her baby,
And in her apron folding it, to bury it she hastened.
A Partridge met her on the way, at four cross-roads she
    met her :
  Where goest, Bourgára, with the child—the child where
    wouldst thou bury?
Say, is it not a cruel sin, thou rock'st it not in cradle ?
Twelve birdlings have I in my nest, and I have not
    killed any;
And one, an only one is thine, and him wilt thou not
    cherish?'
'But thou, twelve birdlings if thou hast, thou hast them
    with thine honour;
And I, if I have only one, it is without a husband.'
'Alas for her who murder does that she her shame may
    bury!'

THE ROSE-TREE.

Grévena.

Η ΤΡΙΑΝΤΑΦΥΛΛΙΑ.

Τριανταφυλλιά μου κόκκινη ;
τὸ ποῦ νὰ σὲ φυτέψω ;
κ. τ. λ..

(*Aravandinos*, 408.)

O LITTLE Rose-tree mine, so red,
O say, where shall I plant thee?
I dare not plant thee in the sea,
For I should fear the sailors ;
I dare not plant thee on the hill,
For fear thou shouldst be frozen.
Oh, I will plant thee in a church,

In beauteous monastery;
And just between two apple-trees,
Between two orange-bushes;
That down the oranges may fall,
And in thy lap the apples;
And all their blossoms flutter down
In showers upon thy roses;
And at thy roots I'll lay me down,
Lie there, and sweetly slumber.

THE GREEN TREE.
Dancing Song.
ΤΟ ΠΡΑΣΙΝΟ ΔΕΝΤΡΙ.

Ποιός είδε πράσινο δεντρί,
—μαυρομματούσα καὶ ξανθή,—
κ. τ. λ..

(*Aravandinos*, 406.)

WHOEVER did green tree behold—
Thine eyes are black, thy hair is gold—
    That with silver leaves was set?—
    Jet black eyes, and brows of jet—

And on whose bosom there was gold—
O eyes that so much weeping hold—
    At its root a fountain flowing—
    Who can right from wrong be knowing?

There I bent, the fount above,
To quench the burning flame of love;
    There I drank that I might fill me,
    That my heart I thus might cool me.

But my kerchief I let slip—
O what burning has my lip!—
    Gold-embroidered for my pleasure;
    'Twas a gift to me, the treasure.

That one it was they broidered me,
While sweetly they did sing for me :
  Little maids so young and gay,
  Cherries of the month of May.

One in Yannina was born,
Robe of silk did her adorn;
  T'other from Zagórie strayed,
  Rosy-cheeked this little maid.

An eagle one embroidered me—
Come forth, my love, thee would I see!—
  T'other a robin-redbreast tidy,
  Thursday—yes, and also Friday.[1]

Should a youth my kerchief find,—
Black-eyed with gold tresses twined—
  And a maiden from him bear it,
  Round her slim waist let her wear it.

[1] Literally ' Monday and Tuesday ;' but as these words are merely brought in for the rhyme, I have taken a similar liberty.

SECTION II.—DOMESTIC.

SUB-SECTION I.—EARLY MARRIED LIFE.

FOR THE THRONING[1] OF THE BRIDE.

Parga and Préveza.

ΕΙΣ ΤΗΝ ΕΝ ΤΩ ΘΡΑΝΙΩ ΤΟΠΟΘΕΤΗΣΙΝ ΤΗΣ ΝΥΜΦΗΣ.

Εἰς τὸ σκαμνὶ ποῦ κάθησες, ξηρὰ ἤτανε τὰ ξύλα,
κι' ἀπὸ τὴν ωμορφαδα σου ἀνθοῦν καὶ βγάνουν φύλλα.
κ. τ. λ.

(*Aravandinos*, 285.)

THOU didst but sit upon the stool, when lo! its wood all lifeless
Thy beauty quickened into leaf, and flushed all o'er with blossom.
The very deer made holiday the day thy mother bore thee.
For dowry the Apostles Twelve bestowed on thee thy beauty.
Of all the Stars of heaven so bright one only thee resembles—
The Star that shines at early dawn, when sweet the morn is breaking.
From out the heavens Angels came, the Saviour's orders bearing:
The brightest radiance of the Sun they brought thee on descending.
Thou hast the hair of Absalom, the comeliness of Joseph;

[1] Literally, however, θρανίον is but a 'stool,' and a 'throne' is θρόνος.

He'll fortunate and lucky be, the youth who thee shall
  marry.
The Bridegroom's mother should rejoice, gay be the
  Bride's new mother,
Who such a noble son has borne, a mate for such a
  maiden.
What *proxenétés* made the match, who cinnamon has eaten,[1]
When such a Partridge was betrothed, and wed to such
  an Eagle !

FOR THE BRIDE'S DEPARTURE.
Ioánnina.

ΕΙΣ ΤΗΝ ΑΝΑΧΩΡΗΣΙΝ ΤΗΣ ΝΥΜΦΗΣ.

Κάτου 'ς τὰ λιβάδια,
καὶ 'ς τὰ λιβαδάκια
κ. τ. λ.

(*Aravandinos*, 299.)

Down among the meadows,
'Mong the little meadows,
Come the mules a-grazing,
Cool, and quiet gazing ;
One is not a-grazing,
Cool, and quiet gazing.
' Mule, why art not grazing,
  Cool, and quiet gazing ?'
' What enjoyment can I have ?
Or what grazing can I crave ?
I am going from my father,
And am wan and withered ;
I am going from my mother,
And am wan and withered ;
I am going from my brother,
And am wan and withered.'

[1] The eating of cinnamon by the προξενητὴς, or matchmaker, and the mothers of the couple, is one of the ceremonies of betrothal.

FOR THE YOUNG BRIDEGROOM.
Epeiros.

ΕΙΣ ΝΕΟΝΥΜΦΟΥΣ.
'Εδῶ σὲ τούταις ταῖς αὐλαίς, ταῖς ὠμορφοσττρωμίναις,
σὲ τοῦτο τ' ἀρχοντόσπιτο, τὸ μαρμαροχτισμένο,
κ. τ. λ.
(*Aravandinos*, 331.)

WITHIN these sumptuous lofty halls, with carpets fine, and cushions,
Within this lordly, princely house, this palace built of marble,
A youthful bridegroom lies asleep, he like a lamb is sleeping ;
And there's a maiden well beloved, and fain would she awake him.
Should she upon him water throw, she fears that it might chill him ;
And should she sprinkle him with wine, she fears 'twould make him tipsy.
Sweet sprigs of basil now she takes, and marjoram she gathers;
Therewith she hits him on the face, and on the lips she strikes him :
' Awake, O golden comrade mine, and sleep thou not so soundly ;
The sun is high within the sky, the nightingales are silent.'

THE WIFE'S DREAM.
Epeiros.

ΤΟ ΟΝΕΙΡΟΝ.
Κοιμᾶται ἡ ἀγάπη μου, καὶ πῶς νὰ τὴν ξυπνίσω ;
πῆρα ζαχαρομύγδαλα 'ς τὸν κόρφο της τὰ ρίχνω.
κ. τ. λ.
(*Aravandinos*, 337.)

O SOUNDLY my belovéd sleeps, and how shall I awake her ?

I take of sugared almonds now, and throw them on her
  body.
' My Partridge, thou dost soundly sleep !' ' My lord,[1] I
  have slept soundly ;
And in my sleep I've dreamed a dream—I pray thee now
  expound it :
All saddleless I saw thy bay, and broken saw the
  saddle ;
Thy gold-embroidered kerchief, too, all in the mud was
  trodden.'
' My bay—it means the road I take ; my saddle—
  foreign countries ;
My broidered kerchief all besoiled—it is our separation.'
' Where thou art going, my hero, now, O let me ride
  beside thee !
That thou may'st have me ever near, before thine eyes
  for ever !'
' Where I must go, my dearest girl, there beauty may
  not venture ;
For I'd be murdered for thy sake, and thou'dst be taken
  captive.'

THE HUSBAND'S DEPARTURE.
Zagórie.

Ο ΞΕΝΕΤΕΥΟΜΕΝΟΣ.

'Στὰ ξένα πᾶς, λεβέντη μου, κ' ἐμένα που μ' ἀφίνεις ;
Πάρε κ' ἐμένα, βάλε με σὰν φοῦντα 'ς τ' ἄλογό σου.
                                                  κ. τ. λ.

(*Aravandinos*, 336.)

' My hero, wilt to foreign lands, and wilt thou leave me
  lonely ?
Oh, take me with thee ! let me cling, a tassel, to thy bridle !'
' What can I do, my well-beloved—what can I do, dear
  lassie ?

[1] 'Αυθέντε (αὐθεντικὸς, lordly, authentic), in Turkish, *Effendi*.

Thy hands are made of precious gold, thy bosom is of silver.
If thou wert but an apple red, thee in my breast I'd carry;
But thou'rt a full-grown mortal now, nor canst hang like a tassel!
And should we pass the hills across, the klephts I would be fearing;
And should we travel through the towns, the Turks I'd aye be fearing.
At monastery, or at church, the very prior would scare me!
At morn will I a goldsmith bring, and he shall twice refine thee;
A silver cup he'll make of thee, a ring and cross he'll fashion.
The ring I'll on my finger wear; the cup I'll ever drink from;
And on my breast the cross I'll wear, by day and night suspended.'

THE EXILED BIRD.

TO ΞΕΝΙΤΕΜΕΝΟ ΠΟΥΛΙ.

Ξενιτεμένο μου πουλί,
Καὶ παραπονεμένο.
κ. τ. λ.

(*Oikonomides, B.* 35.)

MY bird in exile far away,
And lonely and sad-hearted,
The foreign lands give joy to thee,
And I'm consumed with longing.
What shall I send thee, exile mine,
And what shall I prepare thee?
Should I an apple send, 'twould rot;

A quince, 'twould dry and shrivel.
Oh, I will send my tears to thee,
Upon a costly kerchief;
My tears are such hot, burning drops
That they will burn the kerchief.
Arise, O exile, and return!
Thy family awaits thee;
Thy sister longs to see thee come;
Thy wife awaits thy coming,
Her eyes all wet with weeping.

THE ABSENT HUSBAND.
Malakassi.
Η ΣΥΖΥΓΟΣ ΑΠΟΔΗΜΟΥΝΤΟΣ.

'Ηθέλησε τ' ἀηταῖρί μου 'ς τὰ ξένα να πηγαίνη.
'Ανάθεμά σε, ξενητειά, καὶ σὲ καὶ τὸ καλό σου,
κ. τ. λ.

(*Aravandinos*, 343.)

'O HE would go, my comrade dear, away to foreign countries.
O be ye cursed, ye foreign lands, you and your wealth be curséd,
Which take from us our blooming boys, and send them back when married;
Ye take the husbands when they're young, and send them back when agéd!
O exile mine, thy kerchief fine, why soiléd dost thou keep it?
O send it me, my wanderer, O send me thy white kerchief;
I'll wash it thee in water warm, with soap I'll wash it for thee.'
'The water warm where wilt thou find, and where the soap, my lassie?'

'For water warm I have my tears, for soap I have my spittle;
My slab shall be the marble black—send, let me wash it for thee!'

THE HUSBAND'S RETURN.
Parga.

Ο ΠΑΛΙΝΟΣΤΩΝ ΣΥΖΥΓΟΣ.

Γλυκοχαράζ', ἡ 'Ανατολὴ καὶ γλυκοφέγγ' ἡ Δύσι,
πᾶν τὰ πουλάκια 'ς ταὶς βοσκαίς, γυναῖκες πᾶν 'ς τὸ πλύμα,
κ. τ. λ.

(*Aravandinos*, 348.)

DAY sweet in Anatolia dawns, and sweet the West is shining;
The birds unto the meadows go, the women to their washing,
And I go with my good black steed, I go to give him water;
And there, close by a deep well's side, I find a darling woman.
'My girl, for my black steed and me, I prithee draw some water.'
Twelve pailfuls from the well she drew, and yet her eyes I saw not;
But as the thirteenth pail she drew, her head at length she lifted;
Then loudly neighed my good black steed, and sadly sighed the woman.
'Tell me, my girl, why art thou sad, why sorrowfully sighing?'
'My husband's gone to foreign lands, and ten long years he's absent;

But two years more I'll wait for him, three more will I
    expect him;
And comes he not on the thirteenth, I'll hide me in
    a nunn'ry.'
' Now tell me what your husband's like, it may be that
    I know him.'
' Oh, he was tall, and he was slim, himself he proudly
    carried.
A travelling merchant, too, was he, in all the country
    famous!'
' My girl, your husband he is dead, five years ago was
    buried.
I lent to him some linen then—he said thou wouldst
    return it;
And tapers, too, I lent to him—he said thou wouldst
    repay me;
A kiss I lent to him besides—he said thou wouldst return
    it.'
' If thou hast linen, tapers lent, be sure I will repay thee;
But if a kiss thou'st lent to him, that he himself must
    pay thee!'
' O lassie, I am thy goodman; see, am not I thy
    husband?'
' If thou art he, my husband dear, himself, and not
    another,
Tell me the fashion of the house, and then I may believe
    thee.'
' An apple-tree grows at thy gate, another in thy court-
    yard;
Thou hast a golden candlestick that stands within thy
    chamber.'
' That's known of all the neighbourhood, and all the
    world may know it;
Tell me the signs my body bears, and then I may believe
    thee.'

'Thou hast a mole upon thy chest, another in thine armpit;
There lies between thy two soft breasts a grain, 'tis white and pearl-like.'
'Thou, thou my husband art, I know—oh, come to my embraces!'[1]

SUB-SECTION II.—LULLABIES AND NURSERY RHYMES.

LULLABIES.[2]

I.

Parga.

Κοιμήσου, χαϊδεμένο μου
καὶ μοσκαναθρεμμένο μου·
κ. τ. λ.

(*Aravandinos*, 163.)

SLEEP, my little darling one;
Sleep, my sweet musk-nurtured one—
Náni-nani, náni-nani—
On his eyes, Sleep, softly lie—
Nani-nani, nani-nani,
Or be whipped by mammy dear,
Or scolded by his daddy dear.

---

[1] Compare the recognition of Odysseus by Penelópé, and of Laertes by his son in the *Odyssey*, ψ.
[2] Νανάρισμα, from ναναρίζω, to lull to sleep, singing Νάνι νανι, the equivalent of the English *By-by*, or the (far sweeter?) Scotch *Ba-loo*.

II.

Parga.

Κοιμήσου, σαββατόλουστο,
τὴν Κυριακὴ ἀλλασμένα.
χ. τ. λ.
(*Aravandinos*, 164.)

O SLUMBER, washed on Saturday,
On Sunday dressed in clean array,
On Monday morn to school away,
As sweet as apple, bright and gay.
Sleep, the nightingale has flown;
To Alexandria she has gone.
Náni, thou canary bright,
Who my brain bewilders quite.

III.

Parga.

Κουνιέται τὸ γαρύφαλο,
κουνιέται καὶ τ' ἀσῆμι,
χ. τ. λ.
(*Aravandinos*, 170.)

O ROCK the sweet carnation red,
And rock the silver shining,
And rock my boy all softly too,
With skein of silk entwining.
Come, O Sleep, from Chio's isle;
Take my little one awhile.
Náni, though no nightingale
Sweeter is in any vale;
White as curd, or winter snows,
Delicate as any rose.

IV.
Parga.

Κοιμήσου, χαϊδεμένο μου,
κάτι νὰ σοῦ χαρίσω,
κ. τ. λ.

(*Aravandinos*, 165.)

Go to sleep, my darling one!
Something would I give to thee;
Yea, a gift I'd make to thee:
Arta fair and Ioannina,
Arta fair and Ioannina.
Give thee Chio with its vessels,
And Stambóli with its jewels.
Náni-nani, shut that eye!
Or with rocking I shall die.
For Ralli's son, Sleep, do not tarry,
He a General's child shall marry.

V.
Parga.

Τὸ δικό μου τὸ παιδὶ
εἶν' ἀσῆμι καὶ φλωρί,
κ. τ. λ.

(*Aravandinos*, 171.)

My dear child, my darling boy,
Is silver and gold without alloy;
Other children of the street
Are money false and counterfeit.
My good child fain would I see,
When a bridegroom he shall be;
I'll rejoice when by his side,
I shall see his own dear bride.

VI.

Parga.

Ὕπνε, ποῦ παίρνεις τὰ μικρά,
ἔλα, πάρε καὶ τοῦτο,
κ. τ. λ.

(*Aravandinos*, 169.)

O SLEEP, who takest little ones,
Take to thee my darling!
A tiny one I give him now,
A big boy bring him to me;
As tall as any mountain grown,
And straight as lofty cypress;
His branches let him spread about;
From the West to Anatólia.

VII.

Parga.

Κοιμήσου, ποῦ νὰ σὲ χαρῇ
ἡ μάνα ποῦ σ' ἐγέννα,
κ. τ. λ.

Aravandinos, 166.

O SLUMBER now, and she'll thee bless,
  The mother dear who bore thee;
He too, thy sire, who hopes to see
  Thy children grow before thee.

O Slumber, come; come softly now,
  And lie upon my wee one's brow;
O come, and in thine arms now take him,
  And in the morning sweetly wake him.

VIII.
Ioánnina.

Τὸ παιδί μου τ' ἄσπρο, τ' ἄσπρο
τὸ καλέσανε 'στὸ κάστρο,
κ. τ. λ..

(*Aravandinos*, 174.)

My dear boy, so white, so white,
The Kadi's daughters fair invite :
They ask him to the Castle, where
They honey-cakes for him prepare.
Honey-cakes with almonds spread,
Sweetmeats too with sugar red.
Going, going; he's going, he's going!
May the Panaghía guard him!
Going, going; he's going, he's going!
May the Christ watch o'er and ward him!

IX.
Parga.

Πάρτε το, κρατεῖτέ το
κι' ὅλψ τραγουδεῖτέ το.
κ. τ. λ.

(*Arabantinos*, 179.)

Take you him, and keep you him,
All sing gaily songs to him;
He'll fly light as any bird,
Like a lamb leap,'pon my word;
Stare like any peacock proud,
Laugh as any angel loud.
Take him, dance him on your knee,
Softly dandle him for me;
Bid him live, grow strong and tall,
So to win the maidens all.

NURSERY-RHYMES.

I.

'Ηταν ένας γέρος
κ' είχ' ένα πετεινί.
κ. τ. λ.

(*Passow*, 274.)

THERE was an old man,
And he had a cock,
That crowed in the morn,
And awoke the old man.

But there came a cat
And ate the cock, etc.

And there came a fox
That ate the cat, etc.

And there came a wolf
And ate the fox, etc.

And there came a lion
And ate the wolf, etc.

And there came a river
And drowned the lion, etc.

II.
Salonica.

Μιὰ γρηὰ, κακή γρηὰ
Μὲ ταῖς κότταις μάλωνε
κ. τ. λ.

(*Passow*, 276.)

ONE old dame, a bad old dame,
Quarrelled with her cocks and hens,
Quarrelled with her little cat.
  Tsit! and *Xoo!*
  I say, old woman, where is your spouse?

One old dame, a bad old dame,
Quarrelled with her cocks and hens,
Quarrelled with her little cat,
Quarrelled with her little dog.
  Oust! and *Tsit!* and *Xoo!*
  I say, old woman, where is your spouse?

One old dame, a bad old dame,
Quarrelled with her cocks and hens,
Quarrelled with her little cat,
Quarrelled with her little dog,
Quarrelled with her little pig,
Quarrelled with her little ass,
Quarrelled with her little cow,
Quarrelled with her little hut.
  Phoo! Oo! Aa! Youtz! Oust! Tsit! Xoo![1]
  I say, old woman, where is your spouse?

III.

Salonica.

Νάχαμε, τί νάχαμε;
Νάχαμ' ἕνα γέροντα,
                        κ. τ. λ.

(*Passow*, 275.)

WE will have—what shall we have?
We will have an old, old man,
Who shall dig our little garden,
Where the roses gaily grow.

We will have—what shall we have?
We will have a little donkey,
For our old, old man to ride on, etc.

---

[1] In the Levant there is a special exclamation for driving out each of the domestic animals. *Tsit!* for a cat; *Xoo!* for poultry; *Oust!* for a dog; *Youtz!* for a pig; *Aa!* (with nasal sound) for a donkey; *Oo!* for a cow; *Phoo!* for things in general.

We will have—what shall we have?
We will have a little wasp,
That shall sting the little donkey,
That shall throw the old, old man, etc.

We will have—what shall we have?
We will have a little cock,
That shall eat the little wasp, etc.

We will have—what shall we have?
We will have a little fox,
That shall eat the little cock, etc.

We will have—what shall we have?
We will have a clever dog,
That shall kill the little fox, etc.

We will have—what shall we have?
We will have a little stick,
That shall beat the little dog, etc.

We will have—what shall we have?
We will have an oven big,
That shall burn the little stick, etc.

We will have—what shall we have?
We will have a river wide,
That shall quench the oven's fire, etc.

IV.

Parga.

βρέχει, βρέχει, καὶ χιονίζει,
κι' ὁ παπᾶς τυρομυρίζει.
κ. τ. λ.

(*Aravandinos*, 188.)

IT rains, it rains, and soon 'twill freeze,
And the parson smells of cheese;
Where shall we put our lady bride?
Beneath the chickpea-stalk she'll hide.
Where shall we put our bridegroom gay?
Beneath the cross he'll sit all day.

V.
Ioánnina.

Λέλεκα, παπᾶ χατζῆ !
μὴ, εἶδες τά πρόβατα;
κ. τ. λ.

(*Aravandinos*, 197.)

'STORK, O father pilgrim, say!
Did you chance to see my sheep?'
'Yes, I saw them yesterday,
Grazing by the lakeside deep.
A wolf came up and on them fell,
A fox stood by in great delight;
The dogs did bark and bay right well.
The shepherd cried with all his might.'

VI.
Ioánnina.

'Στὸ κελί μιανῆς καλόγρηας
πού'χ' ἀνώγηα καὶ κατώγηα,
κ. τ. λ.

(*Aravandinos*, 195.)

I WENT to a good nun's storehouse,
Which has upstairs and has downstairs,
Oped the door and in I entered.
There I found a wolf a-dancing,
And a fox who food was cooking,
A hare who on the lyre was playing,
A weasel on a pipe was whistling,
And a giant of a hedgehog
At a tortoise eyes was making.
And the tortoise was quite shamefaced,
And within her hole she hid her.
Then upon her bed I mounted,
Found a cake and a round biscuit;
Milk beside them in a pitcher.

VII.

Ioánnina.

Ἄναψα κλωνὶ δᾳδί,
κ' ἔκαψα τὴν τσέπη μου,
κ. τ. λ.

(*Aravandinos*, 198.)

I A PINE-TORCH lighted me,
To my pocket I set fire,
Which has echoes, which has wheels,
Which has fields and mountains high.
Trees upon the mountains grow,
Branches on the trees, I trow,
In the branches nests abound,
In the nests the eggs are found ;
From the eggs young birds come out,
On the birds will feathers sprout.

VIII.

Ioánnina.

Κατίβα, μῆλο,
νὰ σ' ἐρωτήσω,
κ. τ. λ.

(*Aravandinos*, 191.)

' COME down, O apple,
And tell me true,
What does the maiden
That I love, do ?'
' Braid she is plaiting,
By night and day.'
' For whom does she plait it ?'
' For Yanni, they say.'

SUB-SECTION III.—LATER MARRIED LIFE.

THE PARSON'S WIFE.

Η ΠΑΠΑΔΙΑ.

Κορίτσια, μπᾶτε στὸ χορὸ νὰ μάθετε τραγούδια,
Νὰ 'δῆτε κεντισταῖς ποδιαῖς, πράσιναις καὶ γαλάζιαις.
κ. τ. λ.

(*Oikonomides*, B. 7.)

O MAIDENS, to the dance come out, and learn our lays and ballads,
And see the broidered aprons gay, green aprons and blue aprons;
And see, too, how the Parson's Wife comes out among the gallants.
The Parson follows close at hand, and at her side goes begging:
'O most shortwaiting *papadiá*,[1] two words I want to ask thee:
How canst thou leave our house unkept, and all alone the children?'
'Go, Parson, go, do thou go home—go stay thou with thy children,
And I with the young men will go, and with the *pallikaria*.'
'I say, where are the *Hierá*, that I may chant the service?'
'The fire may burn the *Hierá*, the house, and thee within it!'

[1] Παπαδιά, the title given to the wife of a Παπάς, or parish priest.

THE FORSAKEN WIFE.
Zagórie.

Η ΣΥΣΥΓΙΚΗ ΕΥΚΑΤΑΛΕΙΨΙΣ.

Μάνα μ', γιατί μὲ πάντρεψες καὶ μᾤδωκες Βλαχιώτη ;
δώδεκα χρόνους 'ς τῆ Βλαχιὰ καὶ τρεῖς βραδυαὶς 'ς τὸ σπίτι.
κ. τ. λ.
(*Aravandinos*, 340.)

WHY didst thou, *mána*, marry me, and give me a Vlach husband?[1]
Twelve long years in Wallachia, and at his home three evenings.
On Tuesday night, a bitter night, two hours before the dawning,
My hand I did outstretch to him, but did not find my husband;
Then to the stable-door I ran: no horse fed at the manger.
I sped me to the chamber[2] back, I could not find his weapons;
I threw me on my lonely couch, to make my sad lamenting.
'O pillow, lone and desolate; O mattress mine, forsaken,
Where is thy Lord[3] who yesternight did lay him down upon thee?'
'Our Lord has left us here behind, and gone upon a journey—
Gone back to wild Wallachia, to Bucharest unhappy.'

---

[1] The population of the secluded mountain valleys of Zagórie (see *Introd.*, pp. 26, 27) is, in considerable part, Vlach, and the men are famous for their energetic enterprise in commerce during their customary years of exile.

[2] Ὄντα, Turkish *Oda*. Rooms are made into bedrooms by simply bringing the mattress, etc., out of the cupboard.

[3] See *above*, p. 160, n. 1.

THE SALE OF THE WIFE.
Epeiros.
Η ΠΩΛΗΣΙΣ ΤΗΣ ΣΥΖΥΓΟΥ.

"Ένας κοντός κοντούτσικος, πού'χ' ώμορφη γυναίκα,
τοῦ τὴν ζηλεύ' ἡ γειτονιά, τοῦ τὴν ζυλεύ' ἡ χώρα·
x. τ. λ.
(*Aravandinos*, 280.)

A MANNIE, a wee mannikin, once had a wife so bonnie,
That all the neighbours envied him, and all the town was jealous;
But many debts the mannie had, and he would go and sell her.
He washes her on Friday well, on Saturday adorns her,
And when the Sunday morning comes, to the bazaár he takes her.
'I have a damsel dear to sell, she's fair-haired, and she's black-eyed!'
The Widow's Son comes forth to see, and he the seller questions:
'Say, Stumpy, what's the beauty's price—how much will cost the black-eyed?'
'Two thousand for her upper lip; two thousand for the lower;
Her precious body has no price, and it cannot be valued.'
'Hold, Stumpy, hold thy cap in hand, and I will count the money.'
He leads her to the sea-beach down, and in a boat embarks her;
The Darling seats her in the stern, and all the sails are swelling;
And that gay youth, the Widow's Son, embarks, too, for a frolic.

MAROULA, THE DIVORCED.

Η ΜΑΡΟΥΛΑ.

Σήκου, Μαρούλ', ἀπὸ τὴ γῆς, καὶ τίναξε τὸ χῶμα,
σύρε, καὶ στρῶσε τὸν ὀντᾶ 's τὸ πέρα σαχνισάνι,
κ. τ. λ.

(*Aravandinos*, 241.)

'ARISE, Maroúla, from the earth, and shake the dust from off thee;
Arise, and on the balcony now spread for us thy bower.
Go hasten, make us coffee, too, bring wine and fill the beakers;
And take and bathe thyself, and change, and don thy brightest raiment;
Then hie thee to the dance away, then hie thee to the village,
That all the belles may gaze on thee, and all the *pallikária;*
There will thy husband see thee, who another wife has taken.'
'And if I am divorced, what then? 'Twas he who had the worst o't!
At two o'clock I'll to the bath, at four I'll change my raiment;
And out of fourteen *pallikars* I'll choose another husband.
And then I will my house set up right opposite his dwelling;
And there beside his garden gay will I plant me my garden;
I'll come, and go, that he may see, and boil with rage, and burst him!"[1]

---

[1] *Him* thus used for *himself* is common in English *patois*, and may be allowable in translating this Greek *patois*.

THE OLD MAN'S BRIDE.[1]

Η ΣΥΖΥΓΟΣ ΤΟΥ ΓΕΡΟΝΤΟΣ.

Τρεῖς αδερφάδαις ἤμασταν κ' ἡ τρεῖς παντρευθηκάμαν,
ἡ μιάν ἐπῆρε βασιληά, ἡ ἄλλη τὸ Βεζύρη.
κ. τ. λ.
(*Aravandinos*, 206.)

O WE were once three sisters dear, and all we three did marry;
A King one to herself did take, and his Viziér the other,
And I, the fairest of them all, I took a rich old fellow.
They roasted at the Palace sheep, at the Vizieri's, poultry;
But rams and calves they roasted whole to grace the Ancient's[2] wedding.
Uncounted flocks I found were his, and his were herds of oxen,
Unmeasured vineyards, countless casks, and grain in great storehouses.
But what, unhappy orphaned one, want I with all these riches,
Who on my mattress by my side such company must suffer?
Thou oldest man,[3] thou stinking-mouth'd, thou skeleton, thou blear-eyed!
Curst may my mother be; and Earth, dissolve not in thy bosom
The go-between[4] whom she employed to settle my betrothal!

[1] Compare BURNS, 'What can a young lassie do wi' an auld man?'
[2] Παληόγερος.   [3] Πρωτόγερος.
[4] The consequence of which would be that, after death, the προξενήτρα would become a Vampire.

THE OLD MAN'S SPOUSE.
Zagórie.

Η ΣΥΖΥΓΟΣ ΤΟΥ ΓΕΡΟΝΤΟΣ.

Δε μὲ βαροῦν τὰ ξένα καὶ τὰ μακρυνά,
μόν' μὲ βαροῦν τῆς κόρης τὰ μηνύματα·
κ. τ. λ..

(*Aravandinos*, 207.)

I WEARY not of foreign lands, of journeys long ;
I'm wearied only by the message of the girl,
Who sends me word by birds, and by the eagles swift :
' Where'er thou art, my Exile, quickly, quickly come !
Because they have betrothed and married me, alas!
A husband me they've given, slothful, oh ! and old.
About the mattresses I'm scolded every night ;
At morn he drives me forth the water cold to draw ;
A heavy pail he gives to me, too short a rope ;
No water can I reach, though low I stoop and strain ;
Of wool nine fathoms I have cut, a cord to make :
Where'er thou art, my Exile, quickly, quickly come !'

YANNAKOS, OR THE ASSASSINATED HUSBAND.

Ο ΓΙΑΝΝΑΚΟΣ Η Ο ΔΟΛΟΦΝΗΘΕΙΣ ΣΥΖΥΓΟΣ.

Τ' ἄκουσμα πούχ' ὁ Γιαννακός, πούχ' ὤμορφη γυναῖκα,
πούταν ψηλή πούταν λιγνή, πούταν καγκελοφρύδα.
κ. τ. λ.

(*Aravandinos*, 481.)

THE fame that Yannakós enjoyed—a lovely wife he'd married,
Who slender was, and who was tall, and who had thick dark eyebrows,

And white as swan's was her fair neck, her eyes like eyes of partridge,—
Syrópoulo made to set forth from Yannakós to take her.
As on the road alone he went, to God he said a prayer,
That he might Yannakós surprise upon his mattress lying,
Barefooted and ungirded too, clad only in his singlet.[1]
And as he prayed, so it fell out; for Yannakós was sleeping.
'Health, joy to thee, O Yanniké, I wish thee health, good morrow.'
'Syrópoulo, thou welcome art, now eat and drink thou with me.'
'I came not here to eat and drink, I came here for thy fair one;
Give her to me of thy free will, thy life if thou dost love it.'
'To keep my head in safety, I five fair ones good would give thee;
I'd give to thee my mother first, I'd give thee my two sisters;
For fourth one I'd my cousin give, my much bepraiséd cousin;
And last of all my crown I'd give, she who of all is envied.'
But as he spoke ran Yannakós, he ran his sword to fetch him;
Ill-fated man! he reached it not, before his head was severed.

[1] Ποκαμισάκι, a diminutive from the Italian *camisa*.

THE CHILD SLAYER.

Η ΠΑΙΔΟΚΤΟΝΟΣ.

Τρίτη Τετράδη θλιβερή, Πέφτη φαρμακωμένη,
Παρασκευή 'ξημερώανε νὰ μ' εἶχε 'ξημερώση,
κ. τ. λ.

(*Aravandinos*, 455.)

O SAD is Tuesday, Wednesday too, and bitter, bitter Thursday;
And Friday now is dawning, would that it had dawned never!
Forth Kostas wends at morning light, and for to go a-hunting;
And to his teacher Johnny goes, that he may learn his letters.
A paper he at home forgets, and turns again to fetch it.
And in the house a youth he sees, who's with his mother playing.
'Unfaithful mother, who is this? And what wants here this stranger?
At evening when my Lord[1] comes home, all this I shall relate him.'
His mother laughed, and mocked at him, and dragged him to the cellar,
And like a lamb she slew him there, the b——, just like a butcher.
And now is Kostas coming home, home from a hard day's hunting,
A living deer he brings with him, he brings a stag he's wounded;

[1] See note, p. 160.

And in a leash a little fawn, for little John to play with.

'My darling, health and joy to thee! where is our son now, tell me?'

'He went at morning to the school, and has not yet returnéd.'

He mounts his mare and rides away, and hies him to the teacher.

'Ho, teacher, where's my little John? are not yet done his lessons?'

'To school to-day no Johnny came; I have not seen your Johnny.'

Back to his house he then returns, but there he finds no Johnny.

He runs and seizes on the keys, and hies him to the cellar,

And there he finds his little son, like lambkin finds him slaughtered.

In pieces small he chops her up, chops up that she-dog mother,[1]

And gathers up the pieces all, and puts them in a wallet.

Away he bears them to the mill, like any madman running:

'Grind now, my mill, O grind for me the bones of this adult'ress!'

[1] 'He cuttit him in pieces sma'
On fair Kirkconnel lee.'

SECTION III.—HUMOURISTIC.[1]

THE DANCE OF THE MAIDENS.

Ο ΧΟΡΟΣ ΤΩΝ ΝΕΑΝΙΔΩΝ.

'Εμπᾶτε τσιούπραις, 'ς τὸ χορὸ,
τώρα ποῦ ἔχετε καιρό,
κ. τ. λ.

(*Aravandinos*, 410.)

'OUT, now, maidens, to the dance!
Out while you have still the chance;
For very soon you'll wedded be,
From household troubles never free;
When children round you 'gin to grow,
How to neighbours' can you go?'

'We shall beat them well, I trow;
Leave them all at home, I vow!'

'Time to dance how can you take,
When you have to cook and bake?'

'We will leave the bread to burn,
All the meat to smoke may turn!'

---

[1] The most humorous Folk-songs are almost always too coarse for reproduction in translations—compare, for instance, Bishop PERCY'S *Loose and Humorous Songs*. But even omitting these, the Songs in this Section appear to be sufficient to refute the Rev. Mr. TOZER'S remark (*Highlands of Turkey*, vol. ii., p. 257) that 'of real humour . . . there is hardly any trace in their composition.' This fancied fact Mr. TOZER attributes to, or rather deduces from, the 'sad and serious condition of a people conscious of living under oppression.'

'You must sit at home and spin ;
Weaving, too, will keep you in.'

'Both we laugh at gaily, pooh!
Loom and twirling spindle too!'

'Your husband you indoors will close,
And with his stick he'll give you blows.'

'The stick should have two ends, he'd see!
And we would have a second key!'

THE FEAST.

TO ΣΥΜΠΟΣΙΟΝ.

Πίναμαν καυχιὰ γιομάτα
χ' εἴχαμαν καὶ μαυρομμάτα.
κ. τ. λ.

(*Aravandinos*, 411.)

DRINK we beakers filled to brim,
With us black-eyed maidens trim ;
Black eyes with us at our wine ;
Black eyes from the windows shine..

If I were a klepht I'd steal them,
Or were cunning, I'd beguile them !
To the market they should go,
While the crier went to and fro ;
I would sell them, I'll be bound,
Sell them for five hundred pound !

But these eyes can not be sold,
Nor can trafficked be for gold ;
Truly given they ever are,
To a worthy pallikar !

THE JANISSARY.
Salonica.

Ο ΓΙΑΝΙΤΣΑΡΟΣ:

'Στὴν πόρτα τοῦ Σαλονικιοῦ
Κάθετ' ἕνας γιανίτσαρος,
κ. τ. λ..

(*Aravandinos*, 424.)

AT Salonica's gate of yore,
There sat a Janissary;
A Janissary boy was he,
And in his hand a lute he bore.—

A lute of gold. He strikes its strings.
'Play little lute,' to it he sings :
'And tell me, for thou know'st, I wis,
What is the value of a kiss ?'

'A matron's, sequins twelve will cost ;
For widow's, just fourteen you'd pay ;
To kiss a sweet unmarried maid,
Venetian sequins five are lost.'

THE TREE.
Eperios.

ΤΟ ΔΕΝΔΡΟΝ.

Δέντρον ἤτον 'ς τὴν αὐλή μου,
μιὰ παρηγοριὰ δική μου.
κ. τ. λ..

(*Aravandinos*, 415.)

A TREE within my courtyard grew,
To me 'twas pleasure ever new ;
I gave fresh water to its root,
That it might thrive and bear me fruit.

Its leaves were all of gold so bright,
Its branches all of silver white;
Fair pink and white the flowers it shed,
Its fruit was like the apple red;
And I believed it was for me
That they had made it fair to see.

When the apples from the tree
Gathered were, the housewife (she
Was a b——) would give me none;
Into stranger's hands they're gone.

THE WINESELLER.
Epeiros.

Η ΟΙΝΟΠΩΛΙΣ.
Πέρα 'ς τὴν 'Ανατολὴ
καὶ 'ς τὴν Αντριανούπολι,
κ. τ. λ..

(*Aravandinos*, 421.)

IN Anatólia, so they tell,
In Adrianople town as well,
Sweet wine, red wine, there they sell.
There the Turks come every day;
Drink, and then their reck'ning pay.
One old Koniár[1] who's drunk his wine,
To pay his score refuses.
'O give me, Turk, my *aspra*,[2] now,
And I'll to thee a lady bring,
Who has sequins by the string.'
'Thou no lady need'st me bring,
Who has sequins by the string;
But a Vlácha, mountain-bred,
One who wears an apron red.'

---

[1] An Asiatic Turk, settled in Europe, and so called from the ancient Turkish capital, Konieh (Quonya), *Iconium*, in Asia Minor.
[2] See *Trans.*, p. 109, note 1.

THE GALLANTS.
Zagórie.

ΟΙ ΓΥΝΑΙΚΟΠΛΑΝΟΙ.
Τζελέπιδες[1] περνούσανε
και ταμπουρά λαλούσανε.
κ. τ. λ.
(*Aravandinos*, 390.)

ALONG are passing gallants gay,
And on their lutes they sweetly play.
'O play, my little lute, an air!
Who knows? we may entice some fair,
As through the quarter down below,
Or lordlier *mahallá*,[2] we go!'
A high-born maid awakes from sleep,
And from her mattress off doth leap;
Her casement gains with hurrying feet,
And glances down into the street.
'O lordly little window high,
What song wouldst hear as I pass by?
It is a sin, if e'er was one,
So fair a maid should sleep alone!'

THE DREAM.
Zagórie.

ΤΟ ΟΝΕΙΡΟΝ.
Μέσ' την αγιά Παρασκευή,
κόρη κοιμώνταν λυγερή,
κ. τ. λ.
(*Aravandinos*, 405.)

DOWN in St. Paraskeví
Sleeps a maid, and fair is she.

[1] *Chelebis*, a commonly used Turkish word for 'Gentlemen.'
[2] 'Quarter.'

Sleeps she soft, and dreams a dream—
Sees her wedding, it would seem.
This has turned the maiden's head;
She decks her when she leaves her bed,
Bathes herself, and combs her hair,
Gazes in the mirror fair;
Throws her eyes about and plays,
Casts them down, and to them says:
'Little eyes, I'll bless you so,
To the dance as now we go,
If you there yourselves will use,
Husband for me well to choose.
Age and gold I don't desire;
Youth and beauty I require.
An old man's hard to satisfy;
One may not laugh when he is by;
Soft on his mattress must he lie;
His pillows one must pile up high;
And all the night he's snoring lying,
While by his side the maid is sighing.'

THE REFUSAL.[1]
Ioánnina.
II ΜΑΥΡΟΜΜΑΤΑ.

'Απόψε, μαυρομμάτα μου, ἰδῶ θέλω νὰ μείνω.
—'Εδῶ κι' ἄν μείνῃς, ξένε μου, ὄξω θὰ ξενυχτίσῃς.
κ. τ. λ.

(*Aravandinos*, 389.)

'TO-NIGHT, to-night, my black-eyed one, 'tis here that I'd be biding.'
'And if thou bidest here, my guest, thou'lt pass the night outside there.'
'Outside it rains, I shall be drenched; it snows, I shall be frozen.'

[1] Compare BURNS, 'O Lassie, art thou sleeping yet?' and her answer.

'Within, my guest, there is no room; my house it is too narrow.'
'A knife I'll take, and slay myself; thou'lt of the crime be guilty!'
'If thou shouldst wound and slay thyself, 'tis little I'd be caring.'

THE LEMON-TREE.

Ioánnina.

Η ΛΕΜΟΝΙΑ.

Λεμονιᾶς ζητῶ, λεμόνι ἕνα,
κι' αὐτὴ μοῦ ἔλεγε—τάχει ἄλλος μετρημένα·
κ. τ. λ.

(*Aravandinos*, 418.)

Of the Lemon-tree ask I one lemon alone.
She answers—'They've counted them every one!'

Of the Lemon-tree ask I for lemons but two.
She answers—'Not one even is there for you!'

Of the Lemon-tree ask I, I ask lemons three.
She answers me—'*Poüsté!*[1] I owe none to thee.'

Of the Lemon-tree ask I, four lemons I claim.
She answers—'Who art thou? I know not thy name.'

Of the Lemon-tree ask I, five lemons so bright.
She says—'Hold the candle and show me a light!'

Of the Lemon-tree ask I, six lemons I pray!
She says—'Hold it still till it's all burnt away.'[2]

[1] See *above*, p. 140, n. 1.
[2] Compare such Children's Rhymes as
'Oranges and lemons say the bells of St. Clements,' etc., etc.;
which suddenly ends with
    'Here comes a candle to light you to bed,
    Here comes a chopper to chop off the last one's head.'

THE HEGOUMENOS AND THE VLACH MAIDEN.
Ioánnina.

Ο ΗΓΟΥΜΕΝΟΣ ΚΑΙ Η ΒΛΑΧΟΠΟΥΛΑ.
'Σ τὸν ἀπάνου μαχαλᾶ
καὶ 'ς τὴν κάτου γειτονιὰ,
κ. τ. λ..

(*Aravandinos*, 383.)

To the upper quarter go,
Or the neighbourhood below;
Vlach girls sit, and wash them there—
Sit and wash, and comb their hair.
This a '*goúmenos*[1] was told,
Breathless ran he to behold.
' Vlachopoúla, thee I love;
This I've come to tell my dove.'
' *Goúmené*, if thou lov'st true;
Go and fetch a boat, now do;
' Handsome let its boatmen be,
To pull the oars for thee and me.'

THE BULGARIAN GIRL.
Epeiros.

Η ΒΟΥΡΓΑΡΟΠΟΥΛΑ.
Δώδεκα χρόνους ἔκαμα
'ς τῆς Πόλης τ' αργαστήρια,
κ. τ. λ..

(*Aravandinos*, 425.)

LONG years a doz'n I toiled and moiled,
Within Stambouli's workshops;

---
[1] 'Ηγούμενος, Hegumenos, or Abbot.

Sequins a thousand there I earned,
Piastres earned five hundred ;
All of them in one night I spent,
With one Bulgarian damsel.
Give me, O Bulgar, back my coin,
And give me back my sequins ![1]

THE WOOER'S GIFT.
Parga.

ΤΟ ΔΟΡΟΝ ΤΟΥ ΜΝΗΣΤΗΡΟΣ.

'Αγουρος μῆλο μῶστειλε καὶ κόκκινο γαϊτάνι,
—καὶ κόκκινο γαϊτάνι,
κ. τ. λ.
(*Aravandinos*, 384.)

A YOUNGSTER me an apple sent, he sent a braid of scarlet—
He sent a braid of scarlet.
The apple I did eat anon, and kept the braid of scarlet—
And kept the braid of scarlet.
I wove it in my tresses fair, and in my hair so golden—
And in my hair so golden.
And to the sea-beach I went down, and to the shore of ocean—
And to the shore of ocean ;
And there the women dancing were, and drew me in among them—
And drew me in among them.

---

[1] This Song recalls the story of that famous satire of Sappho's, in which she ridiculed her brother Charaxas for having lost all his profit on a cargo of wine with the beautiful Thracian hetaira, Doricha, usually called 'Rosycheeks' (Ροδῶπός), once the fellow-slave of 'Æsop, the fable-writer,' and brought to Navkratis, at the eastern mouth of the Nile, by the Samian merchant, Zanthes.— See ATHENÆUS, *Deipn.*, xiii. 596.

The youngster's mother there I found, and there, too,
  was his sister—
    There was his eldest sister.
And as I leapt and danced amain, and as I skipped and
  strutted—
    And as I skipped and strutted—
My cap fell off, and ev'ryone could see my braid of
  scarlet—
    Could see my braid of scarlet.
'I say, the braid you're wearing there was to my son
  belonging—
    My dearest son belonging.'
'And if the braid that now I wear was to your son
  belonging—
    Your dearest son belonging—
He sent an apple, it I ate, my hair the braid I wound
  through;
    And I will soon be crowned, too.[1]

THE SHEPHERD'S WIFE.
Epeiros.

Η ΤΣΟΜΠΑΝΙΣΑ.

Μι ἀγυναῖκα ἐνοῦ τζομπάνη,[2]
οὔτε τὸ γιαγοῦρτι φτιάνε.
              κ. τ. λ.

(*Aravandinos*, 354.)

A SHEPHERD once a wife had he,
To curdle milk she'd ne'er agree;
His cheese to him she'd never bear,
To leave him was her only care;

---
[1] That is, married. For, in the Greek marriage-service, the priest places garlands on the heads of the bride and bridegroom, saying : Στέφετε ὁ δοῦλος τοῦ Θεοῦ τὴν δούλην τοῦ Θεοῦ. 'Servant of God, So-and-so, crown the servant of God, So-and-so.'
[2] *Choban*, a commonly used Turkish word for 'Shepherd.'

And to the town she fain would go,
And she would be a lady O!
'O leave me not, my partridge dear;
Still with me bide—live with me here.
I'll sell the pig that's in the sty,
A fur-lined cloak for thee to buy;
I'll sell the goats, and have a ring,
Made with the money that they bring;
And all the kids for thee I'll sell,
To buy thee earrings fine, as well;
I'll sell the sheepfold for thy sake,
So I a dress can for thee make;
I'll sell the farm, and land I'll lack,
So thou mayst have a mantle black."[1]

THE KLEPHTS.
ΟΙ ΚΛΕΦΤΑΙ.

Βγῆκαν κλέφταις ϛὰ βουνὰ,
Γιὰ νὰ κλέψουν ἄλογα·
κ. τ. λ.

(*Passow*, 507.)

To the hills the klephtës came,
Stealing horses was their game;
But no horses did they find,
So my little lambs they took,
Flocks of kids from 'neath my crook.
All gone, all gone, all gone, all!
Alack, alack, alackaday!
Little lambs of mine,
Little goats of mine,
    Ohone![2]

---

[1] The ordinary outer garment of shepherd's wives is of unbleached and undyed wool.

[2] Βαι! an exclamation either of mere surprise, or of distress and dismay.

They took from me my milk-pail new,
In which my flocks' sweet milk I drew ;
They took from me my reed-pipe true—
From out my hand they took it, too.
All gone, all gone, all gone, all !
Alack, alack, alackaday !
Little pipe of mine,
Little pail of mine,
    Ohone !

My wether's gone, too, from the fold ;
He had a fleece as bright as gold,
And horns of silver on his head.
All gone, all gone, all gone, all !
Alack, alack, alackaday,
Little flocks of mine,
Little wether mine,
    Ohone !

Panaghía, I pray of thee,
Punish all these klephts for me !
Ay, and on them sudden fall ;
Take away their weapons all.
In their strongholds punish them,
Yea, and all the like of them.
Alack, alack, alackaday !
Little flocks of mine,
Little wether mine,
    Ohone !

Panaghía, if heard by thee,
And thou smite the klephts for me ;
And again within the fold
I my ram, with fleece of gold,

See; when comes Good Friday round,
Lambs I'll roast thee, I'll be bound,
Till from spit they fall to ground.
Alack, alack, alackaday!
Little flocks of mine,
Little wether mine,
Ohone!

THE THIEF TURNED HUSBANDMAN.
Epeiros.

Ο ΑΠΟ ΛΗΣΤΟΥ ΓΕΩΡΓΟΣ.

Ἄφηκε ὁ Γιάννης τὴν κλεψιὰ κ' ἔπιασε τὸ ζευγάρι,
κ' ἔκιασ' αλέτρι ἀπὸ συκιὰ καὶ τὸ ζυγὸ ἀπὸ δάφνη,
κ. τ. λ.

(*Aravandinos*, 352.)

THE robber's trade had Yanni left, and now would be a farmer;
His plough he made of figtree-wood, the yoke he made of laurel;
He made of bullrushes his team, an old spade was his ploughshare;
As for his goad, it was a stick, cut from a branch of olive.
He sowed, and when the autumn came, he reaped his corn nine measures.
The five he owed, and paid them back, three by the Turks were taken,
The one, poor one, that's left to him, he to the mill will carry.
He finds the clapper on the mill, and cut off is the water;
And while he makes the water run, and sets the mill agoing,
The rats come out on every side, and gnaw his sack to tatters.

'I say, boo, boo, my little sack! Ah me! I am unlucky!'
And while he's twisting him his thread[1] to mend his torn sack's tatters,
A wolf comes out from t' other side, and kills and eats his donkey.
'I say, boo, boo, my donkey dear! Ah me! I am unlucky!'
Away he goes and climbs a hill, and sits him in the sunshine ;
And takes him off his breeches wide, to rid them of the vermin.
From high above an eagle swoops, and carries off his breeches.
'I say, boo, boo, O breeches mine! Ah me! I am unlucky!'
He sets out down the hill again, and soon his children spy him.
'O *mana*, here *Effendi*[2] comes, and from the mill he's coming,
Without the sack, without the ass, and oh! without his breeches!'
Yannóva to the door came out—she for the flour was waiting—
And called to him : 'Come, hurry now! the cakes I must be kneading;
For hungry all the children are, and for their food they're screaming.'
'Now hold thy tongue, thou featherbrain ![3] I'm deafened with thy chatter ;
For unbreeched home thou seest I've come, and come without the donkey!'

[1] Unspun yarn, which is dexterously twisted with the hands as required for use.
[2] See *above*, p. 160, n. 1.
[3] Ζαλιάρικα, from Ζάλη, giddiness.

CLASS III.
HISTORICAL FOLK-SONGS.

SECTION I.—PASHALIC.[1]

THE SACK OF ADRIANOPLE.
(1361.)

ΑΔΡΙΑΝΟΥΠΟΛΙΣ ΚΟΥΡΣΕΥΜΕΝΗ.

Κλαίγουν τἀηδόνια τῆς Βλαχιᾶς καί τὰ πουλιὰ στὴν δέσιν,
Κλαίγουν αργὰ, κλαίγουν ταχυὰ, κλαίγουν τὸ μεσημέρι.
κ. τ. λ.

(*Passow*, 193.)

WALLACHIA'S[2] nightingales lament, the birds within the forests;

[1] The most natural division of these Historical Folk-songs seems to be into three Periods—the First extending from the Ottoman Conquest to the first Greek Insurrections in the last quarter of the Eighteenth Century—those, namely, of the Cypriotes in 1760, of the Mainotes in 1770, and of the Souliotes in 1787; the Second Period extending from about 1760 to the Greek War of Independence in 1821; and the Third, from the latter date to the present time. The First Period and Section of the Songs may be distinguished as the Pashalic; the Second, in at least Northern Greece, as the Souliote; and the Third as the Hellenic. For it was only in this last Period that the idea of Hellas was developed, and that Greeks fought as Hellenes, and not merely as Mainotes or Souliotes, etc., or, at best, as Christians against Muslims.

[2] Wallachia here means Thrace, not the Trans-Danubian country now known by that name. Thessaly was for long a semi-independent principality under the name of *Great Wallachia*, Μεγάλη Βλαχία. See *Introd.*, p. 28; also p. 29, n. 26.

13—2

They weep at morn, they weep at eve, and weep they too at noontide.
They're weeping for the pillaged town, sore pillaged Adrianople,
That at the year's three festivals the Turks despoil and pillage.
At Christmastide they tapers take, the palms on Passion Sunday,
And on the morn of Easter Day, break up our 'Christ is Risen!'[1]

THE CAPTURE OF CONSTANTINOPLE.
(1453.)

ΑΛΩΣΙΣ ΤΗΣ ΚΩΝΣΤΑΝΤΙΝΟΥΠΟΛΕΩΣ.

Πῆραν τὴν πόλι, πῆραν τὴν, πῆραν τὴ Σαλονίκη,
Πῆραν καὶ τὴν ἁγιὰ Σοφιὰ, τὸ μέγα μοναστῆρι.
κ. τ. λ.

(*Passow*, 194.)

THE city's taken, it is lost, they've taken Salonίca!
Ayiá Sofiá they've taken too, the Minster great they've taken,
Which has three hundred wooden bells[2] and sixty-four of metal;
And every bell has its own priest, and every priest his deacon.
With them come out the holy Saints, the Universal Ruler,
A message comes to them from heaven by mouths of holy Angels—

[1] The reference is to the Resurrection Song, of which a translation is given *above*, p. 104.
[2] Perhaps 'wooden gongs' would be a better translation of the Greek σήμαντρα, which are simply suspended boards struck with a wooden clapper hung beside them.

'Cease ye that psalmody, and lower the Saints down from their niches,
And send word to the Frankish lands that they may come and take them,
That they may take the golden Cross and take the Holy Gospels,
The Holy Table let them take, that it may not be sullied.'
The Virgin heard the words and wept, all tearful were the Icons;
'O hush thee, Virgin! Icons, hush! mourn not, and cease your weeping;
Again, with years, the time shall come when ye again shall dwell here.'

THE CHILD-TAX.[1]
(1565-1575.)

ΤΟ ΠΑΙΔΟΜΑΖΩΜΑ.

'Ανάθεμά σε, βασιληά, καὶ τρὶς ἀνάθεμά σε,
μὲ τὸ κακὸν ὀπώκαμες, μὲ τὸ κακὸ 'ποῦ κάνεις!
κ. τ. λ.

(*Aravandinos*, 1.)

O CRUEL King, accurs'd be thou, and be thou thrice accursed,
For all the evil thou hast done, the ill thou still art doing!
Thou send'st and draggest forth the old, the primates and the parsons,
The tax of Children to collect, to make them Janissaries.
The mothers weep their darling sons, and sisters, brothers cherished;
And I am weeping, and I burn, and all my life I'll sorrow;
Last year my little son they took, this year they took my brother!

[1] The Child-Tax was enforced till 1675, the last year of the Vizierate of Achmet Kiuprili.

DROPOLITISSA.

Μωρὴ Δροπολίτισσα,
αὐτοῦ ποῦ πᾶς τὴν ἐκκλησιά,
κ. τ. λ.

(*Aravandinos*, 420.)

DROPOLÍTISSA, I say,
As to church you go to-day,
Apron all in front so gay,
And with cap worn all sideway,
Now at church you're going to pray,
A little prayer for us you'll say,
That the Turks take us not away
To be enrolled as Jan'serai,
Nor take us to the Kislar Bey[1]—
Like the lambs on Easter-Day!

NIGHT-SCHOOL SONG.

Φεγγαράκι μου λαμπρὸ
Φέγγε μου νὰ περπατῶ,
κ. τ. λ.

(*Passow*, 278.)

LITTLE moon of mine so bright,
As I walk now shed thy light
On my way to school to-night;
To learn my letters now I go,
To learn to broider and to sew,
And the things of God to know.[2]

---

[1] Literally 'Bey of the Women,' the Chief Eunuch of the Sultan, who was Governor of Greece.

[2] τοῦ Θεοῦ τὰ πράγματα. That is to say, the old Aryan myths of a Trinity, a God-man, and a Resurrection, instead of the unmythologic Semitic monotheism adopted by the Turks.

THE SEA-FIGHT AND THE CAPTIVE.
1574.

Η ΝΑΥΜΑΧΙΑ ΚΑΙ Ο ΕΚΛΑΒΟΣ.

Νὰ ἤμουν πουλὶ γλυκαηδονί, νὰ ἤμουνα χελιδόνι,
νὰ ἤμουν καὶ χρυσοφάναρο 'στο φάρο της Μεσσήνας.
κ. τ. λ.

(*Aravandinos*, 2.)

WOULD that I were a nightingale, or would I were a swallow,
Or golden lantern I would be that's in Messina's beacon,
That I might see, that I might spy when Ríga spreads his canvas!
They joyful sail, and as they row, all gaily sing the sailors;
They seek no port to enter in, no harbour where to anchor;
Their quest is for Alí Pashá, they long to give him battle.
When in mid-sea meet those two fleets, those battle-ships so many,
Then roar the guns above the deep, and day is quenched in darkness.
One prow is with another locked, and mast with mast entangled;
The blades are flashing in the air, and loudly crack the muskets;
With feet and hands the ships are filled, filled all with bleeding corpses.
Alí Pashá's among the slain, that worthy pallikári.
Astern of him comes Riga now, with his great galliot, Riga;
Within, a hundred prisoners all lie with fetters laden.
One pris'ner groaned so heavily the vessel sailed no longer,

And Riga feared, and called to him the captain of the galliot :
' He who has groaned so heavily that still has stood the vessel ;
If he be of my followers, I will increase his wages ;
And if he of my captives be, he shall receive his freedom.'
' I am the man who groaned so sore the vessel sailed no longer ;
For I a horrid dream have dreamt, a dream as here I slumbered.
I saw my wife whom they had crowned and married to another.
A bridegroom only four days old the Turks took me a captive,
And ten long years I've passed since then on Barbary's soil in durance ;
Ten walnut trees I planted there within my dreary prison,
Of all of them I ate the fruit, but Freedom found I never.'

SERAPHEIM OF PHANÁRI.
(1612.)

Ο ΦΑΝΑΡΙΟΥ ΣΕΡΑΦΕΙΜ.

Τοῦ Φαναριοῦ τὸν 'πίσκυπο τον Γερο Σεραφείμη
'ς την ἀζανιὰ τὸν ἔρριξαν οἱ Τοῦρκοι των Φαρσάλων.
x. τ. λ.

(*Aravandinos, 3.*)

THE Bishop of Phanário, the aged Serapheimë,
By calumny the Turks o'erthrew, the Kóniars of Pharsália ;
They chained him in the pillory, and cruelly they tortured ;

Serapheim of Phanári. 205

And near to a dark cypress tree his reverend head they severed.
The roots of the sad cypress tree all faded soon and withered.
To keep the bishop company they slew with him three Klephtës,
And on the spot where their four heads had all been thrown together,
A light was seen to shine at night, seen by a simple shepherd,
Who ran to bring his master word and tell him of the wonder.
His master bade him go again and steal the head from thither,
That head from which the bright light shone, and bear it down to Doúsko.
The shepherd took it, and he ran unto Salambria's margin.
But follow swiftly at his heels two Yánniniots pursuing,
And in his fright the simple swain has dropped it in the river,
Then back unto his master runs to tell of his adventure.
They two, when midnight dark had come, went down to the Salambria;
They search, and soon its radiance bright the head to them discovered,
And running joyfully they came, as morning broke, to Doúsko.
And hurried there both young and old, the men of the White River;[1]
With holy rite they buried it within the sanctuary.
The folk of Agrapha were told; they wrote and prayed the Patriarch

[1] Ασπροποτάμος.

To send an order that the skull the Doúskiots should give them.
They took it and they placed it high upon the hill Korona,
That they might hold a feast to it, and build a roof to shelter.
A picture too they made of him, limned by a skilful painter;
Above was seen the Yánniniots the shepherd swain pursuing;
And at the foot the Plague was crouched, the Plague with aspect dreadful,[1]
Whom he was piercing with a sword and under foot was treading;
And since that time in Agrapha the Death has never entered.[2]

THE SLAVE.

Ο ΔΟΥΛΟΣ.

'Εμένα ὁ ἀφέντης μου μὲ βάνει καὶ κερνάω,
κι' ἀπὸ τὸ συχνοκέρασμα κι' ἀπ' τὰ ψηλὰ τραγούδια,
κ. τ. λ.

(*Passow*, 49a, 1.)

My Master bade me pour the wine and fill for him the winecup.
From often pouring it, and from the high songs that I sang him,
I'd weary grown, my trembling hand the cup could hold no longer.
It fell not on the marble floor, nor on the pebbled pavement,

[1] The Plague is represented as a hideous old hag.
[2] This song is still sung on his Feast-day in the Church dedicated to the martyred Bishop.

The Slave.

But on my Master's lap it fell, and in my Lady's apron.
Sore wrathful waxed my Master then, and he would go
  and sell me ;
And criers he sent round about in all the neighb'ring
  country:
'Who wants to buy a handsome slave, to pour wine for
  his drinking ?'
'O sell me not, Effendi mine, make not of me a bargain;
For am I not thy handsome slave, and thy experienced
  servant ?'
' But I shall sell thee now, my slave, and make of thee a
  bargain.'
' It is not just, Effendi mine, to such a pallikari ;
For I am known of all the world, and everybody knows
  me !'
'Go, go, my slave, good luck to thee ; but come thou
  never nigh me !'

METSOÏSOS.[1]
1690-1715.

Ὁ Μετσοΐσος 'στὰ βουνὰ, ψηλὰ 'στὰ κορφοβούνια,
ἐμαζῶξε κλεφτόπουλα, ὅλ' Ἀρβανιτοπαίδια.

κ. τ. λ.

(*Aravandinos*, 31.)

BRAVE Metsoïsos on the hills, high on the mountain-
  ridges,
Has gathered round him gallant klephts, and they are
  all Albanians.

[1] This robber-chief, whose real name was Mustaphá, was the great-grandfather of Alí Pashá, and the son of Hussein Kapoudji, who is said (though probably really an Albanian) to have come from Constantinople about the middle of the Sixteenth Century, and settled at Tepeléni.

He gathered them, he counted them, he counted them three thousand.
'Now eat and drink, my brave boys all! rejoice, and let's be merry;
This lucky year that's with us now, who knows what next will bring us,
If we shall live, or if we'll die, to t' other world be going?[1]
Now list to me, my pallikars—now list to me, my boys all:
'Tis not for eating I want klephts, I want no klephts for mutton;
I want the klephts for their good swords, I want them for their muskets.
For three days' marching must we do, and do it in one night too;
That we may go, and set our feet within Nikólo's houses;
Which have of coin a right good store, and which have plates of silver.'
'Nikólo, may thy day be good!' 'Thou'rt welcome, Metsoïsos.'
'The boys want lodging here with thee, the pallikars want dinner;
And I myself want five fat lambs, I want two good fat wethers;
A damsel fair besides I'd have, to pour the wine out for me.
No, no! I want no damsel fair, nor mutton killed and roasted;
Piastres[2] in my lap I want, and sequins[3] in my pocket.'

[1] 'ς ἄλλον κόσμο πᾶμε. [2] Γρόσια. [3] Φλωριά.

CHRISTOS MILIONIS.
(1700-1710.)

Ο ΧΡΗΣΤΟΣ ΜΗΛΙΟΝΗΣ.

Τρία πουλάκια κάθουνταν 'στην ράχη στο Ͻημέρι ;
Τ'ονα τηράει τον 'Αρμυρό, τἄλλο κατὰ τὸν Βάλτο.
κ. τ. λ.

(*Passow*, I.)

THREE little birds perched on the ridge hard by the Klephtes' stronghold,
One looked towards fair Armyró, the other down to Válto;
The third, the best of all the three, a dirge was singing sadly:
'Lord Jesus! what can have become of Christos Miliónis?
No more in Valto is he seen, nor yet in Kréavrisi.[1]
They say he has gone far away and entered into Arta,
And taken captive the Kadí, and made the Agas pris'ners.
The Mussulmans have heard of it and sorely are they troubled;
They've called the Mavromáta out, and called Mouktar Kleisoúra.
" If you your bread would have of us, and if you would be leaders,
First must you Christos execute, kill Captain Miliónis:
So has our Sultan ordered it, and he has sent a firman."
When Friday dawned, and when the day had broke and morn was shining,
Then Soulieman set forth in quest, for he would go to find him.
At Armyró they met as friends, as friends they kissed each other ;

[1] *Introd.*, p. 28.

And all the livelong night they drank, until the day was
  dawning.
And as the dawn began to shine, they passed to the
  leméria ;[1]
And Soulieman loud shouted there to Capitán Miliónis:
"You're wanted, Christos, by the King, and wanted by
  th' Agádes!"
"While life and breath in Christos are, to no Turk will
  he yield him!"
With gun in hand they run to meet, as one would eat
  another;
Fire answers fire, they fall, and, dead, both lie upon the
  mountain.'

SYROS.

(1750-1760.)

Macedonia.

'Ο Σύρος ἀπὸ τὴ Σερβιὰ, κι' ὁ Νάννος ἀπ' τὴ Βέῤῥοια
Κονάκια 'χουν τὴν Τσαπουρνιὰ, κονάκια 'στὰ Κανάλια,
                                            κ. τ. λ.

(*Passow*, 30a.)

FROM Servia[2] has Syros come, and Nanno out from
  Vérrla;[3]
They houses have in Tsapourniá, and houses in Kanália,[4]
A lodging-place at Kerosiá, within the Parson's dwelling.
'Now bring forth, Parson, bread and wine, and fodder for
  the horses;

---

[1] The hiding-places of the klephts, supposed to be derived from ὄλη 'μέρα, 'all day.'
[2] The stronghold defending the pass of the Sarandáporos, and originally occupied by the Servians settled in the valley of the Haliacmon, by the Emperor Heraclius, about 620.
[3] The *Bérrhœa* of St. Paul. See *Introd.*, p.37.
[4] Identified by M. Heuzey with the Olympian Sanctuary of the Muses. See *Introd.*, p. 35.

Bring, Parson, too, thy daughter out, our Capitan demands her.'
'I'll give you bread, I'll give you wine, and fodder for your horses ;
But I have not my daughter here, she's gone out to the vineyard.'
The words had hardly left his mouth, the words he'd hardly uttered,
When lo! his daughter dear is seen, with apples heavy laden.
She apples bears, her apron full, and quinces in her kerchief.
He bends, from her the apron takes, and then her hand he kisses.
'Come, maiden mine, upon my knee, and wine now pour out for me ;
I'll drink until the morning break, and birds go seek their breakfast.'
'I am a Parson's daughter, sir—I am a Parson's daughter ;
And for no Captain of them all have I e'er filled a wine-cup.
For it would be a shame to me, a shame to all my lineage ;
A shame 'twould to my father be, who is a man of rank, sir.'
'Then will I take thee with my hand, and with my sword I'll take thee ;
Of no Pashá am I afraid, me no Vizier can frighten ;
For I am Syros the renowned, the celebrated Syros.
By night and day I am at war, at early morn in ambush ;
And famous captains, too, are mine, and chosen men my soldiers—

And mine is Tséghi the renowned; and mine brave
    Captain Tásos;
For when they see my hand and seal, and when they see
    my writing,
They turn the night to day to come, to come apace and
    join me.'

SATIR BEY.
(1760-1780.)

ΣΑΤΗΡ ΜΠΕΗΣ.

Σαββάτο ἡμέρα, κυριακὴ προτοῦ νὰ ξημερώσῃ,
Κίνεσαν ὁ Σατίρμπεής 'ς τὸν πόλεμο νὰ πάνῃ.
                                            κ. τ. λ.
(*Aravandinos*, 45.)

IT happened on a Saturday before the dawn of Sunday,
That Satir Bey from his konak fared forth to battle going.
But as he travelled on the road, and on the road was riding,
A little Bird did cross his path, and sadly him accosted:
'Turn back, my Bey, I pray of thee, turn back, for Death
    will meet thee!'
'Where didst thou learn, thou little Bird, that Death
    would come to meet me?'
'Up in the sky, but yesterday, among the holy Angels;[1]
They wrote thy dwelling desolate, they wrote thy wife a
    widow,
They wrote thy young beys fatherless, they wrote them
    poor and beggars.'
The words had hardly left his mouth, the words he'd
    hardly uttered,
A rattle's heard, and Satir Bey lay dead upon the
    highway.

[1] Compare with 'The Moirai, or Fates,' *above*, p. 111.

THE CAPTURE OF LARISSA AND TIRNAVO.

(1770.)

ΥΠΟΤΑΓΗ ΤΟΥΡΝΑΒΟΥ ΚΑΙ ΛΑΡΣΗΣ.

'Απόψ' εἶδα στὸν ὕπνο μου, στὸν ὕπνο ποῦ κοιμώμουν,
Σὰ μάτ' ἱκάη ὁ Τούρναβος, σὰ μάτ' ἱκάη ἡ Λάρσα.
                                                   κ. τ. λ.
(*Passow*, 199.)

LAST night a dream there came to me, a vision as I slumbered,
In flames did Tírnova appear, and burning, too, was Lár'ssa;
They took the mothers with their babes, and wives took with their husbands;
They took with them a youthful wife—but three days born her baby.
A thousand went in front of them, behind them marched five hundred.
'O wait awhile, my pallikars! O wait awhile, leventës!
My babe in swaddling bands I'd bind, milk from my breast I'd give him.'
The pallikars awaited her, and waited the leventës:
'O Peter, thee I leave my child, O guard him well, and tend him;
For ere I go, and come again, and back can be returning,
The raven shall have feathers white, and shall become a pigeon!'

SOULIEMAN PASHINA.
(1786.)

Η ΣΟΥΛΕΙΜΑΝΠΑΣΣΙΝΑ.

Ηοιὸς θέλ' ν' ἀκουση σκουσματα καὶ μαῦρα μοιρολόγια,
ἅς πάγη μεσ' τὰ Γιάννενα, ἀντίκρ' ἀπὸ τὸ κάστρο.
κ. τ. λ.

(*Aravandinos*, 6.)

WHOEVER mournful cries would hear, and doleful lamentation,
O let him go to Yánnina, before the lofty castle,
And to the great Pashína list, to Soúlieman Pashína,
Who cries and loud laments her lord, and bitter tears is shedding.
'Ye women all of Yánnina, and ladies of the castle,
Now put off all your garments red, and in the black array you,
For they have slain my Soúlieman—have slain the great Viziéri,
The Viziér of all Yannina, and Voïvode, too, of Arta!'[1]

NOUTSO KONTODEMOS.
(1798.)

Ο ΝΟΥΤΣΟΣ ΚΟΝΤΟΔΗΜΟΣ.

Ψηλὰ 'ς τοῦ Βίκου τὴν κορφή, 'ς τὴ μέση ἀπ' τὸ Βραδέτο,
μιὰ πέρδικα κατάμαυρη ἐπικροκελαϊδοῦσε.
κ. τ. λ.

(*Aravandinos*, 7.)

UPON the breast of Bikou high that is within Vradéto,
There had a black-plumed partridge perched, and sang full sorrowfully.

[1] This Soulieman was the predecessor of the famous Ali, the 'Lion of Ioánnina'; and his widow built to his memory a sculptured Fountain, and a large Khan, called the Khan of Kyria, or the Lady, on the other side of Mount Metzikeli from Ioánnina, and on the road across Pindus to Mezzovo—a Khan where I spent a memorably stormy night.

She sang not as a bird should sing, but a sad dirge was
    wailing:
'What is this evil that has fall'n upon deceived Zagóri?
The primate they have massacred, good Noútso Konto-
    démos,
Who was the greatest 'mong the great in all the Vilayéti.
O Noútso! said I not to thee—My brother, with me
    tarry.
Thou wouldst not hear me, wouldst set out, to Yannina
    wouldst hasten,
That Turkish woman to salute, that Souliemán Pashína.
And she, to thank thee, thy poor head did sever from
    thy body,
And on the dunghill cast it forth, and let the dogs
    devour it.
On thee be curses, Páshina, and thrice be he accursèd,
Thy husband, Alisót Pashá,[1] whom to thy side thou'st
    wedded.'

[1] Her second husband.

SECTION II.—SOULIOTE.

KOUTSONIKA.
(1792.)

O ΚΟΥΤΖΟΝΙΚΑΣ.

Τρία πουλάκια κάθουνταν στὸν "Αϊ Ἐλιὰ στή ῥάχη,
Τὄνα τηράει τὰ Γιάννινα, τ' ἄλλο τὸ Κακοσοῦλι.
κ. τ. λ.

(*Passow*, 203.)

THREE birds were on a summit perched—the ridge of St. Elias;
To Yannina did one look down, and one to Kakosoúli;
The third, the best of all the three, a sad dirge sang and chanted :—
' Albania has gathered her, and gone to Kakosoúli,
Three companies are on the road, all three drawn up in order.
One's headed by Moukhtar Pasha, and one by Mitsovónos,
The third, the best of all the three, the Selikhtár is leading.'
And from the mountain opposite, a parson's wife was gazing;
'Where are ye, sons of Métzovo, and Kakosoúli's children?
The Albanians have come down on us, they want to make us captives.
To Tepeléni we'll be dragged, and there they'll make us Muslims.'
And Koutonsíka answered her, from Avaríko answered :

'Fear not, *Pápadia*, have no fear, and far from you be terror,
For now you shall the battle see of Klephtës' long tophaikia—
See how the valiant Klëphts can fight, and they of Kakosoúli!'
But scarce had Koutsoníka said, his say he'd hardly ended,
When, see! the Turks are flying fast, on foot and horseback flying.
One fled, and, flying, another said : 'Pashá, be thou accurséd!
Much evil hast thou wrought for us, hast brought to us this summer ;
Thou'st wasted many Turkish swords, and many of Albania.'
And Bótsaris cried out and said, while his good sword he brandished :
'Come now, Pashá, why art thou grieved, that thus post-haste thou fleest?
Turn here again unto our land, to desolate Kiápha ;
There thou mayest raise thy throne again, and there thou may'st be Sultan.'

LAMBROS TZAVELAS.
(1792.)

Ο ΛΑΜΠΡΟΣ ΤΣΑΒΕΛΑΣ[1]

'Εφώναξε μιὰ παπαδιὰ μὲς απ' τὸν 'Αβαρίκο·
" Πούστε τοῦ Λάμπρου τὰ παιδιά; πούστε οἱ Μποτσαραίοι.
κ. τ. λ.

(*Passow*, 207.)

THERE called aloud a parson's wife in Avaríko's village :
'Where are ye, Lámbro's boys, and ye, the followers of Botsáris?

[1] This song commemorates the great Souliot victory of the 20th July, 1792, over the forces of Alí Pashá of Ioánnina, who is said to have killed two horses in flying from the field of battle.

A cloud has fall'n upon us now; on foot and horseback
    soldiers;
They are not one, nor are they two, but nineteen thousand
    are they.'
'Let come the Turks, those worn-out Turks, for they
    can never harm us!
Let come the battle, let them see the long guns of the
    Soúliots!
And let them know our Lámbro's sword, and Bótsaris'
    tophaiki—
The weapons of the Soúliot maid, the celebrated Haidee!'
The fight began, and loud around the guns their rattle
    opened.
To Zervas and to Bótsaris cried loudly brave Tzavélas:
'Out with your swords, my gallant boys, and let your
    guns be silent!'
''Tis not yet time,' said Bótsaris, ''tis not yet time for
    sword-play.
Keep ye within the fortress still, nor from the walls yet
    sally;
For without number are the Turks, and few, alas! the
    Soúliots!'
'What is it, fellows, that ye fear?' Tzavélas boastful
    answers:
'Our craven heads still must we hide before those dogs
    th' Albanians?'
Each man his scabbard takes in hand, in pieces twain
    he snaps it;
They fiercely fall upon the Turks, like rams they fall
    upon them.
Calls to his men Velí Pashá—'Turn not your backs like
    cowards!'
And thus they answer him again, while they their guns
    are firing:

'This place it is no Délvino, nor is it yet Widini;
But it is Soúli the Renowned, whose praise the world
   has sounded!
It is the sword of Lámbros brave, with Turkish blood 'tis
   stainéd—
The sword that's caused Albania's folk in mourning to
   array them.
The mothers mourn their fallen sons, and wives their
   slaughtered husbands.'

THE CAPTURE OF PREVEZA.[1]
(1798.)

Η ΠΡΕΒΕΖΑ.

" Βάστα καϋμένη Πρεβέζα τ' 'Αλῆ πασᾶ τ'άσκέρια."
" Τί νὰ βαστάξω, δὲν μπορῶ καὶ τί νὰ νταγιαντίσω,
                                                                       κ. τ. λ.
(*Passow*, 201.)

'YIELD not, sore leaguered Preveza, to Ali Pasha's
   soldiers!'
'How sayest—yield not, dost thou not see I cannot
   hold out longer?
Ali Pasha is pelting me with soldiers twice five thousand;
His cannon pierce me like the rain, his shot are like the
   hailstones;
And those small arms shower down on us like still rain
   in the springtime!'[2]
The captives go to Yannina, as slaves to Tepeleni;
They've taken dame Yorgákaina, and all her sons' wives
   with her.

[1] 'Remember the moment when Preveza fell,
   The shrieks of the conquered, the conquerors' yell,' etc.
                                          BYRON, *Childe Harold*, c. ii.
[2] Compare *Il.* xii. 278 : 'But as flakes of snow fall thick on a winter's day when Zevs the Counsellor hath begun to snow, showing forth these arrows of his to men.'

The youngest daughter lags behind, she walks not with the others.
'Walk faster, my brave daughter dear, behind us do not loiter ;
It is, perhaps, thy many coins, thy many pearls oppress thee ?'
'My strings of coins oppress me not, nor do my pearls oppress me;
It is my child oppresses me, I've left him in the cradle.
O cradle! rock my little babe, O rock and feed him for me,
Till I can go and come again, and back can be returning,
To where they slew my husband dear; upon my knees they slew him,
Cut off his hands, which bleeding fell—they fell upon my apron!'

THE MONK SAMUEL.
(1803.)
Ο ΣΑΜΟΥΗΛ.

Καλόγερε, τί καρτερεῖς κλεισμένος μὲς τὸ Κοῦγι ;
Πέντε νομάτοι σώμεεναν κ' ἐκεῖνοι λαβωμένοι.

κ. τ. λ.

Valaorites, Μνημόσυνα.

'KALÓYER, what art thou waiting for, imprison'd within Kounghi?
Five men alone are left to thee, and all the five are wounded,
And thousands are the enemies that are encamped around thee.
Come out, give up the keys to us, and give in thy submission ;
Our general, Velí Pashá, will make of thee a bishop!'
Within the church's lofty walls is Samuel beleaguered,
And on the wind are borne to him the words of traitor Pélios.

The Monk Samuel.

No psalms are sung, no incense burnt, no holy tapers
  lighted ;
But mournful 'fore the sacred gates, five Soúliots are
  kneeling.
They speak not, motionless they kneel ; yet see, anon
  and ever
A hand is raised, that reverent makes the sign of their
  salvation.
And still, upon the marble floor, their blood-stained
  swords are lying,
Swords that so well have fought and striven for their
  belovéd Soúli !
Not with them there is Samuel seen ; alone before the
  altar,
The mystic offering he prepares, and there, alone, he
  worships.
And firmly in his aged hands he holds the sacred vessel,
While many, many secret words he murmurs to his
  Maker.
His undimmed eyes, though heavy grown, red-rimmed
  with many vigils,
Intently contemplate the feast, the Sacred Blood and
  Body.
An ocean they, of which the waves, with secret hopes
  are surging !
Hushed be ye now, ye thundering guns ! and cease, ye
  cries of battle !
For Samuel will celebrate on earth his last Communion.

And as upon the Flesh Divine the priest in rapture gazes,
Falls from his eye the cup within, one tear, like dew
  transparent.
' My God and Father, buried here within Thy house, I
  thirsted ;

Unmixed with water, incomplete would be Thy Holy
    Supper ;[1]
Accept, Creator, this sad tear, and do not Thou despise it,
From my heart's leaves, all clean and pure, Thou seest
    that forth it floweth ;
Accept it, my Creator, now ; I have no other water.'
A ray of sunlight streaming in, illumed the sacred vessel,
And warmed the Blood, until, at last, it rose in wreaths of
    vapour.
And when the grace divine he saw, then Samuel exulted.
The sacred cup he trembling held, and to his bosom
    pressed it :
And as he kissed, with reverent lips, he heard, like
    heart's pulsation,
That soft, with newly given life, the Sacred Blood was
    throbbing.
And lowly bend the pallikars, as ope the Holy Portals,
So low that on the marble floor they strike their valiant
    foreheads,
And thus await, immovable, the words of the Kalóyer.

Unmoved the priest approaches them, upon his face a
    glory,
As bright as snowy mountain-top, illumined by the moon-
    beams.
A barrel in his hand he bears, those hands so maimed
    and wounded ;
Imprisoned in its staves are death, and fire, and
    desperation.
That one alone is left to him, and that alone suffices.
Before the Holy Portal, now, he sets it up unaided,
Three times he consecrates it there, three times he prays
    before it,

[1] This is the Orthodox, which differs from the Catholic version.

As if the Holy Table 'twere, or as it were the Platter.
The priest above the Sacred Cup extends his hands in
    blessing,
And calmly, silently he lights the match to fire the barrel ;
Then violently his knees resound upon the marble pave-
    ment.
His hands he lifts, his countenance with light celestial
    kindles ;
Then raise their eyes the Soúliots, and gaze on the
    Kalóyer.

THE PRAYER.

My Father, I have done Thy will,
Right faithfully, for years two-score ;
And now my race is nearly run,
Thou givest to me trouble sore !
Thy Will be done, not mine, O Lord !
Let us Thy mercy now obtain ;
Have pity, and Thy wrath restrain.

An orphan, whom the world forsook,
I gave my youthful soul to Thee ;
I Souli to my bosom took,
My only child on earth to be.
Alas! my Souli I have lost,
And now my latest hour has come,
Receive me in Thy heavenly home.

O count, and see how few remain ;
The others slain and slaughtered fall ;
In valleys lone, upon the plain,
They're dead and wounded, scattered all !
Untombed and unlamented strewn,
Their bones are rotting in the shade
Of rocky pass, or grassy glade.

Fierce wolves by night and birds by day
Upon our blackened flesh have fed ;
Have pity, Father, Thee we pray;
Forgive our sins, for Thee we've bled.
And now that we to Thee draw nigh,
And to Thy bosom hasten home,
Oh! let us as Thy children come!

Behold, O Lord, our wounded hands,
That unto Thee we raise on high,
From blood of the unfaithful bands
They've ta'en this stain of crimson dye.
And sanctify us, Thee we pray,
And say to each,—Thou hast well done,
My faithful, blessed, valiant one.

Now Soúli has expired indeed!
And not a single valiant hand
Is left of all the Soúliot breed,
That can with finger grasp his brand.
Almighty Father, be to us
A Fatherland. Of life bereft,
To us no other hope is left!

Above, in heaven, around Thy throne,
Among the many mansions fair,
Give, Father, to Thy servants lone,
Such mansions, and such dwellings there,
That Soúli still we may recall.
And cliffs and crags, too, let there be,
That still my Koúnghi I may see.

Of Soúli free no soil remains
Enough for her defenders' grave.
Have pity, Father, heed our pains ;
O Father, hear us, hear and save,

And unto me this favour grant—
That Koúnghi mine, this holy dome
And altar, may be Samuel's tomb.

Here infidel, with foot of scorn,
Shall never, though he triumph, dare—
Shall never, I have said and sworn—
To tread my Koúnghi's rocky stair.
With me to heaven the keys I bear ;
No man the keys shall take from me,
Nor will I give them up to Thee.

There high in heaven before Thy face,
Still will I wear them at my side ;
Thy servant Samuel asks this grace,
That with him still they may abide.
Grant him this favour, gracious Lord ;
Be not Thou angry, but forbear,
For I alone the keys would wear.

And now that in Thine ears we've poured
Our pain and all our grief and woe,
To Thee we come : accept us, Lord.
From our sweet Soúli we must go.
Ah, Soúli ! thou art lost to me !
Be still, my soul ! thou must not weep ;
The time has come when thou may'st sleep.

Then to his five companions his outstretched hands extending—

O Thou, my God, all-merciful,
From earth I, a poor fugitive,
Must to Thy holy shadow flee,
And in Thy presence come to live.

One favour grant, Creator mine—
That these brave five with me may come,
And share with me that heavenly home.

Within my arms they've nurtured been,
None have they loved but Thee and me,
No other master have they served ;
They martyrs are for liberty.
Then take from me my blessing now;
And fear ye not, my children dear,
With me ye'll live—be of good cheer.

Drop after drop, drop after drop, their bitter tears are falling,
Where they bedew the marble floor they crack and rend the pavement.
'Tis sorrow deep that tears their hearts, death has for them no terror ;
And weeping rises Samuel too, and from the Holy Table,
In one hand takes the Blessed Cup, the Spoon takes with the other,
To celebrate the Sacrament of his belovéd Saviour.
He gives the first, the second too, the third and fourth receive it,
And it suffices for the last, and now to him is offered.
Then, as the *papas* sweetly sang, the holy service chanting,

'Of thy mystic supper,
To-day, O Son of God. . . .'

Resounded with redoubled cries the blows and war's contention.
The Infidels surprise thee, Monk ! what is it thou art doing ?

His eyes he lifts as loud the blows upon the door are
  falling,
And from the Spoon within his hand lets fall upon the
  barrel,
Of Christ's pure Blood one flaming drop, one drop alone
  has fallen.
'Tis struck as with a lightning-flash, and the whole earth
  is thund'ring.
One moment shines the unsullied church, one moment
  glitters Koúnghi.
Ah! what a consecration dire she's at her death re-
  ceiving!
Black Souli the unfortunate—what smoke, what incense
  burning!
The monk's black cassock, floating still, towards the sky
  ascended,
And spread, and spread upon the wind in wide and fearful
  darkness,
And rising with the smoke it soared, and with it on was
  sailing.
And sailing, floating on it went, and still like death was
  poising;
And where its flaming shadow fell, upon the hills and
  valleys,
Like mystic fire it burnt the groves, and scorched the
  wooded hillsides.
But with the first rain-storms of spring, and with the
  showers of summer,
Shall spring again the freshest grass, with laurels, olives,
  myrtles;
With slaughters, victories, and hopes shall spring fresh
  joys and Freedom!

EVTHYMIOS VLACHAVAS.[1]

ΕΥΘΥΜΙΟΣ ΒΛΑΧΑΒΑΣ.

Βλαχάβα, πειὸς δ' ἐγέννησε, ποιὰ μάνα, πειὸς πατέρας ;
* * * * *
'Ο ῎Ολυμπος ἀγάπησε τὴν ὤμορφη τὴν ῎Οσσα,
κ. τ. λ.

Valaoritis, Μνημόσυνα ἄσματα.

VLACHAVA, son of whom art thou, what mother, and what father?
* * * * *
Olympus loved the much-desired, the proud and lovely Ossa ;
For many years he gazed on her, his eyes with love's fires burning ;
And she would blush beneath his gaze, and she in fear would hide her.

One night, one night of spring, the joy of gods, serene and tranquil;
In heaven the stars all glorious shone, from very fulness trembling,
As though they held love's hidden flame, love's burning, love's heartbeating.
No sound was heard but bleating flocks, or sheep-bell's muffled tinkle,
As wandered o'er the fields the sheep, and grazed within the meadows.

[1] Nothing was ever known of the parentage of this hero of Olympus and Pindus, and hence the following splendid myth. After many victories over the troops of Ali Pasha, his band was attacked by ten times their number, and he himself was taken prisoner, diabolically tortured, and put to death. The heroic monk Demetrius, who had been his friend and constant companion, was soon afterwards taken prisoner, and built into a cell with his head only free, in order thus to prolong his agonies.

Anon and ever, on the ear sweet strains of woodland music
From shepherd's pipe lulled lovingly to sleep the trees and flowers;
And fragrant from the laurels blew the breeze, and from the myrtles,
And from the joyful lily who from out the stream had risen,
As white as purest maiden's face the Sun has ever gazed on.
The lily curved his slender neck, and darted loving glances,
To woo his shadow in the wave, within the deep blue water.
O sweetly, sweetly, Echo brought upon the ear the carol
Of Klepht, who calls to mind the deeds of Christos Miliónis.[1]
And winds and trees and waters now stand still, all else forgetting,
And breathless listen to the praise of him their ancient comrade;
While softly falls the crystal dew, pure as the tears of children,
As if a sudden grief had seized upon the new bride's being,
While listening to the dirge he sings for Christos Miliónis.
Why, hills, surrounded by such wealth of love, and joy, and gladness,
Girt with a life so manifold, with harmonies so varied,
Why hear I not 'mid rustling leaves, and willow's swaying branches,

[1] Singing probably the ballad, given *above*, p. 209.

And in the rippling of the streams, the voice of Freedom whisper?
Such was the night Olympus chose to tell his love to Ossa ;
To show the love he bore for her, and tell her of his passion.
See how the lover is adorned! across his ample shoulders,
All white and wide his beard is spread, in soft and waving billows,
That combed are by the moonbeams rays, and tinged with mellow radiance;
Around him snowy clouds he draws, like foam-flecks freshly gathered ;
The opal mist of sweet May dew he wears, as fustanella.
And brightly gleams, girt round his waist, and glitters on his shoulder—
The lightning-flash for his good sword, the thunder-bolt for musket.
Joy to the maiden who is loved, loved by the Klepht Olympus!
The mountains whispered all night long, and one another questioned ;
And when the Morning Star arose, and woke from sleep the roses,
That with the Dawn sprang up the hills, and to the highest summits,
On Ossa, lovely Ossa, still Olympus fond was gazing,
And saw her blush beneath his glance, blush like a bashful maiden.
He stooped, he bent his crest to her, and on her lips he kissed her ;
And quick that kiss, that kiss alone, like life and flame commingled,

Thrilled through the veins of the new bride, and all her
    being kindled.
Ere many years had come and gone, ere many months
    and seasons,
A sound was heard on Agrapha, and in the lofty
    Pindus—
The footsteps of the Armatole, the terrible Vlachavas;
The voice of eagles too that cried, the voice of falcons
    screaming:
'Ye forests, open wide a path, and gather up your
    branches;
And let the Stoicheiò pass by, the Drákontas of Ossa!'

Fallen into the power of Ali Pasha, Vlachavas, after being cruelly tortured, is dragged through the streets of Ioánnina for three days, and dies. He is then decapitated by a Gipsy, who places his head on a stone pillar. But his faithful dog has followed unnoticed in the crowd.

The night had fallen, and, satiate, the wild beasts had
    departed.
The dog alone remained behind; upon the earth he
    stretched him,
And moaned, and moaned incessantly, poor hound, from
    his great sorrow.
But when the midnight dark had come, he sudden leapt
    and bounded,
And in his mouth, and with his jaws, to seize the head
    he struggled;
But, maimed and bleeding, his poor claws upon the stone
    slip, broken.
It is too high, he cannot reach. Yet still he clings, and
    stretches,

And slips, and falls; but, eagerly, again he leaps undaunted;
And with a last, wild, hopeless bound, he stands upon the summit.
That head, that head so terrible between his teeth he seizes;
And with it swift he flees away, across the hills and valleys.
And as their rapid course they take, the forest trees, all startled,
Ask one another, 'Who is this?'—the pine-tree asks the plane-tree,
The willow asks the cypress tall, the elm-tree asks the laurel—
'Who is this who is passing by? say, is it not Vlachavas?'
And with their eyes they follow them, but they are fleeing ever.

When, near the dawning of the day, they reach the heights of Ossa,
Upon her topmost, topmost ridge, among the deepest snow-wreaths,
The faithful dog a deep bed digs, and there the head he buries,
And by its side he stretches him, and lays him down expiring.
O happy be the snowy bed where buried lies Vlachavas!
The mother who the hero bore again her bosom opens,
And spreads a couch that he may rest, like babe within the cradle.

MOUKHTAR'S FAREWELL TO PHROSÝNE.[1]

Σὰ φύλλο κίτρινο καὶ μαραμμένο
Μὲ πέρνει ὁ ἄνεμος μὲ τὰ φτερὰ
Μακρ' ἀπὸ σένανε, παραδαρμένο,
Φροσύνη, ἀγάπα με, στην ξενιτειά.
κ. τ. λ.

(*Valaorites*, Η Κυρὰ Φροσύνη.)

TOSSED like a yellow leaf, withered and waning,
Now on the wind's restless wings must I rove;
Far, far away from thee, sadly complaining,
To foreign lands wand'ring, Phrosýne, my love.

The wavelets e'en now the lake's margin were kissing,
Lapped in a slumber so tranquil and deep;
Boreas has blown—they are surging and hissing,
And high 'gainst the white cliffs in thunder they sweep.

Phrosýne, I'm sent to the land of the stranger,
Afar 'mid the fire of fierce battle's array;
Send from thy loved lips, 'mid strife and 'mid danger,
Sweet kisses a thousand to cheer on my way.

For then, if my hour come, while still I'm a rover,
On soil of the stranger, my heart and my life—
There, if, to drink my blood, vultures should hover,
To gorge in the desert with gluttonous strife,

[1] Moukhtar, a son of Alí Pashá, had an intrigue with the beautiful and accomplished young wife of a Greek of Ioánnina. When Moukhtar had been sent to a distant command by his father, she and a number of other ladies, accused of infidelity to their husbands, were drowned in the Lake by command of the tyrant, who is said to have made advances to the beautiful Greek, which were repulsed. Her tragic fate caused her sins to be forgotten, and transformed the adulteress into a heroine and martyr.

Who knows, my belov'd, but those kisses might give me
The life I had lost, and I'd rise at thy hest,
And come like a dream to the arms would receive me,
And lull me, unhappy, Phrosýne, to rest!

The winter clouds come, and the snowstorms will follow,
The flowers are all faded, their fragrance is flown;
Away, too, is flying, Phrosýne, the swallow—
Beware! for around us night's darkness is thrown!

Phrosýne, I go where the fierce battle rages,
To lands of the stranger I'm sent far away;
Who knows what is written on Fate's hidden pages?
Farewell, my Phrosýne—farewell I must say.

THE CAPTURE OF GARDIKI.
(1812.)

ΑΛΩΣΙΣ ΓΑΡΔΙΚΙΟΥ.

Κοῦκκοι, νὰ μὴ λαλήσετε, πουλιὰ νὰ βουβαθῆτε
Καὶ σεῖς καϋμέν' Ἀρβανιτιὰ οὖλοι νὰ πικραθῆτε.

κ. τ. λ.

(*Passow*, 219.)

O CUCKOOS sing your song no more, and all ye birds be silent!
And ye Albanians everyone, be ye o'ercome with sorrow!
The citadel has given in, and fallen is Khoúmelitza;
Gardíki still is holding out, and she will not surrender;
But she to battle fain would go, she fain would go to battle.
Alí Pashá has heard of it, and greatly hath it vexed him.
And furious he with both hands writes, and sends abroad his mandates:

The Capture of Gardíki.

'To thee, Lieutenant Yousoufí; to thee, Yousoúf the Arab;
Now when thou shalt my letter see, and thou shalt see my mandates,
Demítri shalt thou take alive, the same with all his children.
I want, too, Moustaphá Pasha, with all his generation.'
'I, joyfully, Pashá, will go; I go to bring them to thee!'
And up arose Yousoúfi then, and went forth to Gardíki.
And as he went to war against and fight with the Gardíkiots,
Ismáil Delvíno called to him, and shouted from Gardíki:
'Where go'st, dear Yousoufí Agá, dear Yousoufí the Arab?
This place it is not Yánnina, nor is it Tepeléni—
It is Gardíki's famous town in all the world renownéd,
Where little children even fight; and women too, give battle;
Where fights the brave Demír Agá, a worthy pallikári;
Three days, three long, hard days they fight, three days and nights they struggle,
Ere they surrender to Yousoúf, and to his hands submit them;
And only Ismáil still holds out, holds out within Gardiki.'
'Come, 'Smaïl Bey, and thou shalt see the eyes of our Viziéri!'
'I never will submit to thee, and ne'er will I surrender!
I have a deadly gun to wield, and I've with me picked soldiers.'
But they are scattered, sword in hand, Yousoúf has made them pris'ners.
Ismaïl Bey he's captive made, brave Ismaïl Delvíni,
And prisoner made Demír Agá, with him Demítri Dostè;

And taken them before the gate of Yannina's Vizieri.
Low bend they there, his skirt they hold, and kiss his
    hand so humbly.
'We are to blame, my Lord Vizier; we pray thee now
    forgive us!'
'There's no forgiveness here for you, nor mercy will I
    show you!
Here! take these men, and drag them out unto the
    broad lake's margin;
Take you stout planks with you, I say; of stout nails
    take you plenty.
Off with you! nail them to the planks, and in the
    waters throw them;
There let them swim the livelong day, the long day let
    them row there!'

THE KLEPHT VRYKOLAKAS.
(1815.)

ΒΡΥΚΟΛΑΚΑΣ.

"Ενα πουλάκι ξέβγαινεν ἀπό την "Αγια Μαύρα,
Νύχτα σε νύχτα πέταγε, νύχτα σε νύχτα ψάχνει.
                                        κ. τ. λ.

(*Aravandinos, 73.*)

THERE flew, flew out a little bird, flew out from Santa
    Maura;
Night after night he flew along, night after night was
    searching,
The klepht Vrykólakas he sought, and Thémio Baláska.
At last he found them, and unearthed them down by
    Skouliána.
'Your health, my boys, and luck to you!' 'Thou'rt
    welcome here, my birdie!

My little bird, tell us some news, tell us some joyful
    tidings.'
'What shall I tell you then, my boys, what tale shall I
    be telling?
'Fore yesterday, and yesterday, I passed by Tsioúnga's
    palace,
Their conversation there I heard ; oft, too, your name
    they mentioned.
The 'guemenos the traitor was, as in his throat he took
    you,
And to the kapitan you know he wrote and sent a letter:
" Again comes forth Vrykolakas, and with him klephts a
    dozen ;
He's going to be crowned and wed, he's going to take
    Yannoúla." '

DESPO OF LIAKATA.
(1816.)

Μεσα 'ςτὸ κάστρο, 'ςτὰ ψηλὰ σεράγια τοῦ Βεζύρη,
ὅπου εἶχε χίλιας πέρδικες κλεισμέναις κ' ἐλαλοῦσαν,
                                                  κ. τ. λ.

(*Aravandinos*, 74.)

WITHIN the Castle's[1] lofty walls, the great Vizier's
    seráglio,
Where are a thousand partridges, in chains, yet sweetly
    calling,
They yet another captive bring, a partridge all adornéd,
Among the folds of Liakatá they've hunted and en-
    trapped her ;
And every partridge sweetly calls, and she alone is
    silent.

[1] Alí Pashá's Castle at Ioánnina. See *Introd.*, p. 26.

'Why, Despo, speak'st thou not to us, and why art thou so sullen?
Go in, the chamber to prepare, and change the mats and bedclothes,
And I will come and gaze on thee, and we'll converse together.'
'I am not sullen, my Pashá, but I, Pashá, have never
Been taught to spread the mattresses, and lay the sheets in order;
I'm from the folds, a shepherdess, and this is all I ken, sir—
The flocks and herds to feed and tend, and morn and eve to milk them;
The shepherd's gaiters coarse to knit, and curdle the *yiaoúrti*.'[1]

THE EXILE OF THE PARGHIOTS.
(1819.)

Η ΜΕΤΑΝΑΣΤΑΣΙΣ ΠΑΡΓΙΩΝ.

Μαῦρο πουλάκι πῶρχεσαι ἀπὸ τ'ἀντίκρυ μέρη,
Πές μου τί κλάψαις θλιβεραῖς, τί μαῦρα μυρολόγια,
κ. τ. λ..

(*Passow*, 222.)

'BLACK little bird that comest out, from other regions comest,
O say what weeping sore it is, what doleful lamentation
They send from Parga's city out? it rends the very mountains!
Say, do the Turks attack her now, or does the battle burn her?'
'The Turks have not attacked her now, nor does the battle burn her;

[1] A kind of curd, usually eaten uncooked and with sugar, and thought particularly wholesome in spring and early summer. But the Armenians cook it with an herb called *roka*, and serve it with toast and butter. This *roka*, a plant with small green leaves, is also used as a salad.

The Exile of the Parghiots. 239

But all the Parghiots are sold, are sold as goats and cattle.[1]
Ill-fated folk! now they must go, in exile must they sojourn!
They leave their homes, they leave the tombs, the graves of their forefathers;
They leave their holy place of prayer, by Turks it will be trodden;
And women tear their long black hair, and beat their fair white bosoms;
And all the aged loud lament with bitter lamentation;
The priests with weeping eyes take down the Icons from their Churches.
Seest thou those lurid fires that burn, what black smoke from them rises?
There are they burning dead men's bones, the bones of those brave warriors
Who put the Turks in mortal fear, the Vizier in a fever;
They are the bones of ancestors their children now are burning,
That the Liápës find them not, nor Turks upon them trample.
Hear'st thou the wailing of the town which echoes through the forests?
And hearest thou the sounds of woe, the bitter lamentation?
It is because they're driv'n away from their ill-fated country:
They kiss her stones, they kiss the earth,[2] and to her soil Farewell say!"[3]

---

[1] The conduct of the British High Commissioner of the Ionian Islands, Sir Thomas Maitland, in reference to Parga, was certainly, to say the least, open to very severe criticism.

[2] Compare *Il.* iv. 522: 'And as he (Agamemnon) touched his own land, he kissed it.'

[3] They have now, however, returned; and I had the pleasure of making the acquaintance of prosperous merchants belonging to old Parghiot families.

SECTION III.—HELLENIC.

ZITO HELLAS!

ΖΗΤΩ ΕΛΛΑΣ.
'Ω λιγυρὸ καὶ κυφτερὸ σπαθί μου,
Καὶ σύ, τουρέκι μ', φλογερὸ πουλί μου !
κ. τ. λ.

(*Kind*, Τραγώδια, 12.)

O THOU, my sword belov'd, so keen, I gird!
And shoulder thee, my gun, my flaming bird!
O slay ye, slay the Turks again,
The tyrants scatter o'er the plain!
 Live thou, O sword I gird!
 Long life to thee, my bird!

And when, O my good sword, I hear thy clash,
And when, O my black gun, I see thy flash,
That strew the ground with Turkish slain,
And 'Allah!' cry those dogs amain,
 No sweeter music's heard ;
 Long life to thee, my bird!

Now skies are dark, and thunder-clouded o'er,
And tempest, rain, and flood, with Boreas roar ;
I climb the hills, and leave the plain,
The mountain-passes wild I gain ;
 My country rises free—
 Long life, my sword, to thee!

For the most holy faith of Christ ; for thee,
Hellas, my fatherland, and liberty—
It is for these that I would die ;
Only while these live, live would I.
 If not for them to strive,
 Why longer should I live?

The hour has come, and loud the trumpets sound ;
Now boiling is my blood, with joy I bound ;
The *bam*, the *boom*, the *glin, glin, gloun*
Begin, and loud will thunder soon ;
 While Turks around me die,
 Hellas, Hurrah! I cry.

KOSTAS BOUKOVÁLAS.

Χρυσὸς ἀϊτὸς ἐκάθουνταν στὸν ἥλιο κ' ἐμαδιόνταν,
Κι' ἄλλος ἀϊτὸς τόνε ῥωτάει καὶ τὸν βαρυοξετάζει·
                                              κ. τ. λ.
(*Passow*, 8.)

A GOLDEN eagle in the sun sat sad, and plucked his feathers.
Another eagle questioned him, and earnestly he asked him :[1]
'Hullo, what is't has crossed thee now, thou sittest all so faded?'
'Last night I saw, saw in my sleep, while tranquilly I slumbered,
That I to the Pashá flew off, to Berat, into Koúrtè ;
And, while his guest, I heard him say the Albanians all were coming,
Were coming down to Agrapha, to crush the klephtës coming.'

[1] Compare *Od.*, xix. 545 : 'But he (the eagle) came back, and sat him down on a jutting point, and with the voice of a man he spake.' . . .

The eagle Boukoválas heard, and to the fields descended,
His followers he gathered round, his retinue assembled.
To them he told the evil dream, and by an oath he bound them,
No more to trust to word of Turk so long as life was in them.
He further charged and said to them, and called them round in council,
And to the stronghold cried, and said to them within the loopholes :
' Boys, take your weapons in your hands, and all comb out your tresses ; [1]
The Turks are going to fall on us—an army of twelve thousand.'
And Metromáras then arose, and to his men he shouted :
' Take heart, my warriors! and show that ye are men and Christians! [2]
We'll clear the Turks from out the land ; here on this spot we'll slay them !'
As lions roar they loud and long, as lions they make their sortie ; [3]

[1] This recalls the story told by HERODOTUS (vii. 208—9) of the Persian spy who, on the eve of the battle of Thermopylæ, reported that he had found the Spartans combing out their tresses ; and the reply made to Xerxes by Demaratus, that this meant that they would fight to the death. Compare PLUTARCH, *Lycurg.* c. 22, and XENOPHON, *Rep. Lac.* xii. § 8.
[2] Compare *Il.* v. 529 : ' My friends, quit you like men, and take heart of courage.' The term Christian is, among the Greeks, popularly applied only to members of the Orthodox, or Greek, Church, and other Europeans are called, not Christians, but Franks. An old hermit of Mount Athos, whom I visited in his cave, was unable to believe that, as an *Anglos*, I could be a Christian ; and, to please the poor old maniac, I performed the Orthodox rite of kissing an Icon of the Panaghía. The true equivalent of the Χριστιανοί of the text would, therefore, be ' Greeks ' rather than ' Christians.'
[3] Compare *Il.* v. 782 : ' In the semblance of ravening lions.'

They rush upon the Turkish ranks, like goats abroad they're scattered ;
They slaughter and make prisoners as many as two thousand.
But Kostas in the fight has fall'n, fall'n are his two companions,
Who'd been in Goúra Armatoles, and Klephts had been in Zýgos.
The fields lament them, and the hills, and all the vales are weeping ;
The maidens of Phourná lament, for arts and wiles so famous;
And mourn the young Klephts for their Chiefs within the lone leméria.[1]

THE KLEPHT'S FAREWELL TO HIS MOTHER.

Ο ΑΠΟΧΑΙΡΕΤΙΣΜΟΣ ΤΟΥ ΚΛΕΦΤΟΥ.

Μάνα σοῦ λέω δὲν ἠμπορῶ τους Τούρκους νὰ δουλεύω,
Δὲν ἠμπορῶ, δὲν δύναμαι, ἐμάλλιας' ἡ καρδιά μου·
κ. τ. λ.

(*Passow*, 153.)

'I TELL thee, mother, never will I be to Turks enslavéd ;
I cannot, it is not for me—my heart would die within me.
My gun I'll take, and I will go—I'll go and be a klephtë,
And on the mountains I will rove, and on the highest ridges.
I'll for companions have the groves, with wild beasts I'll hold converse ;
The snows I'll for my covering take, for couch the rocky ridges ;
And with the young Klephts all day long, I'll hide in a leméri.
I go, my mother ; weep thou not, but give to me thy blessing,

[1] See p. 210, n. 1.

Yea, bless me, little mother dear, that many Turks I
    slaughter.
And plant for thee a rose-bush fair, and plant a clove
    carnation;
With sugar thou must water them, musk-water pour
    upon them;
And when they blossom, mother mine, and when they
    put forth flowers,
Know that thy son is living still, and 'gainst the Turk is
    fighting.
But when that sad, sad day shall come, when comes
    that bitter morning,
The morn when both those plants shall die, and faded
    hang their blossoms,
Know that thy son all wounded lies—in weeds of black
    array thee.'
Twelve years, twelve long, long years had passed, twelve
    years and fifteen months gone,
And all that time the rose had bloomed and blossomed
    the carnation,
Till dawned a morning bright of Spring, till dawned a
    May-day morning;
Sweet sang the birds within the groves, and all the
    heavens were laughing—
One lightning-flash, one thunder-clap, and all was
    turned to darkness!
Then sadly the carnation sighed, the rose-tree tears
    was weeping;
At once they faded both and died, and fading shed their
    blossoms,
And with them faded, too, and died, the Klepht's unhappy
    mother.

THE KLEPHT'S WINTERING.

Ο ΚΛΕΦΤΗΣ ΠΑΡΑΧΕΙΜΑΖΩΝ.

Ἐμαραθῆκαν τὰ δεντριά, τὰ κορφοβούνι' ἀσπρίζουν,
Κι' οἱ Βλάχοι πᾶν 'ς τὰ χειμαδιά, πᾶνε να ξεχειμάσουν,
κ. τ. λ.

(*Aravandinos*, 128.)

THE trees are faded, withered all, the hills with snow are glistening.
The Vlachs into the lowlands go, they go for winter pasture.
The Klepht, where shall he shelter find? He leaves the mountain-ridges,
His garb he changes,[1] through the woods all silently he's stealing.
No smile is there upon his lips, with head bent low he's striding;
He counts the passing days and nights, and waits the hour impatient,
When spring shall open, beeches bud, and he gird on his weapons,
With gun on shoulder, run again along the rocky ridges,
And climb into the mountains high, and reach the Klephts' leméri,[2]
To mingle with his company, and ply again his calling,
To slay the Turk wherever found, to strip bare every trav'ller,
And wealthy captives seize upon, to hold them fast to ransom.

[1] Exchanging the black kerchief and dirty-white kilt of the Klepht for the white fez and baggy breeches of the Peasant.
[2] See p. 210, n. 1.

THE KLEPHTS AWAITING THE SPRING.
ΟΙ ΚΛΕΦΤΕΣ ΑΝΑΜΕΝΟΝΤΕΣ ΤΟ ΕΑΡ.

"Ησυχα που εἶναι τὰ βουνά, ἥσυχοι που εἶν' οἱ κάμποι !
Δὲν καταροῦνε θάνατο, γεράματα δὲν ἔχουν,
κ. τ. λ.
(*Aravandinos*, 127.)

How peaceful all the mountains lie, how peaceful lie the meadows!
It is not death that they await, old age does not afflict them ;
The spring-time only they await, and May, and summer sunshine,
To see the Vlachs upon the hills, to see the fair Vlach maidens,
And listen to the music sweet that with their pipes they'll waken.
While graze their sheep, around whose necks the heavy bells are tinkling.
Again they'll set their sheepfolds up, and set up their encampment.
Again the young Klepht boys will come for frolic and for dancing.
The Klepht bands, too, will scour again the fields of fair Pharsália,
Their Turkish foes to catch alive, and when they're slain to strip them,
And golden sequins carry off, and then divide and share them ;
And give, perhaps, some two or so to fair and kind Vlach maidens,
When stealing from them kisses two, with sweetest fun and frolic.[1]

[1] Γλυκοπαιγνιδάκι.

HAIDEE.

ΧΑΙΔΩ.

Ποιὸς εἶδε ψάρι σε βουνὸ καὶ' αλάφι σε λιμάνι ;
Ποιὸς εἶδε κόρ' ἀνύπαντρη μέσα στὰ παλληκάρια ;
κ. τ. λ.

(*Passow*, 305.)

WHO fishes on the hills has seen, or deer upon the waters?
Who an unwedded girl has seen among the *pallikária*?
For twelve long years had Haïdée lived an Armatole and Klephtë,
And no one had her secret learnt among her ten companions,
Till Eastertide came round again, the feast of Easter Sunday,
When all went forth with sword to play, to fence, and throw the boulder.
Once Haïdée threw, and only once; ten times the *pallikária*.
So tightly prisoned was her form, her shame and her confusion
Did burst the fastenings of her vest, and showed her lovely bosom.
One cries that it is gold he sees, another says 'tis silver;
One little Klepht has caught a glimpse, he knows what 'tis full rightly.
'That is no gold that ye have seen, nor is it even silver;
'Tis Haïdée's bosom, nothing else—'tis Haïdée's hidden treasure!'
'O, hush thee, hush thee, little Klepht! and do not thou betray me;
And I for thee my life will give, I'll give thee all my weapons!'

THE LOVELORN KLEPHT.[1]

Ο ΕΡΩΤΕΜΕΝΟΣ ΚΛΕΦΤΗΣ.

'Απόψε δὲν κοιμήθηκα, καὶ σήμερα νυστάζω,
λιὰ δυὸ ματάκια γαλανά, γιὰ δυὸ γλυκὰ ματάκια·
κ. τ. λ..

(*Aravandinos*, 142.)

THE livelong night sleep fled from me; to-day I'm all aweary
For two sweet eyes, for two sweet eyes, two eyes of sweetest azure.
But I will steal them some dark night, some dark and moonless midnight,
And to the hills I'll mount with them, high to the mountain-ridges.
At midnight I will kiss them there; at morn again I'll kiss them.
Oft have I heard the partridge call, the nightingale oft warble;
Three times the cocks have crowed aloud, five times has screamed the peacock.
Awaken, O my partridge-eyed! Awake, and with me hasten!
And I will kiss the olive brown that on thy cheek's imprinted!

THE DEATH OF THE KLEPHT.

Ο ΘΑΝΑΤΟΣ ΤΟΥ ΚΛΕΦΤΟΥ.

Σαράντα κλέφταις ἤμαστε σαράντα χαραμίδες.
Κ' ἐκάμαμ' ὅρκο στὸ σπαθί, τρεῖς ὅρκους στὸ τουφέκι,
κ. τ. λ..

(*Passow*, 146.)

ONCE we were forty gallant Klephts, we numbered forty Robbers,

[1] Placing it here, instead of in the *Erotic Section*, may, perhaps, be excused by the completion thus given to the Song-picture of Klephtic life.

Who'd made an oath upon the sword, three oaths on the tophái̇ki,
That when a comrade should fall sick, then would we all stand by him ;
Stand by him when the Fates should call, or Destiny[1] demand him.
The best of all the band fell ill, the richest and most valiant.
One to another signs did make, and said to one another,
'What, comrades, shall we do with him—a stranger in a strange land ?'
And he replied and answered them, with lips all dry and parchèd :
'Boys, take me in your friendly arms, and bear me in your bosoms,
And dig me with your hands a grave in th' Earth that must devour me.
Throw earth by handfuls, kisses throw, throw tears, and earth by handfuls ;
But lay me on my face, your path I shall not then discover.
And when you see my mother dear, my long-expecting mother,
Who always looked for my return three times a year impatient—
The first, Annunciation Day; the second, Passion Sunday;
The third, the saddest time of all, was at the Resurrection—
Say not to her that I am dead, say not that they have killed me ;
That I am married only say, and in a far, far country.'

[1] See 'The Moirai or Fates,' *above*, p. 111.

SABBAS THE ARMATOLE.
(1821.)
ΣΑΒΒΑΣ.

Δὲν κλαῖτε, δέντρα καὶ κλαριά, καὶ σεῖς, κοντοραχούλαις,
δὲν κλαῖτε τοὺς ἀρματωλοὺς καὶ τὸν καπετὰν Σαββα
κ. π. λ.

(*Aravandinos*, 81.)

OH, weep ye not, ye trees and boughs? oh, weep ye not, low ridges?
Weep ye not for the Armatoles, and their brave Captain Sábbas?
Lord Jesus! what will happen here, the summer that is coming?
In Goúra they're no longer seen, nor yet in Armyriótë.
They say, to Yannina he's gone to give in his submission.[1]
'Effendi, many be your years!' 'Ah, Sábbas, thou art welcome!
How didst thou come? how dost thou do? how fare thy pallikaria?'
'Effendi, they submit themselves; they've to the fields descended,
And I'm to thy protection come, to take hold of thy garment!'

DIAKOS THE ARMATOLE.
(1821.)
ΔΙΑΚΟΣ.

Τρία πουλάκια κάθουνταν κάτω στὴν 'Αλαμάνα,
Τὄνα τηράει τη Λειβαδιὰ καὶ τ' ἄλλο τὸ Ζητοῦνι.
κ. τ. λ.

(*Passow*, 235.)

THREE little birds had perched themselves, and sat in Alamána;

[1] To Ismail Pashá, who was then victoriously besieging Alí Pashá, whose hour was now come.

Diakos the Armatole. 251

One looked down to Livadia, another to Zetoúni,
The third—the best of all the three—a lamentation warbled :
' Arise and flee, Diákos mine, and let us to Livádia.
Omér Pashá's attacking us—Omér the Bey Vrióně.'
' Why, let the cuckold come along, and show himself, the apostate !
We'll let him see the battle of the Armatole's topháiki ;
We'll let him see Diákos' sword, how in red blood it revels !'
When furiously the fight had waged from morning until evening,
Their guns they threw aside, and drew their swords from out the scabbards,
And like wild lions on the Turks they made a desperate onset.[1]
Three times the Othmans count their dead, three thousand find they missing.
When call their roll the Armatoles, they miss but three Leventës ;
No one has gone to keep a feast, or gone to keep a wedding.
Then cried Diákos unto them, with all his might he shouted :
' My brother, Basil, where art thou ? thou, Ghiórghi, my belovèd ?
Their blood ye shall require from him, from that Omér Vrióně ;
Meantime go ! hither bring the Cross, and we'll all kiss't together !'

[1] Compare p. 242, and note 3.

THE SIEGE OF MISSOLONGHI.
(1826.)

Η ΠΟΛΙΟΡΚΙΑ ΤΟΥ ΜΕΣΟΛΟΓΓΙΟΥ.

Σαββάτο ἡμέρα πέρασαν ἀπὸ τὸ Μεσολόγγι,
Τὴν Κυριακ᾽ ἦταν τῶν Βαϊῶν, Σαββάτο τοῦ Λαζάρου.
κ. τ. λ.

(*Aravandinos*, 15.)

ONE Saturday, as journeying, I passed by Missolonghi—
It was Palm Sunday's eve, it was the Saturday of Laz'rus—
I heard within a sound of woe, of tears and lamentation.
Not for the slaughter did they mourn, nor for the dead were weeping;
'Twas only for the bread they wept, for which the flour was lacking.
Then from the Church a priest proclaimed, and called to all the people:
'My children, young and old, approach; come here to St. Nikóla;
Come for the last time and partake of the Communion holy!'
But from the rampart Bótsaris was calling to them loudly:
'Whoe'er is brave, and swift of foot, a worthy pallikári,
Let him to th' Isles a letter take, to Hydra and to Spezzia,
That they provision bring of corn, and we drive out our hunger;
And drive away the Arabs, too; that dog Ibráhim with them.
Where goest, I say, 'Brahím Pashá, with thy worn-out old Arabs?
This place they call it Kárleli, they call it Missolonghi,
Where fight the valiant Héllenes still, like worthy pallikária!'

NASOS MANTALOS.
(1828.)

ΝΑΣΟΣ ΜΑΝΤΑΛΟΣ.

Τὸ λέν οἱ κοῦκκοι 'ς τὰ βουνὰ κ' ἡ πέρδικες 'ς τὰ πλάγια,
Τὸ λέει κι' ὁ πετροκότσιφος 'ς ἕνα ξερὸ δεντράκι.
κ. τ. λ.

(*Aravandinos*, 98.)

THE cuckoo sings it on the hills, and on the shore the partridge,
And on a withered little tree our Peter-blackbird[1] sings it;
And as a funeral dirge they chant and sing the mournful ditty:
'The noise of many guns I hear, and dismal is their knelling,
Perhaps 'tis for a wedding, or perhaps 'tis for a feast-day?'
'They neither for a wedding fire, nor do they fire for feast-day,
But Náso's battling, fighting hard against Hassáni Ghíka.
Three days the fighting's lasted now, three days and nights the battle;
No water have they, bread they've none, no friend has come to aid them;
And now at break of day, at dawn, with sword in hand arising,
A red-wet road[2] he opens wide, 'Farewell,' they say to Khásia.

[1] This name given to the blackbird recalls the lines read long ago somewhere or other:
'Art thou the Peter of Norway boors?
Their Thomas in Finland,
And Russia far inland?
The darling of children and men,
The bird who, by some name or other,
All men who know thee call their own brother?
Our dear little English Robin!'

[2] Κόκκινον δρόμον, literally a 'red road.' But Burns has 'red-wat-shod.'

THE BATTLE OF KALABAKA.[1]
(1854.)

Η ΚΑΛΑΜΠΑΚΑ ΚΑΙ Ο ΧΑΤΖΗ ΠΕΤΡΟΣ·

Τ' ἔχεις, καϋμένε κόρακα, καὶ σκούζεις καὶ φωνάζεις,
Μήνα διψᾷς γιὰ αἵματα, μήνα διψᾶς γιὰ λέσια ;
x. τ. λ..

(*Oikonomides*, A. 32.)

WHAT aileth thee, O wretched crow, that thou art crying and screaming?
It may be thou dost thirst for blood, or thirstest thou for carrion?
Come out high over Kósiako, high over Kalabáka,
And down towards the river look, and down to Krea-Vrissi;
There Turkish bodies thou shalt see, thou shalt see headless bodies,[2]
Where they have shut up Aliá Bey, and with him troops four thousand.
The bullets fall as thick as rain, and cannon-balls as hailstones,
And see, those muskets pour their shot like to the small rain falling.
Hold out, O Hadji Petros mine, against the Liáp[3] topháikia!

[1] This was the last battle of the futile Greek Insurrection during the Crimean War. See *Introd.*, p. 30, n. 27.
[2] They were really Arab mercenaries over whom the Greeks gained the victory in the Upper Glen of the Peneiós which preceded their defeat at Kalabáka, where the forces of Abdi Pasha and Fuad Effendi formed a junction, as, of old, those of Cæsar and Domitius.
[3] It was the Albanians of this tribe who turned the fortune of the day against the Greeks.

KAPITAN BASDEKIS.[1]
(1878.)

ΤΟΥ ΜΠΑΣΔΕΚΗ.

Τα παλληκάρια τὰ καλὰ, ἀδίκως τὰ σκοτώνουν,
Μὲ μπέσα καὶ μὲ πλάνημα καὶ μὲ βαρὺ σικλέτι.
x. τ. λ..

(*Oikonomides*, A. 85.)

THE pallikars, so gallant all, unjustly have been slaughtered,
With lying words and treachery, with great and grievous suff'ring.
Upon the cross-roads there they lie, so many headless bodies;
Each traveller that passes by, stands still and thus he asks them:
'O bodies, say, where are your heads? O say, where are your weapons?'
'O may that leader be accursed, that Kapitan Basdékis,
Who did not shame to sell himself at Volo, in the fortress!'
'May you live long, Hobárt Pashá!'[2] 'Thou'rt welcome, my Basdéki.
Ho, there! make ready coffee, quick, and fill a long chiboúki;
And send two ladies here to us, to talk to and amuse him,
And he'll relate his grievances, and tell us all his troubles.

[1] One of the leaders of the Pelion Insurrection in which Mr. Ogle perished—killed or murdered. See *Introd.*, p. 30, n. 29.
[2] I wonder whether our Turcophile Admiral is aware that his interview with the Insurgent has been thus graphically described in Greek Folk-song?

How many rebels were with you, how many *Boulouk-djídes?*[1]
'Insurgents forty once were we, and had ten *Bou-loukdjídes*,
And ne'er a one of all our band who was not strong and healthy,
Until the time when sickness seized our first, our eldest brother.
For forty days we carried him, and bore him on our shoulders,
Till worn out had our shoulders grown, and ragged was our clothing;
And one unto the others said, and to his fellows murmured :
" Boys, shall we go and leave him here, here in this ditch bestow him ?"
And the poor wretch heard what he said, and then he fell a-weeping.
"My boys, my boys, don't leave me here, within this ditch don't leave me ;
But take me hence, and carry me up to the ridge that's yonder,
That nightingales may be my mates, and I with birds may gossip,
Until the spring shall come again, and come once more May's summer,
When mountains dress them in the green, and gay are the leméria,
When come th' Insurgents on the hills, and Vlachs their black sheep leading."'

[1] Commanders.

THEMISTOCLES DOUMOUZOS.[1]
(1880.)

ΘΕΜΙΣΤΟΚΛΗΣ ΔΟΥΜΟΥΖΟΣ.

Πουλάκι 'πηγε κάθησε 'στὸν 'Αϊλιὰ 'στὴ 'Ράψαν,
Ὁληιμερὴς ἀπ' τὸ πρωῒ πικρὰ λαλεῖ καὶ λέγει.
κ. τ. λ.

(*Oikonomides*, A. 89.)

A LITTLE bird had perched itself on Aïlià in Rápsan,[2]
And all the day, from early dawn, a bitter song was wailing:
'Olympus have I wandered o'er, the country round Kissávos,
And now from Hellas am I come, nor there could I discover
That Kapetan Themistocles, the gallant pallikári;
But bitter tidings gathered I, as on the road I travelled:
By faithless Rapsaniots he's slain, for they have given him poison.
Accursed be thou, O Rápsanè, thou who hast done this evil!
With treachery thou hast destroyed the Chief of all the Captains.
Hoar are the ridges for his sake, for him the towns are weeping.
The Koniárs he made to quake, for fear of him they trembled,
And ne'er a one was there who dared to meddle with a Christian.

[1] *Domouz* is the Turkish for a 'pig.'
[2] A famous village on the Lower Olympus. I spent several days, before Christmas, 1880, boar-hunting in its neighbourhood. But I am unable to say whether the accusation here brought against its inhabitants is well founded or not.

Katarrachiás, Kalóyeros, the Chief of the Klepht Captains,[1]
These too bear witness to his worth, and talk of all
    his bravery;
They vaunt his swiftness in the chase, and greatly praise
    his freedom.
Upon Olympus he was famed, a stag in all his glory;
With silver ornaments he shone, like snow upon the
    mountain.
Said I not, my Themistocles, to Rápsanè, O go not;
For very faithless are its folk, and evil will befall thee?'
'I went to see my native town, I went to see my
    kinsfolk;
The thought had never come to me, nor could I ever
    fancy,
That they who were my dearest friends would seek to
    give me poison.'

[1] To capture these gentlemen, and their bands, a *corps d'armée* was organized in the autumn of 1881; and by the favour of Salyh Pasha, the Commander-in-Chief, I was permitted to accompany it for six weeks—this being the only way in which it was then possible to ascend Olympus, or explore its environs.

APPENDIX.

BIBLIOGRAPHY OF GREEK FOLK-LORE.

ARAVANDINOS.—Συλλογὴ δημωδῶν Ηπειρωτικῶν ᾳσμάτον. 1880.
BLACKIE.—*Horæ Hellenicæ.* 1874.
BLANCHARD.—*Poèmes patriotiques de Valaorites.* 1883.
CHASSIOTIS.—Συλλογὴ τῶν κατὰ τὴν Ἤπειρον δεμοτικῶν ἀσμάτον. 1866.
CONZE.—*Reise auf den Inseln des Thrakischen Meeres.*
Χρονογραφία τῆς Ἠπείρου. 1856.
DROSINUS.—*Ländliche Briefe—Land und Leute in Nord-Euböa.* 1884.
EVLAMPIOS.—Ὁ Ἀμάραντος. 1843.
FAURIEL.—*Chants populaires de la Grèce moderne.* 1824.
FIRMENICH.—Τραγούδια Ρωμάϊκα. 1867.
GELDART.—*Folk-Lore of Modern Greece.* 1884.
GLENNIE.—*Samothrace and its Gods, Contemporary Review.* May, 1882.
HAHN.—*Griechische und Albanische Märchen.* 1864.
HEUZEY.—*Le Mont Olympe.* 1860.
IATRIDOS.—Συλλογὴ δημοτικῶν ᾳσμάτων. 1859.
IKEN EVNOMIA.—Vols. I. and II.
KIND.—Τραγούδια τῆς νέας Ἑλλάδος. 1833.—Μνημόσυνον. 1849.—*Anthologie.* 1844.
LEGRAND.—*Chansons populaires grecques.* 1876.—*Recueil de Poemes historiques.* 1877.
LELEKOS.—Δεμοτικὴ Ἀνθολογία. 1868.
MACPHERSON.—*Poetry of Modern Greece.* 1884.
MANASSEIDOS.—Διάλεκτος Αἴνου, Ἴμβρου, καὶ Τενέδου. Ποικίλη ὅλη εξ Αἴνου καὶ Ἱμβρα.
MANOUSOS.—Τραγούδια ἐθνικά, κ. τ. λ. 1850.
MARCELLUS.—*Chants du Peuple en Grece.* 1851.
OIKONOMIDES.—Τραγούδια τοῦ Ὀλύμπου. 1881.
OPPENHEIM.—*Volks und Freiheitslieder.* 1842.
PAGOUNOS.—Ἠπειρωτικὴ διάλεκτος.

260 Bibliography of Greek Folk-Lore.

Pandora, Εφεμερίς τῆς Ελλάδος.
Panhellenic Annual.
PASHELY.—*Travels in Crete.* 1837.
PASSOW.—*Popularia Carmina Græciæ Recentioris.* 1860.
Parnassos, Νεοελληνικὰ ἀνάλεκτα. 1870—71.
Φιλολογικὸς συνέκδημος. 1849.
POLITOS.—Γλοσσολογικὴ συμβόλη.
ROSS.—*Reisen auf den Griech. Inseln des Aegaeischen Meeres.* 1840.
SANDERS.—*Das Volksleben der Neugriechen.* 1844.
SCHAUB.—*Poèmes grecs modernes.* 1844.
SCHMIDT.—*Das Volksleben der Neugriechen.* 1871.
SHERIDAN.—*The Songs of Greece.* 1826.
STAMATELLOS.—Σὐλλογὴ τῶν ζώντων μνημείων ἐν τῇ γλώσσα τοῦ Λευκαδίου λαοῦ.
TEPHARIKI.—Λιανοτράγουδα. 1868.
TOMMASEO.—*Canti popolari.* 1841.
TOZER.—*The Highlands of Turkey.*
VALAORITES.—Μνημόσυνα ᾄσματα. 1861.—Ἡ κυρὰ Φροσύνη. 1859.
ZAMBELIOS.—Ἄσματα δημοτικὰ τῆς Ἑλλάδος. 1852.
ZANNETOS.—Ἡ Ὁμερικὴ φράσις. 1883.

THE END.

Elliot Stock, Paternoster Row, London.

www.ingramcontent.com/pod-product-compliance
Lightning Source LLC
Chambersburg PA
CBHW032057220426
43664CB00008B/1041